EARTH DANCE DRUM:
A CELEBRATION OF LIFE

WHAT OTHERS ARE SAYING

Blackwolf and Gina's new book is nothing short of brilliant! It is a 'must read' for those who wish to know more about Native American philosophy, and should be required reading for everyone who works in the field of Counseling and Human Development. This is storytelling at its best! The lessons about life, and the deep understanding of native cultures shared in these pages are rare gifts, to be treasured and read again. I am forever changed by the experience of reading *Earth Dance Drum*.

—Janet I. Jones, M.Ed., NCC, Professional Standards
& Certification Committee, Association for
Multicultural Counseling and Development

This book fills the empty spaces that need healing words of nurture for all relatives living on Mother Earth. Blackwolf and Gina touch the unity of Spirit to live a well-balanced life.

—MEGIZIKWE (Eagle Woman) aka-Tinker, Waaswaagoning Ojibwe Nation,
Lac du Flambeau, Wisconsin

Earth Dance Drum is a poetic masterpiece! After reading this book, one's participation in Powwow will never be the same. What before seemed to be social dances performed for entertainment are now seen as dances with profound spiritual meaning. We owe a debt of gratitude to Blackwolf and Gina for this intimate sharing of Native American wisdom. This is a truly remarkable book that will enrich the reader for many years to come.

—Dr. Paul B. Steinmetz, S.J., author *Meditations with Native Americans:
Lakota Spirituality,* and *Pipe, Bible, and Peyote Among the
Oglala Lakota: A Study of Religious Identity*

Blackwolf and Gina Jones paint the process of healing through a world most non-indigenous people have yet to understand or encompass. Celebrate *Earth Dance Drum* for inviting all people to celebrate without judgment!

—Tony Trupiano, author and host of the radio program,
Your Health Alternatives.

Ultimately practical, *Earth Dance Drum* is overflowing with wisdom and insight. Blackwolf and Gina have made a major giveaway and we are the fortunate recipients of their wealth. They teach us to will live Namaji, to become an active link of love on the Sacred Hoop. This powerful work is applicable to us all.

—Dru Kristel, author of *Breath Was the First Drummer,* founder of the Not Always North American Drum Core.

Earth Dance Drum, is a creative, in-depth and knowledgeable account of our connection to our Mother Earth. Having read this book, it brings to life feelings and emotions which bring me closer to my Native American culture.

—Kenneth R. Ninham, M.S.E., Native American Psychotherapist

Earth Dance Drum is so well-crafted you will want to read each passage over to capture the beauty of the words and their meaning. There is a perfect blend of poetry, stories, exercises and information. It is my hope, as a teacher, to offer students a look into this ancient culture in order for them to think more deliberately about their lives and the choices they make.

—Lori R. Fulmer, M.S.E., teacher

Migwetch, Blackwolf and Gina, for writing of beauty, wisdom and hope. I felt calm and empowered as I read the book. The metaphor of Powwow teaches important Ojibwe life principles: pride, dignity, honor and respect. It is in our power to live with these central Anishinaabe values.

—Robert C. Palmer, M.D., Anishinaabe, Ojibwe descendant.
Child Psychiatrist; Clinical faculty, Stanford University
School of Medicine; consultant to the
Four Winds Lodge, San Jose, CA.

A profound message of spirituality that speaks to your soul!

—Jack Canfield, Co-author of *Chicken Soup for the Soul:*
101 Stories to Open the Heart and Rekindle the Spirit.

In a day when many feel desperate, *Earth Dance Drum,* reassures the reader that everything will work out in life, that we all can live positive again.

—Aught Coyhis, CADC III, Former Tribal Chairman of Stockbridge-Munsee

Earth Dance Drum is like a warm embrace to the world of dancers, of singers, of those who listen to the drum. Written in eloquent, inspired prose, it escorts us all back to the Circle for just one more inter-tribal. Highly recommended!

—Dee Sweet, Poet, White Earth, Anishinaabe

EARTH DANCE DRUM: A CELEBRATION OF LIFE

by
Blackwolf & Gina Jones

Commune-A-Key Publishing
Salt Lake City, UT 84158

Published by:
Commune-A-Key Publishing
P.O. Box 58637
Salt Lake City, UT 84158
(801) 581-9191
(801) 581-9196 Fax

Jones, Blackwolf, 1935-
    Earth dance drum: a celebration of life / by Blackwolf & Gina Jones.
    p. cm.
    Includes bibliographical references and index.
    ISBN: 1-881394-48-4 (pbk. : alk. paper)
    1. Spiritual life.
    2. Healing.
    3. Indians of North America—Rites and ceremonies.
    4. Indians of North America—Medicine.
    5. Powwows.
    6. Dance—Psychological aspects.
    7. self-actualization (Psychology)
    I. Jones, Gina, 1960- .
    II. Title.
    BL624.J646 1996   299' . 7—dc20
                                            96-10757
                                            CIP
    $16.95 USA

Editorial: Caryn Summers and Nancy Lang
Cover Design: Lightbourne Images, Ashland, OR
Typeset Design & Graphics: Bailey-Montague & Associates, Salt Lake City, UT

DEDICATION

To All Tribal Drums and Dancers

This book is not intended to elaborate on Native American teachings or ceremonies. For those seekers wanting more, you are directed to find an individual teacher or lodge. Each dance within depicts one of many interconnecting Hoops and does not presume to reveal the personal experience of individual dancers. As each life-circle is a unique life-experience, we intend only to honor the diversity of Life, while dignifying the essential interconnectedness of all. It is merely the finger pointing. Look beyond to your own understanding and truth.

ABOUT THE COVER

We invite you to encounter the cover of this book, as intimately as you experience the words. Return to this mystery when you find yourself filled, moved, emptied or stilled. Allow this beautiful depiction to enter your spirit. May it honor your questions and settle your answers.

This design respectfully illustrates the balancing of life: the pulse, the song, the dance, the celebration. With deep respect, may you experience the honor of Sky Father and Earth Mother. Enter the possibilities of Grandmother Moon, the Life cycles, the Sacred Hoop of all things. With courage, journey within to discover meaning.

Like the dancer, may you recognize that this is your moment to dance. May your emotions sway as soft fringes, your steps express your values, your mind be as quiet as the night. May you lift Life itself with the joy of your spirit.

Notice the drum. Hear the love vibration of Creation. Feel the strong beat that continues life, that is Life. Understand that your drum, your heart, is dependent on your dance. Likewise, Earth Mother's health is dependent upon our steps. She is a great vibrating drum whose pulse we must return to. Both land and water—two of the four elements—are sounded with Her beat. Listen to Her song. Hear that you and I are nearly three-fourths water and will soon return to Her soil. Can you touch this vibrating truth? Can you feel the world in the palm of your hand? It is up to us to mend the Sacred Hoop. It is our future, that we now face.

Now move between the dancer and the Earth-drum to discover the black vastness of Eternity. The Great Mystery is for you to enter. This is your silence. This is your journey. This is your beginning. This is our beginning.

Behold the brilliance of the Stars. The Star People shine of wisdom, love, respect, bravery, honesty, humility and truth. With this generosity, may you honor the Creator and face difficult situations with integrity. As our relatives celebrate their own dance in the Spirit World, may we always honor the past by preparing a good path for the future.

Have you followed the two shooting stars? We were gifted their presence on two separate occasions while discussing the book, as it was being prepared for you. One trailed into the East. The other into the West. May your journey and presence honor the blessing of Gitchi Manidoo. May our words move into the Universe to be found by you. May you move into the Universe to share with all.

The Sacred Fire, the third element, honors the dancer's color. What is your special color? How do you uniquely connect with the light and the dark, the world and your Self, the visible and the invisible? Honor your moment, for the Breath is the source of life and is the great gift of all. Follow your breath, as air is the fourth element, and you will discover Mitakuye-Oyasin—that we are all related. The Breath is the joining of the Web of Life.

May this design ignite your internal flame. May you open this book to find meaning within. May you honor the Universe with your own sincere design for Life. May *Earth Dance Drum* become you.

Migwetch.
Gina and Blackwolf

TABLE OF CONTENTS

ACKNOWLEDGEMENTS

We would like to express our thanks and love
to everyone who has assisted us on this journey and in particular:

To my sister, Vivian, who lives life with Namaji.
Blackwolf

To my student, Thai, whose sweet smile I will always remember.
Gina

and
To our family and friends.
Blackwolf and Gina

To Bram and Gaelyn, of Lightbourne Images, whose art
beautifully portrays the essence of this work.

To Robert Owen, whose silouette on the cover is the
expression of Mitakuye-Oyasin.

To everyone who offered their skills and understanding in
the creation of this book, we honor your connection.

And, to our dynamic editors, Caryn and Nancy, we say Gitchi Migwetch.

To the
Four Directions,
Four Elements,
Four Races,
and
Gitchi Manidoo,
We offer this gift to the Universe.

PREFACE

HONOR EARTH MOTHER AND DANCE!

Down a blacktop road where the woods try to fulfill their purpose, roots from Sister White Pine push up from under the pavement to reclaim her right to exist. The road looks as though it is a temporary blanket covering a sleeping child who is trying to toss it off with her kicks.

Earth Mother is patient. She knows she will eventually reclaim herself. For humans are the endangered species now. By slashing down Earth Mother's limbs, cutting her locks of hair, ripping up her soft skin, humans are destroying their own home, extinguishing their own flame. Earth Mother's limbs will grow back into forests. Her hair will flow once again in the waterfalls and rivers. Her skin will heal with the colors of her beauty. With or without humans, when time gives her healing, when the axes, the picks and the poisons are no more, Earth Mother will again be whole.

Earth Mother will heal when people live vigorously and honorably, with her once again.

There was a time when this was so. It was a time when people worked hard. I remember my mother dragging brush from the woods as though she were simply combing Earth Mother's hair. She experienced the world where only one can experience it—outside, in nature. Where insects are not pests, but our relatives. Where fresh air and Grandfather Sun's rays are rejuvenating. My mother was strong and healthy. Working hard with Earth Mother was a good gift to her. It made her legs and arms powerful, her laugh hearty, her smile full, and her spirit strong.

Before the idle hum of the washing machine had reached the Reservation, it was like that—people and Earth Mother living together as one great system. As a boy, my mother and I would wash our family clothes with Earth Mother. My mother would first loosen the dirt from the clothing with a wooden agitator. Gathering all the clothes, we would go to the greatest power of all, the Water Spirits of Indian Lake. I would row the redwood boat with yellow birch oars, as Mom dangled each item into the moving water. We rinsed them all clean, my mother, the water, the boat from Sister Tree, and me. It was a concerted effort. An effort of collaboration. We trusted each other to do what each could do well. And together we cleansed our world. There was an order to the universe and a sense of interconnectedness.

In my dream, I have remembered this order. I have seen many dancers, heard many drums and sung many songs. The dancers of my dream were of different colors. The drums were from different lands. The songs were in different tongues. I heard the worldwide drumming that had once resonated together. Then eventually the drums ceased, the people no longer danced and Earth Mother sickened.

Yet, my dream did not end there. With great joy I heard the drums resume! With great relief I watched Earth Mother heal. With powerful understanding I felt the healing medicine vibrations. People of all races danced to the drum, danced for the Earth. Each drumbeat vibrated as one of the many strands of a spider web. The vibrations con-nected all to my dream. Here I saw the Grand Web encase and encircle Earth Mother. I saw this compressed Web of Life become the healing bandage She needs to again become clear, clean, and whole.

This is my dream.

Blackwolf

It is time to dance softly on Earth Mother's back, as the faces of the future are looking up. Look into Her soil. What do you see? Can you see the tears of Earth's children as the pavement is poured over them? Can you see the smiles of Earth's children as you bend to smell the wild rose in the woods? WE are responsible to the future. In the words of Chief Seattle, we do not inherit Earth, we only borrow Her from our children. Our children ask us to prepare a safe and friendly environment for their Grand Entry into the physical dimension. By celebrating Earth Mother, we celebrate with all. The past, the present, and, the future. WE will celebrate as One.

Please, sit close to this book, as you would a fire. You will hear Blackwolf's voice whisper amidst my words. Please, join this Hoop of Love. You will hear the voice of All circling the pages. Please, hear my voice. It sings my prayer. It honors You.

May the Sacred Eagle Feather I hold in my hand elevate this important matter to the heights of the dancing clouds, the soaring eagles, the swaying tree tops. We must all honor Earth Mother. We cannot celebrate our own life separated from her. She is our life. To celebrate life, we must celebrate All Life. We must come to one mind. The time is Now to heal and rejuvenate Her.

Please, hear my celebration as I pass the feather on to you. Hear the Eternal Beat. Hear the Song. Dance this Song with me.

You are invited to Powwow! Pau-wau or pauau is Algonquian for a gathering of medicine men and spiritual leaders in a healing ceremony. Early European explorers mispronounced the name as 'powwow' and believed it meant any large gathering of Native people. Today, Powwow is an outgrowth of the spiritual and social dances of Tribal people[1].

Have you ever seen the elaborate bead work, the beautiful regalia, the animal affinities present at Powwow? If that is all you have viewed, you have glimpsed only the peripheral truth. Like a canoe

---

[1]   May this book bring the Indian and non-Indian world together at Powwow, as the public is welcome to attend all Powwows—all nations, all colors, all people are invited to experience *Earth Dance Drum*.

passing through a mist, see what is beyond the haze. See the clear shoreline that leads to a new horizon. See the meanings more colorful than the colors. See the colors' meanings. We are only the painters of a beautiful design that has already existed. It is time to look and listen with your heart to what Powwow truly is, to see the Earth when the Earth was new.

Here you will find a celebration of drumming, a celebration of singing, a celebration of dancing, a celebration of living! Through drumming, may you hear love vibration that binds us together. Through singing, may you lift your own prayers to Ishpeming[2]. Through dancing, may you surrender completely to Earth Celebration. Through living, may you look at a lavender Iris and see its unparalleled elegance.

This writing has been a gift to me. Like Brother Eagle flying above my celebration, may you transcend with this gift we now pass on to you. And like me, may you feel as though all colors are you, and discover your face wet with tears you have not yet realized you shed.

I invite you to fill with this celebration for all. Come alive with the love of the Spirit World. May the Hoop of Love be your journey. May Earth Dance Drum be You.

Gina

Slow down to hear the steady beat. Then the song can be sung. Inside World Harmony we can celebrate our dance.

To dance is to share both the joy and the pain. We have all been wounded, just as Earth Mother has. To dance is to be able to go beyond one's injuries, to reclaim your right to exist... your right to flourish... the right of all to flourish. To dance is to know the freedom of living fully, of flowing with, rather than against, the tide. To dance is to connect to the Great Pulse with each step. Like newborns first focusing their eyes, see the world around you. See

---

[2] Pronounced: ISH-pe-ming and refers to the High Place.

your sacred role. Once you understand your voice, you can sing your song. Once you realize what your hands can do, touch the wonder of the world around you. You are given hands to drum. You are given a voice to sing. You are given a heart to heal. You are given a spirit to dance.

Through tribal wisdom and dances, poetry and stories, you will strengthen your connections to Earth Mother and the Spirit World. The guidance in this book will allow you to recognize truths that will be echoed joyfully as you explore your personal caverns and climb your mountain peaks.

Earth Dance Drum takes you down the River of Life where the shoreline is the Self. It respectfully floats you into a life-swim with Others, it places you into the current of synchronicity with Earth Mother, and finally, it returns you to the shores of Self once again, to dance as One, never alone. Discover your union of Self, Others and Earth Mother. Dance your entire life experience, from your sunrise to your sunset.

Carry the message of Earth Healing to other Drums, to other parts of your world. From the Four Directions may the Drums resonate! From the East to the South to the West to the North, let the Drums echo this healing globally!

May *Earth Dance Drum* honor you and honor the world. May the Drum beat vibrations, songs, and dance to all corners of the Earth.

Become! Celebrate! Enjoy! Adorn yourself in the colors of yourself! Consciously link your Seventh Direction[3] to All Directions. Dip your hand in paint and imprint it on your Life shield. Celebrate Earth Mother's Life! Celebrate Your Life! Celebrate Our Life! It is time to go to Powwow and dance!

---

[3] The Seventh Direction is You, in both the physical and spiritual worlds. Your hoop intersects with Eternity where all directions of life come together. The Seventh Direction is addressed more fully in Chapter 1.

DANCE!

Hear the Drum beat.
Hear the bells ting.
Hear the wings flap.
Hear the Spirits sing.

See the leaves' dew.
See the feathers felt.
See the child's smile.
See the colors melt.

Smell the sweet grass.
Smell the fry bread.
Smell the freed cedar.
Smell the rain bed.

Taste the blue berry.
Taste the given deer.
Taste your sweat drip.
Taste your own tear.

Feel the cool soil.
Touch the here, now.
Touch the soft fern.
Feel the Powwow.

Dance the Heart Beat!
Dance the Sacred Ring!
Dance the Spirits' Song!
Dance the Eagle's Wing!

DANCE WITH SELF

If you dance, make sure it is you that is dancing.

PART ONE

DANCE REGALIA

*The Dance of Life begins in your heart. In your spirit.
In your silence. It is here where one prepares for the dance,
the Celebration of Life.*

Tribal people understand the silence. In this space of Self we put on our bells, our moccasins, our elaborate bead work, our feathers. Here we gather our eagle-wing fans, prepare our staff or Medicine Wheel[1], and attach our Medicine Bags[2] to our wrists. Men may put on their bustles or roaches, their chokers, bells or breast plates, their arm bands or grass dance regalia, their animal skins or head dresses. Women may put on their jingle dress or traditional shawls, their leggings, their beaded hair pieces or ribbons. We all put on our regalia as a ritual of sacred preparation.

Tribal people present themselves in their dance regalia to express their deepest Self. It is time to express yourself. It is time to find, validate, and celebrate your true essence, your truest Self.

---

[1]   The Medicine Wheel is a Native American healing wheel used to represent balance in one's life, as well as a symbol for life cycles. The Medicine Wheel has three parts: the circumference, (the Sacred Hoop), the center (Gitchi Manidoo) and the Four Directions (East, South, West and North). A more thorough discussion of the Medicine Wheel can be found in *Listen to the Drum: Blackwolf Shares His Medicine* and *The Healing Drum*.

[2]   A Medicine Bag is a Native American healing pouch that contains a variety of herbs, medicines, etc. used to connect the participant to the Spirit World. Medicine Bags may also include personal items that represent themselves and their experiences and is sacred to the individual. A Medicine Bag is an Indian's most prized companion. More can be read of Medicine Bags *in Listen to the Drum* and *The Healing Drum*.

Watch the birds. Are the sparrows merely the colors of their feathers? Are they the songs they sing? Or are they the movement of their wings? The experience of their flight? Are sparrows the hunger and fulfillment they feel inside? Or the winds they ride? Are they what we see and experience them to be, or what they see and experience? Are sparrows all of this? None of this? More than this? Only a sparrow knows what is to be a sparrow.

Our personal regalia expresses our outward feathers, yet is rich beyond the bright colors and elaborate design. Our beautiful regalia is our celebration of Self, manifested for others to see. It is our internal design and colors, our internal patterns. Our outward regalia symbolizes our Seventh Direction, our internal Self.

Listen with your heart to the story of Sing With Birds. Discover for yourself what preparing for the Dance of Life truly means.

SING WITH BIRDS

In the distance, the flute played its solitary song as the young girl, Sing With Birds, looked at the leaf in her hands. It was a beautiful green leaf. A leaf with veins, rivers that had brought it nourishment. But the Wind Spirits had ushered this leaf to the ground to meet the West Door early, before its time, before the time of its sisters and brothers. Sing With Birds turned the leaf over and set it back down on the dry ground. She thought about her brother, Evening Sky, who had died in the swift-flooded river last summer. Evening Sky had died before his time, too, she thought. Before his sisters and brothers.

The clouds overhead came together like the angry waves Sing With Birds had once seen on the Great Water. The sky filled with gray and purple, the colors Sing With Birds had previously chosen for her regalia. Suddenly, as if to carry this beautiful girl into the great mystery, the West Winds lifted Sing With Bird's silky hair. Like plants in a moving sea, her hair curled and twisted and wound around to kiss her lips with its fleeting praise. Leaves and dried grass became restless. The leaf she had just held in her hand did what Sing With Birds wished she could: surrender to the power of Wind-Walking.

Sing With Birds stood up as if to follow the leaf to where it would go, closer to the moving waves of clouds. Back at the encampment, the flute carrier of her people continued to play his song, but sharp notes carried his anticipation into the humid air. It was not his notes, but the thunder overhead that caused her to stop in her path. The wonderful crashing thunder, the honor beats, filled Sing With Birds with joy. As her heart moved to ride its vibration, the rain began to fall and the flute player sang a long note of greeting.

Large warm drops hit Sing With Birds' face as she looked out to Sky Father. First her nose, then her forehead, chin and eyelids. Her arms reached up to funnel in as much rain to her as possible and soon the young woman felt the refreshing cool of the Summer rain. Sing With Birds stood there, watched the leaf follow its own path, and realized it was the path that she could not yet go.

There was no hurry. She knew she would meet her brother again. Instead, the dancing leaf reminded Sing With Birds that tonight she would dance for Evening Sky. Tonight, she would give her dance to her brother. Tonight, she would dance with his memory. Sing With Birds raced to her village, where her mother was busy getting ready for the dance.

"Boo-zhoo[3], Sing With Birds," her mother greeted as the wind blown girl entered her lodge. "I thought maybe you joined the birds and were nesting in the cedars down the

---

3   Pronounced: Bou-zshoo and means hello.

hill." The rain now sounded beautiful, rhythmic, and soft, just as it had felt a minute ago on Sing With Birds face. The canvas welcomed the rain just as the wet girl had.

"No, Mother. See? I am all wet!" the girl laughed as she placed her hands on her mother's soft face.

Pretending to be shocked, Red Turtle Woman turned to the blanket before her and answered, "Ah ho. You should have been named Swim With Fish, I think!"

"May I help?" the girl asked as she watched her mother spread dance articles out on the blanket.

"No. But the comb and I will help prepare you for the dance." Sing With Birds sat down at her mother's feet, ready to receive the gift.

Red Turtle Woman enjoyed combing her daughter's hair. It was as long and smooth as the high grass that dances in the wind. Since Sing With Birds was a little one, her hair had only been cut fourteen times. It was a way to measure her growth as the snow melted each year.

The blue beech wood comb, carved by Evening Sky, had been the best gift Sing With Birds had ever received. She remembered how long he had worked on it, careful to let the wood become separated yet strong enough to comb through Sing With Birds' hair. Now her brother was part of the Drum. The memory of his voice still carried Sing With Birds to her heart, just as it did when she was a little girl and he sang only to her. Tonight his Spirit would sing for all the people, she knew. Evening Sky would help these people return to their hearts, to the beat, to the eternal, to the Great Spirit.

Red Turtle Woman carefully separated her daughter's hair and the girl-woman felt the tingling comfort it brought her.

The familiar warm feeling of caring fingers began to braid her hair. Somewhere in the back of Sing With Birds mind, she heard the rain let up. The afternoon shower would cool Earth Mother for the dancing to come. With her eyes closed in delightful bliss, Sing With Birds rehearsed her dance movements in her mind. She saw her shawl twirling with the wind, like a yellow sparrow, its fringes never touching the ground. She saw her steps, light and quick, touching the ground, touching the beat. She saw her face intent, her body flowing into the songs. She saw her spirit soaring. Sing With Birds knew it was time to prepare her entire Self for the dance.

Her mother's fingers continued to bring in more hair from each side to meet in a rich thick braid. Sing With Birds could feel the gift she received from her mother nearing its' end, as her bottom hair was wrapped with leather. At the braid's end, Red Turtle Woman attached the mink fur piece. Brother Mink would sway tonight with the Wind Spirits, thought her mother.

Giving her mother a big hug, Sing With Birds got up and gently touched the colorful beaded flowers that adorned her moccasins and her dress. The Color of the East Direction accented the purple and gray. Yellow's creating power still startled Sing With Birds each time she looked at it anew. It reminded her of her quiet Self. It reminded her of her not-so-quiet-Self, too, as her heart giggled, remembering the time she had dripped the honey on her sleeping brother's toes. He had many visitors that night, she remembered.

But it was always the purple and gray that brought her to the silent place, the place she stayed when her brother died. The place where she finally found peace. "It is so beautiful," thought Sing With Birds. She thought how her mother had lovingly attached each bead in the winter hours. Sing With Birds remembered how her mother had been strong for her, for all of them. She looked at the beads that had been sewn on with her mother's tears.

Sing With Birds looked to the gift from Brother Deer. "I will be as swift as you, tonight," she promised, as she straightened and separated the fringes on her shawl. "You will see. I will dance for the glory of Evening Sky."

Finally, Sing With Birds was completely dressed. Red Turtle Woman stood admiring her daughter.

"What do you think, Mother?" Sing With Birds asked.

"What I think, is that there is one thing missing." Sing With Birds looked down at her dress. She stretched her neck around to see from behind. She looked at her feet. She could find nothing missing.

"What is it, Mother?" she asked, impatient to dance for her brother.

Reaching behind her back, Red Turtle Woman presented Sing With Birds with the most glorious Eagle plumage. "Here. As this was once gifted me in my clan lodge, in keeping with tradition, I am honoring you with the passing of this gift. Wear it in honor as you dance the Circle."

Looking at the soft white feather, Sing With Birds listened with her heart and felt the soft breeze of the North Door. In her heart she knew Evening Sky had come to dance with her. As Red Turtle Woman attached the feather to her daughter's hair, Sing With Birds was finally ready to dance. Opening the door to the beginning sunset, Sing With Birds opened her Spirit to fly together with her Brother.

Each morning, many of us take the time to find out about the weather, determine what to wear, what the newspaper reports. But do you bother to take your internal temperature? Take time to prepare yourself for the gift of another day. Like Sing With Birds, prepare yourself emotionally, quiet to your Spiritual Self and prepare your regalia. It is time to think about what you will celebrate, or you will celebrate nothing.

PREPARATION FOR THE DANCE OF LIFE

Come to know your uniqueness.
Come to declare your uniqueness.
Come and dance with your Self.

Our regalia manifests four aspects of our Self: physical, psychological, emotional, and spiritual. You can wear the most beautiful clothing ever made, yet it only becomes meaningful when you imprint it with your uniqueness, preen your emotional feathers, smooth out your values and link your Spirit to the Great Spirit. Your regalia is coming home to Self and then expressing the Self. It is a physical, mental, emotional, and spiritual preparation for the Dance of Life. It is an act of deliberate balance. I invite you to now prepare, and then wear with your heart, your own personal regalia.

PHYSICAL PREPARATION FOR THE DANCE OF LIFE

Imprint Your Uniqueness

An easy way to meet your individuality is to find some sand, dirt or clay and make footprints. Many people are probably more familiar with the way expensive tennis shoes imprint the sand than their own foot. Go now and imprint your foot. We have become so accustomed to being distanced from Earth Mother and ourselves, including our own bodies, that this may be a new experience for even a twenty or a sixty year old person. Observe the imprint, the way the granules lift and compress. Earth Mother acknowledges you in this unique way. She responds to you in a way unlike anyone else.

You are unique. When you become familiar with your own footprint you have taken the first step to celebrating your uniqueness.

For thousands of years, people have been celebrating their uniqueness by making hand paintings in cave and rock formations around the world. Their marks still remain to the delightful discovery of archeologists. But has the meaning behind such art been discovered by most people? Establish your place in the Universe with a footprint and a hand print on parchment or in plaster. Frame it and hang it on the wall. Declare yourself! Celebrate your uniqueness!

Each Spring on the Reservation, my parents would trace my feet on butcher paper. My mother would take her time tracing, making sure my foot was outlined to its contour. She would do each foot separately, for she recognized each foot grew differently. Then the paper was given to Nelly[4]. Mrs. Mike would take freshly tanned deer hide and sew two pairs of summer moccasins, the exact size of my feet. One for inside the house and one for outside. The inside mocs stayed soft, while the outside, having gotten wet and dirty, became hard. Sewn with sinew, it would take her only a few days before I would see my new mocs. Actually, I would always smell them before I saw them, as the smell from reddish charred wood used in the tanning process announced their completion.

How does your personal regalia acknowledge your growth? How can you accommodate your regalia for the differences you become, you grow into, from day to day? How can you adjust for the different environments you live in? How can your regalia announce your special gifts?

The Threads of Regalia Begin with Your Feet

Moccasins are a very important part of Native people's attire. We honor our uniqueness by designing and sewing intricate designs on them. Diamond-patterned bead work was always adorned on my moccasins to remind me of my affiliation to the pine snake. In the moccasins, we care for our feet, for we honor all that our feet must do. With our feet, we celebrate life. Your feet honor you by carrying you through life. How will you honor them?

---

[4]   Nelly was the wife of Mike Bostoni, "Moccasin Mike." She was also known as Mrs. Mike.

Massage your feet and honor them[5]. They carry you from Birth's door to Death's door. Take the time to relieve them of their burden. Decide what you can do to help your feet. Consider the effects of high heels, obesity, and neglect. Do for your feet what you would do for a friend. If you question the importance of such honor, ask someone who has lost their feet, due to disease, accident, or war, the importance of such respect. Moccasin Mike, my 80-year-old Anishinaabe[6] friend and neighbor, knew this well. Having lost his leg during a logging accident at the turn of the century, he honored his one foot completely. He was able to go beyond his loss to celebrate his wooden peg-leg gifted by Brother Tree. Yet, Mike's respect did not stop there. He often told me about his dreams and how he dreamt about and honored his lost foot. The celebration of our true Self must begin with our physical self. To fully honor who we are, we must honor *all* of who we are.

Make your own moccasins and design a pattern that will best represent you. Embellish them with beads, paint or bells. Express your true Self in what you wear.

Now consider whatever else covers your body, for either comfort or effect. First care for your body, then wear it for yourself. People who are truly free dress themselves not for what society might say is appropriate, but for what they feel is meaningful to them. I wear wolf tee-shirts. Through my clothing, I am expressing my concern and respect for Brother Wolf. The Anishinaabe Way states that whatever happens to the wolf, happens to people. I know that the celebration of my life, hinges on the celebration of others'.

What is meaningful to you? What can you wear that will express your deepest convictions, your deepest values, your deepest Self? Consider why spiritual people from across the globe wear specific attire. It is more than to simply state their identity. Like the regalia at Powwow, it is an expression of their deepest Self. It is an expression of their convictions. They become walking bill-boards announcing their spiritual awareness. You do not have to go to Powwow, become a priest or a rabbi, to have a cause and express that

---

5   Reflexology is a type of foot massage. Nerve endings from all parts of our body, including organs, eventually end up in our feet. By massaging our feet, we massage our entire body.

6   Pronounced: a-ni-shi-NA-bae. Refers to those who are the ancestors of the tribes now known as Ottawa, Potawatomi, and Ojibwe.

cause. You can wear something as small as a necklace or as large as a printed tee-shirt to make a difference with the people you encounter today.

Sadly, today's streets are filled with people (including children) wearing clothing that screams of hopelessness and escape. The slogans, through sarcastic humor, belittle living and the ability to make a difference. Yet, some people make a positive difference by wearing reminders of what life is truly about. Be deliberate in your choices. What you wear can affect others by either perpetuating the norm's apathy for tomorrow's children or instilling and reasserting Namaji.

Namaji

Namaji[7], the highest of all Anishinaabe principles, is respect, honor, dignity, and pride. Our regalia is woven with these threads. We wear Namaji for all to see. Namaji is for all: one's Self, Others and Earth Mother. How do you show respect for your Self? How do you wear your dignity? What are you proud of? How do you extend Namaji to others?

Namaji is the geyser that lifts all of creation to sacredness. All is elevated and cared for. Discover ways to manifest Namaji. Discover the pure joy it gives you. Discover how you will affect others. Become the mirror of Namaji that others will look into and then become. Celebrate, as you see others look into these reflections and become that which they see and value. Namaji will spread, if we learn to hold onto its worth. Cherish Namaji, just as Earth Mother remembers once being cherished. Care for your Self. It is the first step in giving Namaji away. Namaji is for you.

PSYCHOLOGICAL PREPARATION FOR THE DANCE OF LIFE

Entwined within our physical preparation, our regalia declares our belief system.

---

[7]   Pronounced: NA-MA-GEE.

What Is Important To You?

Identify your values[8]. Come to know what you believe. Come to know what is most important to you. Come to recognize when your values are tested. Only when you can stand up to the test, are your values truly validated and confirmed.

Sister Bear is fully a bear once she has hibernated. Brother Eagle is fully an eagle once he has soared on his own. And Brother Fern is fully a fern once he has unraveled in the Spring. You may value patience, but you are not truly patient until difficult endurance is demanded. You may value honesty, but you are not truly honest until honesty outweighs dishonest gains. You may value strength, but you are not truly strong until asked to be soft. You may value love, but you do not truly love until you have loved your enemy.

What do others see of you? Like the blind spot in your car's side-view mirror, we have a self-observation blind side. The only way you will ever know the part of yourself you cannot see is if you ask someone what they see and they tell you. If they like you, love you, respect you, or simply have courage enough to tell you, you will come to know your blind side. "None are so blind as those who will not see," speaks well to the person who does not look at themselves nor ask others for feedback. What you truly value is often seen by others, without any words. Without any declaration, we declare what we value.

Question what you value and why. What do you collect? Stop and see this about you, as though you are looking at someone else. What we collect tells a lot about our interests, and also about deficiencies from our childhood. Interests or deficiencies may lead to cravings and to obsessive-compulsive behavior patterns which may turn around and bite us where we don't want to be bitten. Make an appraisal of your collectibles. Make an appraisal of your values, both the tangible and intangible (as in attention, affection, recognition, and approval), and see if your gatherings are constructive or destructive.

---

8   Exercises in value identification are taught in *Listen to the Drum* and *The Healing Drum*.

Defend Who You Are

Values are seldom easy to preserve and protect. Those who sacrifice their values for the sake of immediate comfort are plagued with guilt, what ifs, should haves, second guessing and wishing. Consider the bear who never roared, or the eagle who never soared, or the fern who never opened. Tap your Mash-ka-wisen[9], walk through your fear, and embrace your values. Be who you are!

Identify, prioritize, recognize and practice your values. When you follow your beacon at all times there is no remorse. The consequences are acceptable. As a coward follows his head, a warrior follows his heart.

Know where your heart is. Follow your heart rather than your head. Experience who you really are.

EMOTIONAL PREPARATION FOR THE DANCE OF LIFE

Adorned with our regalia, we dance with the colors of our emotions. Our emotions must be honored.

Our emotions are signs to guide us, warn us, and help us celebrate. Although oftentimes deemed positive or negative, emotions simply exist. "What is, is," echoes the wisdom of the Navajo. Accept your emotions for what they are— reminders, helpers, and indicators. Your emotions are the smoke signals of your internal spiritual fire. Pay attention to the signals you are given. Listen to the pain or the joy. Heed their warning. Thank them for their help.

Identify and Care For Your Emotions

Learn to identify your emotional status. In this way, you are able to respond appropriately to what your emotions are telling you. You will be able to recognize patterns that lead to inevitable behaviors. You will be able to intercept these behavior patterns if they are undesirable. You will be able to predict

---

[9]   Pronounced: mash-KOW-sin, and refers to inner-strength. More can be read about Mash-ka-wisen in Listen to the Drum and The Healing Drum.

responses and find ways to change the course they tend to take you. You will be able to change your reactions to responses, your insanity to sanity, your aggression to assertiveness, your passivity to courage, your consequences to deliberate choices.

What do you do when you cut your finger? Think about it. Do you automatically lick your wound? Do you run cool water over it to help it heal? Do you gently compress it? Instinctively, all animals take care of physical wounds. And we are animals. Likewise, we need to take care of our emotional wounds. We need to gently lick them clean and be sure they heal. If we ignore them, they fester, and then we have a bigger problem which, incidentally, still requires healing.

Reflect periodically throughout day. See clearly who you are, what you are experiencing. Like Brother Eagle, preen your emotional feathers throughout the day. They are the feathers that help you fly to greater heights.

Acknowledge Your Growth

Once you have come to the total honesty that exists inside you, please stand up. Place your hands at the height of how tall you feel you are *inside*. How tall do you feel emotionally? How tall do feel psychologically? *How big are you inside?* Take time, now, and determine this. Be honest in this discovery. Totally honest. This will only be as accurate as you are honest.

This examination measures your self-esteem, feelings of adequacy, your degree of insecurity or security, sufficiency, and self worth. Some people will be up to their knees, some to their waist, their shoulders, or their nose. Some people are up to their heads. You can tell by the comfort you feel in their presence. If you are uncomfortable in someone's presence, ask yourself if it is your insecurities you are sensing or their insecurities displaced onto you. If you can say you are as tall psychologically and emotionally as you are physiologically, you are congruent.

Today, many people are not congruent because they have not been taught, as tribal people once were, how to become and remain in balance. As you grow spiritually, emotionally, physically, mentally, at work, and play, 50%

inner focused, 50% outer focused, 90% in the present, 5% in the past, and 5% in the future, you become your own point of reference, able to validate yourself. Your self-esteem will rise to the configuration of your body. If your measurement exceeds your height, you are now going in an egocentric, narcissistic direction. In that event, I suggest you practice humility which is the antidote to arrogance.

Self-esteem cannot be verified by others. You are worthy and sufficient because you say you are worthy and sufficient. If you depend on others' opinions of you then it is "other-esteem" and "other-worth" rather than a self validation of your esteem and worth. If you are secure with yourself, you have no need or desire for other people to be like you, for you understand that that would deplete them of their own uniqueness. Our differences make us each special.

Love and Become

How can Leaf grow if he is not attached to his tree? How can Bee produce honey, if she has no hive? How can Volcano erupt if he has never been inside Earth Mother?

What value would you attribute to your love? If you can't give love how can you open up to receive it? If you consider yourself to be unworthy or unlovable as a person, then giving love becomes impossible. Become rooted, return home and connect to the Great Love Source.

Self acceptance means liking and respecting your physical self. Have positive regard for your natural physical state of being and recognize yourself as a masterpiece of the Creator's work.

By virtue of culture, many people, especially women, fall victim to the dictate of society and respond with behaviors that the culture expects from their bodies: They shave, deodorize, perfume, use lipstick, eyeliner, rouge, fake fingernails, opt for liposuction, breast augmentation, and color their hair. The fallacy is that their natural self is insufficient and unpleasant, that only an artificial self is attractive. The only time they become their natural self is in the safety of seclusion.

How could you ever know if you are acceptable and loved for who you really are, if you never have the courage to present your real and honored self to another person?

If you wish you had a different body, rediscover the gifts your body has given you and strengthen its strengths. This thought automatically weakens the power of the weaknesses. When you see others as better, smarter, stronger, more beautiful than you, remember we are all waves of the same ocean. Some days the wave is big, some days it is small. Surf the wave you are given today and experience the rolling heights it offers. Validate your self, your abilities, your gifts, your understandings. Validate your uniqueness.

The need for approval is based on the false assumption that you cannot validate yourself. Don't allow your worth to be held in other's hands. My dad used to say that life is overcoming resistance. Like a salmon swimming up stream, internal resistance challenges us to move against our fears and doubts. You can experience the same challenges with a positive focus or a negative focus. Find the positive and build on that. It will snowball into greater celebration. Hear this story of internal celebration.

BLUE HORSE

One summer day, Blue Horse ran down to the river, angry at himself for having lost the race. "Everyone was watching," he thought, still feeling the heat on his face. Blue Horse sat down at the shore and threw in some stones, trying to make as big a splash as possible. "The splashes must be bigger! I can make them bigger!" he thought. Bent on throwing handfuls of stones, Blue Horse suddenly noticed a brood of ducklings coasting off the shoreline, directly in the line of Blue Horse's anger. As most ducklings do, they began swimming up the river together, dependent upon the security of each other. But as splashes from Blue Horse's anger reached them, the ducklings veered off as one body. Trying to become ducks, the ducklings would teach Blue Horse a lesson about inner victory that day.

Blue Horse watched as the ducklings paddled their legs like crazy. It was all in vain, he noticed. The current they were swimming against was very strong. Nonetheless, it was clear to the boy that the ducklings needed to get "there," to the other side of the river. For what? he did not know, but he soon became curious about the race the little ones were swimming. Chaotically, they paddled, bumping into one another, the current obviously too strong for their tiny legs. Catching himself laughing at their silly insistence, Blue Horse forgot his anger.

Continuing to watch, Blue Horse noticed there was one duck of another mind. Like the others, this duckling began as part of the brood, swimming up the river with her sisters and brothers. However, once this duckling reached the swift moving current she noticed a rock sticking out of the water, pushed herself up on it, and rested. Basking in the sunshine, preening her feathers and watching the hopeless paddling of her sisters and brothers, Duckling became Duck.

The other ducklings finally floated backwards and got out of the water where they had begun the race of no importance, never making it to the other side.

The boy shifted his own understanding as he became humble enough to learn from Duck. Duck accepted the fate of the moving water. Duck found a harbor of peace in the fast concerns of the day. Blue Horse saw how Duckling raised her own feathers of understanding to become Duck.

Standing up, Blue Horse stopped long enough to hear the babbling river. He felt the tears drying on his dirt-streaked face. He remembered the race once more, but this time he felt the gentle wind. The young man set the rest of the stones down at his feet and ran off to join another game.

Which duck are you?

Many people, like the paddling ducklings, are externally motivated. They obsess about the triumph of the "other side" and material success, and will try in vain to reach it. Forgetting about internal success, they lose the race. Yet some people have found the sweet secret, as the duckling did, and are internally motivated. They realize there is only so much one can realistically do. They are able to let the rushing concerns of the day pass them by. They are able to make the most of their circumstances and win internally.

Work at becoming internally strong. Find the tranquillity inside to give you this strength. Then tap it and become. It will not matter, then, what passes you by, for you will not allow your Self to pass you by.

Rediscover the path to Self Celebration. It is not so difficult to follow. You are now at the deep pool of coming to self. Look at the reflection of you. Discover the values you cherish, the emotions that govern you, the behaviors you can change. Decide to take the journey down the untrodden path with only your Self as company. Befriend your Self and enjoy your gifts. Beyond the climb, find a waterfall of acceptance. Let its' spray blend in with your tears, and heal. Accept yourself for who you are, now. Refreshed, run through the fields of your Spirit. Value your unique fragrance, your special growth, your beautiful budding, your connection to the Spirit World. Value your Self.

Once you have experienced this self-respect, you are ready to become as you are meant to be. Give your Self permission to dive into the River of Life, where currents will take you where they must, where Life will change as you change. Then love your Self. Love what you've become through the discipline of swimming (internally) upstream as well as pausing to rest and celebrating in the light of the Great Mystery. Celebrate the arrival onto the shore of Self. Celebrate your successes and your failures. For both have helped you become.

SPIRITUAL PREPARATION FOR THE DANCE OF LIFE

To prepare and put on one's regalia is a spiritual ritual. Inside the moment, we become keenly aware of all that we are: our values, our emotions, our uniqueness, our entire being. Having listened well, we know our inner world, our internal mazes and caves. We put on our regalia with love for our Self and the Spirit World.

The connection to the Spirit World is one that must be nurtured. It is a link in which spiritual instinct guides us. It is developed with disciplined connection.

Find and develop your connection to the Great Mystery. Prepare for the Celebration of Life, the Celebration of Self. To honor your Self, you must first know where to look.

Find Where You Are

Native people have long understood the wisdom of coming to Center, to Self. They knew where to look and how to develop a heightened sense of awareness. They understood where the Great Mystery abides. The following exercise will show you this path.

Where are you right now? Notice your breath. Where is it? Don't change it. Just notice it. Look inside you. Where is it? Is your breath in your diaphragm? Your lungs? Is it in your back? Your throat? Your stomach? Wherever your breath is, that is where you are. Now lower your breath to your navel. Practice breathing to this center. Consciously bring your breath to this calm place. Soon, it will become automatic, for that is its home, that is where it is intended to go.

The Gift Of Life

Your breath is the gift of life. As such, it will take you to your center, where one truly lives. This is Ain-dah-ing[10]. This is the place of peace. The place where creativity flows. The place of union between Self and the Spirit World. Like

---

[10] Pronounced: AH-da-ning. This is the Anishinaabe word for home. It is referred to as the 'home within our heart.' Greater explanation of this concept can be found in *Listen to the Drum* and *The Healing Drum*.

the fern used to fan the campfire's dying embers, your breath will fan your spiritual flame. Allow your breath to give your Spirit this consuming connection.

So obvious, yet so hidden, the power of the breath continues us. And like the great Wind Spirits, our breath can lift us to heights never reached, views never seen, notes never heard, love never felt before. The Great Mystery awaits where it initiated us... in the gifting of our breath. Return to the source —to your breath—and you will return home, to Ain-dah-ing. No matter where you are on your life trail, no matter what condition your body is in, no matter your age, your intelligence, or your needs, the Breath of Life is for all to celebrate. The breath is the great connector. All people, all of Life, connect through this Gift of Life, as our breath is mingled by the West and East Winds. Our breath is shared with all animals and plants to be re-used, re-honored, re-celebrated again and again.

The discipline of deep-breathing and spiritual connection is the key to life. Practice this. Acquaint yourself with this. Like indigenous people around the world, practice proper breathing techniques and deep breathing exercises.

Breathe Properly

First, learn to breathe properly. Close your lips. Seal them so that you are breathing solely through your nostrils. The old way for Native American mothers was to watch their children carefully to ensure they were breathing through their nose. If the child breathed through the mouth, the mother would pinch the lips together until the child breathed easily and naturally through the nose. If this did not work, the mother would take buckskin and bandaging under the chin around to the crown of the head, so the jaws would be forced together. Covering the lips with another piece of buckskin, the habit of nasal breathing was formed.

The nose is meant to trap germs that would try to invade your body. Let your nose keep your insides clean. Be conscious of closing your lips as you breath. Practice this, until it has become habit for you, as well.

Deep Breathing

For Native people, running great distances was required in order to develop a lung capacity as a source of health, energy, power, and vitality. It was common for boys to run ten, fifteen, or twenty miles on a regular basis in order to develop their lungs. As part of their spiritual training, the connection between breathing and the Spirit World was obvious to Native people. Today, this aspect to training body and spirit can be achieved through vigorous exercise.

Native people understood that deep and rapid breathing rid the body of poisonous gases and replaced it with a fresh supply of oxygen. They knew that challenging the body and the deep breathing which accompanied it, pumped the blood within the organs below the diaphragm and strengthened them, just as their legs were strengthened from daily discipline.

When I run with my German shepherd, I remind myself of these medicinal benefits, of the exchange that is taking place. Always, Mying's effortless enjoyment of the run inspires me to continue and even moves me into forgetting the work involved. Visualize yourself as the fire with a greater access of air supply. Your life can be lived more fully with more intensity. Make a commitment to yourself to exercise regularly. Swim, climb, hike, run, ride a bike! Give your respiratory muscles the opportunity to do what they are intended to do. Find ways to breathe deeply, naturally. Exercise your muscles and you honor yourself. Not only will your lung capacity improve, you will expand your capacity for living fully.

Deep Breathing Exercise

No matter your physical condition, there are simple deep breathing exercises that you can do. Begin by standing with your legs spread comfortably under the width of your waist. Once you have determined the stance that is comfortable and holds you up naturally, locate your breath. Discover its cycles. Discover its effortlessness. Be sure you are breathing through your nose. Relax into this knowing for a few moments.

Once you are relaxed and your breath is natural, you are ready to begin. Make sure your back is relaxed and straight. Allow the structure of your legs to hold you. Remain balanced, your arms resting easily at your side. Bending your knees slightly, allow your weight to drain into the earth below you, lowering your center. As you gradually lower, gradually exhale. Let out the last of your breath as you reach your lowest position.

As you gradually inhale, gradually straighten your knees so that you resume your starting position. Allow your breath to enter into your center, letting your diaphragm expand, stretching the walls of your lungs. Visualize your breath pouring into your Center.

Do this cycle until it has become easily repetitive.

Now, use your arms. As before, lower and raise your body with the inhalation and exhalation of your breath. This time, however, begin with your elbows bent, at your side, the weight of your arms resting in your elbows. Your palms face down, your forearms extending outward. Hands hover out and above your center, distanced about that of your stance. As you lower, allow your arms and hands to lower along with your center. Reaching your lowest position, turn your hands inward, so that the palms are now facing each other. Like scooping up some water, allow your hands to turn over so that now the palms are facing up. Rising to your original starting position, lift the invisible water to the height of your chest cavity, inhaling the good breath into your center. Upon reaching the height of the inhalation, turn your palms downward, letting the water fall. Repeat this procedure, lowering, dumping, scooping up the water, exhaling the breath...to rise again, lift the water, and inhale into your center.

Deep breathing is a way to slow down to Self and plug into the spiritual reservoir of life and energy. From these simple, yet effective exercises, a spiritual wellspring is available to you.

Spiritual transcendence is not reserved for the chosen few. The Breath of Life is an offering for all—it offers spiritual strength, deliverance, and joy to all who accept. It is free. It is freeing. It is the access to spiritual freedom.

Spiritual Freedom

Spiritual freedom is the highest of all Life experiences. It does not take into account your status or your circumstance. It transcends all ties to this world, yet offers gifts to be used while living in this world. You come to see the spiritual in the commonplace. The beauty in the moment.

Spiritual freedom is the understanding that spiritual experiences are accessible to you at every moment. Don't limit Self. Open up to the unlimited. Some people go to religious functions waiting for a spiritual connection to "happen" there. Although the gathering of sincere hearts is a powerful spiritual opportunity, bountiful connections and unlimited opportunities to experience spiritual freedom can be found everywhere, anytime, to anyone.

Spiritual experiences surround you in nature. Acknowledge nature's moments and your spiritual experience will change with each moment. As you develop personal relationships with nature, your spiritual condition remains fluid and alive. Rather than hoping for an idea to move you, connect to the world and allow the vibration of the universe to flow through you. Become the conduit for spiritual experiences and understandings. This is the spiritual freedom that will lift you to the heights of Ishpeming.

Other benefits will permeate your life beyond the joy that spiritual experiences give you. One gift of spiritual freedom is soft focus. Soft focus is the ability to relax your view of life both around you and in you. A way to understand this view is to concentrate very deliberately and intensely on something within your environment.

Begin with something outside yourself. Select an object within your view and concentrate on it. Stay with it for a few minutes. Intensify your concentration. Notice the tension. Notice the limits you have placed on yourself as you focus on one thing. Now relax your eyes. Notice your peripheral vision. Notice the calming inside. Soften your vision and see around you. Gaze into a candle's flame and experience your focus changing from hard to soft.

Now, focus on something within you. It may be a tense muscle, an emotion, or a thought. Concentrate on that single aspect with your total being. Intensify your concentration. Stay with it for a few minutes. Now relax your inner eye. Notice how you suddenly become aware of things that radiate outward from that spot. Notice how its importance melts proportionately into everything else. Practice this way of world viewing. Whether it is your inner world or the outer world, decide how you will see it, or if you will see it. You may have a pounding headache, then someone yells, "Fire!" Suddenly, you are no longer aware of your headache, and your mind looks instead for the fire.

As you practice deep breathing exercises, learn to soften your focus on your breath. Allow your breath to breathe you. In this way, you are free to experience the depths of yourself and join the spiritual realm.

Soft focus is global. Soft focus is neither positive nor negative. It just is. Soft focus is accepting of life circumstances. With this focus, you are spiritually free to see alternatives and solutions. Soft focus will help you visualize your position in the universe and accent your importance as a needed, functional part of an infinite consciousness and existence.

Viktor Frankl spoke to this revelation. As a Jewish psychiatrist who was a prisoner in the Nazi death camps in World War II, he tasted the nectar of spiritual freedom. Survivors of such circumstances understand spiritual freedom. It is a union of Self with the harmony of the Universe. Meaning was born in the death camps of Auschwitz. The prisoners found that love survived death. They could see the beauty in the setting sun and the light in the darkness. Spiritually free, these prisoners triumphed over dire conditions. By saying "yes" to Life, they connected to the All of Life and understood their experience as vital to their Self.

Give yourself a gift today. Gift yourself the freedom to experience the Spirit World, personally. Go outside and find the beauty of your surroundings. Discover the lessons Earth Mother waits to give. Relax and connect to something in nature, recognize the Great Hoop of which it is part. Come to see that you journey this life together. Befriend the world and you will experience the joy of Eagle's flight.

Choose to partake in this nourishment. It will sustain you in times of need. Your spiritual development will gift you the freedom to soar, even in difficult situations.

TO BUTTERFLY WOMAN

She followed Moonlight
To find her path.
She listened to Music-makers
To hear her heart.

But she could not hear.
She could not see.

She walked the stretch of sand
To see where she had come.
She climbed mountain changes
To change herself.

But she could not remember.
She could not change.

She followed bee's circles
To join their understanding.
She dove into cold waters
To awaken her breath.

But it was too cold, too fast.
She could not join.

Then walking amidst the darkness
She saw her shadow,
Following her,
Mirroring her,
Blinding her.

So she stopped,
Reflecting in,
Looking out,
She simply sat.

On wings they came
Discovering her,
Joining her,
Circling her.

Butterflies fluttered about her.

Changing her.

Remembering her.
Seeing her.
Hearing her.

Resting.
They rested with her.
Opening.
They opened to her.[11]

---

[11] This poem is to honor a woman I met. Sitting in the teaching lodge, butterflies entered, circled and
rested upon her. I watched as she taught the tiny-tot children to sit still and speak with their hearts
in order to invite the butterflies in.

LET YOUR BELLS JINGLE AND COMMUNICATE AS "WE"

For thousands of years, Native people knew themselves completely and communicated effectively with themselves and others. If we can't communicate with Self, how can we possibly expect to communicate with someone else? Learn to listen to what your entire self is saying: your emotions, your spirit, your mind, your body. Then sound your celebration. Like the bells and jingles sewn on regalia to invite the spirits in to join the dance, dance with the Spirit World as you celebrate. Attach to your own Self-Celebration.

Live in an internally, rather than externally, controlled world. If you are not in charge of your thoughts, then who is? If you don't control your emotions, then who does? Every emotion that you have ever experienced has evolved from a thought. If you take charge of your thoughts, you take charge of your feelings. Your happiness or misery depends on your thoughts. You go where your head goes.

Why choose misery over happiness if both are available to us? You are responsible for your feelings, not someone else. Learn to be happy. Lead your mind and your center to the light places. Learn to talk to yourself in a way that produces self-health, rather than self-destruction. You can learn to make almost any experience a self-fulfilling event. Use your mind to work *for you* in a positive direction. Your mind tells your body and emotions what to do, so make sure your instructions are productive rather than destructive. In order to take full control of your thoughts, you'll need to remind yourself constantly that you are the sole owner of your thoughts.

Talk to your Self as "We." Listen to your Self as "We." Communicate with your internal team. Recognize that your entire being has separate needs and functions.

Listen to your body and its craving to be exercised.
Listen to your mind and its need for reflection.
Listen to your emotions and their aching to be heard.
Listen to your spirit and its thirst to connect to the invisible.

What do your body, mind, emotions, and spirit say? Do they tell you to exercise? Read? Pray? Cry? Stretch? Laugh? Go to the doctor? Sleep? Eat? Listen? Hug your child? Heal? Whatever it is they are telling you, listen. They speak to you and request attention, affection, recognition, and approval that you seek from your consciousness and others. If you listen to their requests and honor them, what do you suppose they would do for you in return? Honor them, and they will honor you.

When was the last time you got a massage? Meditated in the woods? Laughed until your sides ached? Took a relaxing warm bath? Listened to your child? Ate nutritiously? Inhaled fresh healing oxygen? Floated on the water? Said no? Took a stand? If you want your body, mind, emotions, and spirit to take care of you, you need to take care of them.

Can you contemplate? Can you come to the mind's eye, the place of observance between your eyebrows, just above your nose, from where you have a bird's eye advantage of Self and your circumstance?

Take the time to slow down to Self, develop soft focus and listen to your drum. Inside the silence you will be able to see around you. Picture yourself above, able to view you, your environment, the people and things you interact with. With this global view, you will be able to see further out, recognizing the consequences of your actions. This window to Self will give you an aerial photo of your profile and what adjustments you must make to come into balance. Like adjusting a binocular's focus until the figure and the background come together, our real and "ideal" Self can merge into focus. We must use our mind's eye to become and stay integrated. Our mind's eye is to our inner self-concept, as our conscience is to our value system.

When you practice deep breathing, you bring your body fresh, healing, tranquilizing oxygen. Find the inner center of control where you can experience peace. Here you can simultaneously come to many decision making processes. From here you can "respond" to your outer world circumstance, rather than "react" to it. Here, you can talk to your Self as "We." Here is where you can go when you have intercepted your emotional signals. Drop your center of consciousness to the experiential realm, just as the blue heron drops its center of gravity onto one leg as it scouts its water-world for fish.

Practice returning to Ain-dah-ing by breathing into your center. As you breathe, allow your thoughts to dissolve. As emotions cloud your thinking, drop to your emotional center. This is the place of peace. Rehearse this journey and you will know your way there, even in the darkest moments. When your emotions are in this calm place, your mind will be clear, also. When your mind is clear, your emotions are calm. Here, your entire Self will be attended to.

THE COLOR OF THE SEVENTH DIRECTION

I was walking through an autumn woods when I recognized my color. All around me was gold. Golden dried grasses and ferns. Golden leaves. Golden sand. In a circle I turned, soaking up the feeling it gave me. As though I was at the center of all the golden hues around me, I felt fully complete and balanced. My breathing was slow and deep. My emotions were as calm as the resting of the woods. It was a powerful moment. Like seeing myself in the mirror for the first time, I saw the color of my Seventh Direction clearly. The internal recognition and celebration filled me with unspeakable joy!

Since then, I have seen the power of my color. I have remembered the dreams I have had in which I stood in a room full of rich golden hues. I have noticed another picking out that particular color for me. I have remembered words of songs that touched me intimately as golden colors were evoked in me. I now recognize the feeling of completion, whenever that color unexpectedly turns up.

Like my Seventh Direction, all the Directions are represented by a color.

The color to the East is Yellow. Like the first rays of morning sun, East brings the new light of innocence. It is the filling of the night container. It is birth, the Spring of the year. It is the explosion and creation of life from the darkness. The is from the is not. The something from the nothing. This is the source of all knowledge. East is the beginning of our Sun Trail[12].

---

[12] The journey we take in this life to complete the hoop. Beginning in the East of birth and ending in the West of death, the Sun Trail is a celebration of the life we are gifted.

Next is <u>South</u>, the color Red, the color of Earth Mother. South represents summer and adolescence. Like the birds who go south to bring back seeds to scatter to the Four Directions, life is replenished over the Earth with this Direction and growth is abundant.

<u>West</u> is represented by the color Black. Our Sun Trail takes us to this direction and expresses the place of the Spirit World. As we go deep into the cavern of Self, we grow into adulthood. This is the direction of knowledge where we bundle the wisdom we have collected along our life. We should not be afraid of this direction, as it represents the completion of the life cycle.

The color of <u>North</u> is White. Spirits dance in the Northern sky, teaching us how both light and darkness simultaneously emanate from the same essence, that they are complementary, one in each other. These Northern Lights endlessly empty and fill one another, producing a glorious mystery of separation and connection. As the accumulation of all colors, it is consuming and solidifying. It is a time when our Elders wear the white crown of Elder enlightenment. From this suspended state of consciousness, flow the eternal waters of the Spiritual river of life, the spring waters of new vitality. It is the direction of the Bear, the medicinal healing for our people. From the North all will be renewed.

Some say these four colors—Yellow, Red, Black, and White, represent the four races of man. They teach us that we need to learn to live in harmony.

Next, is green. Green is the color of Earth Mother. We are asked to go in, to this fifth direction, reminding us that Earth Mother nurtures our growth and provides all things necessary for life. She is our connection to life.

The sixth direction is Blue. Blue is for Sky Father, the place of the Star World. Sky Father reminds us of our sacred place in the Universe. This direction connects our present life with the world which we are moving out toward.

The color of the Seventh Direction is you. It is all of you. It is the gentle balancing of all aspects: physical, mental, emotional and spiritual. You are the hoop of life that intersects eternity. Discover the color of yourself, the color that best represents who you are. Your life path links on the Eternal Hoop.

At Powwow, we beautifully represent ourselves, in the now. I invite you to listen in to my silence. Listen in to my choice. See my color. It is the choice of my direction. Here is my preparation for Life's Dance of Powwow.

THE PREPARATION

Inside my quieted skin, I open my regalia case and am ready to open to my Self. I look inside and can hardly wait for the dance to begin! The Celebration is at hand!

My moccasins come out first, for I must secure my footing before anything else. Unraveling the ties, I understand that as the roots bind the forests together, so must our feet and energies root into Earth Mother and bind us to Her energies and nourishment. I think of the tenderness of dancing on Earth Mother's back as I slip into the comfort of my moccasins. I know that occasionally I will step on a Mishomis[13] stone on the Powwow grounds and my fortitude will be tested. I am grateful for the discomfort, for it will lead me to tolerance.

I find my bells and know the Spirits enjoy bell vibrations. My bells will call in the Spirits from the six external directions and stimulate my own spirit—from my seventh internal direction. I fasten the bells' leather strings around my ankles and the jingling begins. I look forward to joining the jingling of the bells as we invite the Spirits into the Powwow Circle[14]. I hear how my bells will salute the Veteran Eagle Staff and Flag Bearers as their names are announced and they post their staff and colors during the Grand Entry.

---

[13] Pronounced: mi-SHOO-mis. Means Grandfather in the Ojibwe language. It is also a term for the spiritual healing stone.

[14] There is an old saying, "Invite the evil spirits to Powwow, so you can keep your eye on them." Occasionally, you will see a dancer, dancing counterclockwise on the perimeter of the Powwow circle. This is usually a warrior dancer who is keeping any evil spirits out of the dance circle proper.

Next, I put on my front and back cloths on which I have
sewn special insignias, meaningful to me. I put on the
megis shell belt that symbolizes the Ojibwe[15] origin story. It
is the story of how Gitchi Manidoo[16] took four parts of
Earth Mother and blew into them using the megis shell. I
straighten the belt and honor the different tribes and their
different origin stories. I remember Elders saying that there
are many roads to the High Place, that all rivers lead to the
same ocean. No one road is better than another. I shift the
belt to the right spot, knowing the Elders are very clear
with these words.

I put on another belt from which my kinnikinnick[17] pouch
hangs. Inside I am already celebrating, knowing soon I will
put this strong medicine down on Earth Mother as I dance
the Circle of Celebration. I will carry this medicine in my left
hand, because it is closer to my heart.

I jingle as I reach in my case to find another bag. It is my
personal Medicine Bag. In it I keep articles to give me mental, emotional, physical and spiritual fortitude. I look inside
and touch the objects. Pausing, I connect and gain strength
with their spiritual energies. I know I will need this Mash-ka-
wisen, as I will dance for many hours.

I adjust the two belts, one of shell and one of leather, that
cover and protect my emotional vulnerability. I am pleased
my mid-section is embellished with medicines to honor
Earth Mother and deflect negative attitudes. I am certain

---

[15] Pronounced: O-jib-wa. Known variously as the Anishinaabe, Chippewa, Ojibway, Chippeway,
Otchipwe, and refers to the large tribal nation residing in upper midwestern states and a large
section of Canada.

[16] Pronounced: GI-chi MON-ee-doo. Means Great Spirit.

[17] Pronounced: KIN-ee-kin-ik and means "much mixed." It is a tobacco based mixture accompanied by
other herbs, primarily, cedar, balsam fir, sweet grass, calamus root, sweet non-fern, sweet gale and
mints. Other mixtures may include bear berry, sweet goldenrod, rose petals, sage, willow bark, red
ooshier bark, sweet clover yarrow and tobacco. Kinnikinnick is used in Native American sacred
ceremonies.

they will encourage positive interaction, both socially and spiritually. The megis shell represents the Spirit World and when Earth Mother was new. The leather belt symbolizes the Physical World and my dependence on our Mother. This reminds me to keep a foot in each dimension.

I put on my breast plate to deflect negative energies which may be approaching my heart area and don my choker of black buffalo bone, whose metal shield is engraved with a black wolf. The choker not only protects my throat, it reminds me that what I say is very important and has long lasting effect. In my heart, I hear Elders say, "Our tongue is to speak with when we know what to say and how to say it, and our teeth are to keep our tongue in our mouth till we figure that out."

The arm bands come next, to honor and respect the warriors who upheld tribal sovereignty with their life and limb. This moment of silence is for them.

The coyote skin now goes over my head and down my back. I marvel at how the coyote has the ability to adapt to any given environment. I think of Los Angeles and the many coyotes that inhabit this city. As the cities have encroached on Brother Coyote's land, Brother has learned to maneuver his way through the maze, continuing to survive and flourish. This is what I need to learn from Brother Coyote, I think now, how to adapt and adjust to Life circumstance. I need to flourish where I am planted, by being flexible and resourceful, by being soft focused and seeing the opportunities within every adversity. I know Brother Coyote speaks these lessons to all who accompany him as he dances on my back in the celebration of Life's Powwow Circle.

I adjust the top of Coyote's head and touch the four Sacred Eagle Feathers. One for each direction. The Eagle Spirit holds the highest part of Brother Coyotes' and my anatomy. I think of how Eagle has nothing between His spirit and the Great Spirit. I must learn from Eagle.

Now I am in harmony: spiritually, mentally, physically and emotionally from head to foot.

In my right hand, I cool myself with my wing fan and I know I will soon hold it high to salute the Eagle Staffs and Drum Beat Recognition. Together, we will honor the Spirit World. In my left hand, I prepare to dance with an Apache pipe tomahawk. Feeling its weight, I discern its purpose: it can be smoked for peace and healing, or it can be turned to repel a hostile attack. There are always two sides, two possibilities in Life, I think.

I look down at the pipe I carry. Its four beads catch my eye: yellow, red, black and white. I think of what it represents, the four directions and the four races. One final look in the mirror and I know I am ready to enter Powwow together with all who will dance. Mitakuye-Oyasin[18]—we are all related, and we all dance and celebrate Life together!

The Seventh Direction is all of who you are. Like the sparrow that only knows sparrow, only you know who you are. The Seventh Direction is you. The you of today. The possibilities of tomorrow. It is you, now. Join the celebration of life and celebrate your Self. Prepare your own regalia. Prepare your Self. That is your privilege. That is your obligation. That is your right. That is your gift.

---

[18] Pronounced: mi-TAHK-wee-a-say or mi-TAHK-wee-es. Means 'we are all related.'

GRAND ENTRY

They dance with me now.

Grandpa's among the bustles,
Dancing proudly like no other.
I see him.
He dances with me now.

And in the jingle dresses' jingle
I hear the laughter of my Mother.
I hear her.
She dances with me now.

I often feel Brother's Spirit sway
In grasses I pass by.
I touch him.
He dances with me now.

While Sister's colors dance again
In the colors of the sky.
I remember.
She dances with me now.

People are truly celebrated for their uniqueness only two times in life ... at birth and at death. At the coming and the going, our Spirit is given honor and respect. It is good. Honor is due. We must respect the moments of life and death. As active spiritual participants, this acknowledgment does matter; it is experienced. Yet, few people will experience such high regard for Self in between these two beginnings.

Tribal people have long recognized that just as our Grand Entry into both the Physical World and the Spirit World is celebrated, a like-celebration needs to take place, here and now, for the uniqueness of Self. We enter new experiences every day. We touch new possibilities. We travel new paths. Every day we need to celebrate our arrival to the new day that we are given.

Powwow is the celebration of Life. Powwow celebrates the Grand Entry of each moment. It is the Grand Entry of Earth Mother. It is the Grand Entry of her children. It is the Grand Entry of Self into a new moment. It is a celebration of uniqueness, of becoming, of living.

Grand Entry begins when it is ready to begin. Indian Time is circular. Past, present and future are cycles of reality, with no beginning and no end. Time is indivisible. You cannot cut liquid water with a knife and you cannot separate time with a second hand. Time is fluid. You are never late nor early within Indian Time, because you cannot divide it. Things begin when things are ready to begin.

Look to the flower. It blooms in its own time and season, not when it is told to. The flower blooms with the Heart of the Giver, not from the mind of the receiver. Look to the fly as it, too, teaches us Indian Time. Its bulging eyes give it circular, 360 degree vision. This is the vision of the Creator. The vision of past, present, and future come into one full eternal circle. This vision is soft focus. Soft focus is the circular vision of the internal eye allowing us to view all at once. The Sacred Hoop[1] honors the seasons of your Self. Remember this when you enter your own moment, your personal celebration. You can not be late, nor early, for the Celebration of your Self.

ALL IS READY

The Grand Entry opens each Powwow celebration. With great anticipation, dance regalia in place, and with all aspects of their being in balance, partici-

---

[1]   The Sacred Hoop is the symbol of our journey in this life, as well as our connection to the Spirit World. It also illustrates the cycle of all things.

pants line up to the rightful place that the Creator has reserved especially for each dancer. Then they wait for their moment.

All stand for this special ceremony. Dancers and spectators recognize that both the unity and sovereignty of Indian people are joyously declared as the Grand Entry opens.

The Eagle Staff is lifted.

The raised staff symbolizes and acclaims Indian people. Made out of sacred cedar, the feather staff signifies the unity of the Indian World. Veterans have carried the Eagle Staffs to the edge of the empty Circle and are honored now as they lead this magnificent dance. The dance is ready to begin. The drum beats. One high-pitched voice announces the song to the rest of the singers. Then these voices amplify the opening phrase, singing the dignified sweeping melody.

In unison, the veterans recognize the beat of entrance and the crooked staff pierces the open space and honors Earth Mother with its wrapped fur and cloth. Prayers are lifted to the Great Spirit with the hung Eagle feathers. The way is prepared for the dancers, as the Eagle Staff is carried in and begins a clockwise path of Namaji[2]. All prayers will be heard. All spirits invited. All hearts and minds as One.

More veterans are honored as the U.S., Canadian, P.O.W., M.I.A., and other military flags, are carried in next. The veterans of military service and their flags remind us of great sacrifice, of great service, of great loyalty, of great Mitakuye-Oyasin. They remind us of our ancestors and their gifting. We honor them at this moment.

The open circle, the dancing arbor, begins to experience filling. Its outside ring has filled with people of all colors and cultures[3]. The drums, at the eye of the circle, are shaded by Grandfather Sun as tree boughs lace an over-

---

[2]   Some dances of some tribes go counterclockwise to welcome a visiting nation, etc. Indians go "with the flow" wherever they dance and honor the traditions and customs of the dance they attend.

[3]   The dance circle may be surrounded by bleachers, lawn chairs or seats of some sort. Often this resting place for dancers and spectators is shaded with cut tree boughs lacing an overhead framework. My favorite is the natural seating made by Earth Mother herself, such as raised Earth or an amphitheater-like environment. The Powwow celebration invites all people to learn more about these traditions. With understanding comes acceptance and unity and dispels fear of the unknown.

head circular wooden frame. Four entrances mark the four directions as yellow, red, black and white ties have been fastened earlier to each entrance pole, and become invitations for the dancers to dance. But at Grand Entry, all must enter from one direction, just as we all enter Life from the same direction. Grand Entry is an entrance of One.

Head (lead) dancers follow our veterans and flags. A male and female dancer are honored for their distinctive person and knowledge. They lead all dances. The community looks to them as honored guests. We naturally bestow the head dancers with Namaji, for we celebrate their integral role. They honor us with their presence.

Royalty follow these honored ones. Royalty are young women who have been highly judged for their communication skills[4], knowledge of culture and customs, talent and poise. As with past generations, these values are regarded highly and are deeply prized. With their beaded crowns and titles embroidered on sashes and shawls, the girls of varying ages enter the Dance Circle proudly and remind us that we must honor who we are. They dance with the energy of youth and their dance-style carries their tribal traditions. With their presence they ensure tribal wisdom continues.

Male traditional dancers enter next[5]. A dramatic, stately dance fills the growing circle, as these older dancers imitate the movements of animals or move in a crouched position as though they are hunting or tracking. In addition to bells, hairpieces, chokers, and breast plates, they may wear animal skins or a traditional bustle tied to their lower back[6]. They traditionally carry decorated fans, weapons, staffs, fur wrapped rings, or other items meaningful to them. Their dance is a reminder of the past, of survival, of honor for our relatives. They tell a story about where we came from. With their dancing, Earth Mother's children are thanked for their gifts.

---

[4] The oral tradition of Native people remains a central cultural adhesive. Tribal tongue, stories, lessons, history and sacred truths depend on the continuance of this tradition. Recently, there has been an upsurge in language acquisition and all oral traditions. As old age wisdom taught, one's "word" is to be treated as truth. In native tongues, there is only one meaning for each word and it is, therefore, a concrete language and cannot have misinterpretations. The European language system and the emphasis upon "written" language as superior, created and still creates, critical problems, politically and culturally.

[5] Elders are often among their ranks.

[6] These bustles are made of hawk or eagle feathers.

Next to enter are the male fancy dancers. They are ignited with vibrant movement, color, strength, and endurance. Their fast style of dancing ignites our own heartbeat. Twirling and spinning, their fancy footwork follows the fast rhythm of the drum and is simply stunning! Two bustles are worn, one at the shoulders and the other at the lower back[7], linking them to the traditional dancers, to the past. Their acrobatic movements touch the invisible and link them to the future, showing us all things are possible.

Male grass dancers enter, and the yarn-fringes cascading from their shoulders, waist, and legs, appear like waterfalls of color[8]. Based on an old war-society dance of the northern plains, the grass dance is another fast step dance in which the dancer spins, twirls, steps, and then appears to almost lose his balance....only to spin, twirl, and step again. Weaving and dipping, their dancing becomes the high grasses swaying in the wind. We listen to their whispered steps to learn of life.

As the dance arbor fills into one complete circle, the veteran dancers move in toward the drum, creating a spiral. More room is made for the waiting dancers to fill the circle. Their moment of celebration will be seen by all. The men have all entered, making the path ready for the women and children[9].

Women traditional dancers lead in the ladies. As dignified as the traditional men, their affinity with nature is revealed in their dress. Their regalia is regal and their poise is proud. Their soft tanned dresses of deer or elk are adorned with porcupine quills, cowrie shells, or beads[10]. The fringe that decorates their worn shawls sways with each beat and does not touch the ground. The traditional women's flowing fringe is hypnotically beautiful and elevates all women's honor.

The dance circle fills and moves to greater balance as the fancy women dancers enter. They are as spectacular as the male fancy dancers and their dance requires as much endurance and strength. Shawls are worn over their

---

[7]   These bustles are usually very colorful due to dyes, ribbons and beads.

[8]   Original grass dance regalia was made out of braided sweet grass and hung from the waist of the dancer.

[9]   The order of Grand Entry may vary from nation to nation.

[10]   Some dresses are more 'modern' using contemporary material and decorations.

shoulders. The ends are held in their hands. Their hands rest on their hips. Their elbows extend. Suddenly, they stretch out their arms and their fancy shawl transforms into an enchanting bird as the women step, jump, and whirl to the fast beat. These young women lift our spirits with their high stepping. They are our joy in flight.

Jingle dress dancers are heard before they are seen[11]. The magnetic tinkling sound follows the beat of the drum. With graceful movements, these women carry an eagle-feather fan in one hand and rest the other hand on the hip. Subtle hops cause the bells to jingle and a line of these dancers entering the arbor creates a sound of near magic. They are soothing to the eye, ear, heart, and spirit of all who see, hear, feel and soar.

The final dancers to enter the Great Circle are the future.

The children enter. It is wonderful to watch the children's energy and maturing movements. Children watch and learn their particular dance style like a bear cub watching his mother fish for supper. The children are becoming their vision even as we watch them dance the Circle of Grand Entry. Their dancing gives us all hope and courage. The children dancers give us our future.

Tiny Tots are last. Little. Somewhat fearful. Excited. Uncoordinated. Delightful. Looking around, they have much to take in. Stumbling, they have much to learn. Smiling, they have much to give back. They look down, back up, and around the arbor. Yet, they connect to the same beat as the most skillful dancer there. They are the tail of the spiral, but it is the same circle, the same dance. Tiny Tots have entered the circle to celebrate the same beat! It is the same celebration of Self!

When all have entered the Dance Circle, the song ends. The bells cease. The movement stops. And the drum waits.

---

[11] See Chapter 9 for more background. Today's dancers wear tin tops from chewing tobacco cans that are rolled into cones and sewn on the dress, one for every day of the year.

AND THE DRUM BEGINS

It is a strong beat. A full beat. Always the beat is steady. Sometimes quick, sometimes slow, but always the beat of our Spirit. The Eternal Beat embraces my heart and connects me to the Great Spirit. Like Brother Eagle who carries our prayers, the Drum sings. The voices follow the rise and fall of the currents of life. The melody trails with the echo of my heartbeat, lingering only long enough to spark a memory without words. It is a memory of old-knowing. It is the call of our ancestors.

My Spirit recognizes their song. I recognize the Way. I remember what had been forgotten. My heart moves to grasp what is not written, what is not said, what is not heard, what is not read. And I know it is not lost. I am the Spirit of my Ancestors. I am the link between the past and the future. I am the now.

I wait for my moment. The celebration dancing inside me is climbing. As the Eagle Staffs fly proudly with Namaji, my prayers float on the wings of Brother Eagle and are lifted to the Creator. I see flags pierce the Circle of Life with integrity and fly the colors of nations, of people, of memory[12]. I see the circle of dancers heal and close. Honoring and healing, the flags soothe and mend. The Drum continues. The song sings itself. And I wait for my moment.

Like a wind storm picking up power, my link to the Spirit World strengthens. I move further into in a world of vibrations and songs that sing to my Spirit. I listen to the drum. I hear the music of my people. I hear the web of life vibrate with strands of goodness. I hear the Silence inside. The drum's downbeat is stressed and I think of what I

---

[12] Visiting countries' flags are also honored. Canada's flag is often posted, as the tribal nations were artificially split by a political boundary. This tribute not only honors the Canadian dancers, it erases the political line drawn and recognizes the inherent unity that cannot be divided.

might otherwise miss. I think of the Great Mystery. I think of the parts of me that I do not see. I think of the songs I have not yet sung. And finally, I think of nothing.

An attendant offers me loose tobacco from his birch bark basket. With gratitude, I accept. Then in my honored moment, I follow my heart's strong beat and enter the dance arena for all to recognize. It is the moment of celebration, here and now, for my Seventh Direction, my personal uniqueness. Penetrating Earth Mother with body vibration, I quiver as a dancing drum. Like a butterfly fluttering its newly woven wings, I transform and I become the drum. I am Earth Dance Drum!

As I join the Grand Entry, I am present and connected to all people who have entered this Dance Circle of Life before me. For thousands of years, they have entered in grand style. Great honor swells inside me as I join the Eternal Circle.

I dance lightly and with respectful awareness, for I do not have the right to abuse our Mother's Skin[13]. I sprinkle the tobacco on Earth Mother as I dance. I thank Her for all She has given us.

With rhythmic beat, I join the dancers before me, sink into Earth Mother, and massage Her. We know She is delighted and my dancing prepares the way for the next dancer. It is a never-ending Circle of Preparation.

As I place my feet softly down, I know that the dance circle has been prepared with Namaji[14]. With Namaji, it is now my turn to honor the Spirits, as the Spirits have honored us. I smell the lingering fragrance of sage and sweet grass

---

[13] It is up to each dancer to look for ways to lessen the impact of their moccasins, just as it is our responsibility to look for ways to lessen our impact on Earth Mother by not crushing plants, roots, or other species.

[14] Tobacco was put down to thank Earth Mother. Sage was released to purify the grounds and the smudging of sweet grass invited the Spirits of our ancestors into the Circle.

and it hints of the Spirit World. As the bells jingle, I hear the beat of the Eternal and realize that our ancestors join us in this celebration. All those who have gone before us—Spirit Energy—dance with me, now.

Grand Entry fills. Our Spirits mingle with our loved ones. The arbor pulses with the good beat of life. Like a snake, the collecting dancers wind around the Drum, the Heartbeat of the Universe. On the regalia of my fellow dancers, the spiritual presence of Coyote, Eagle, Bear, Fox, Wolf, Falcon, Hawk, and Turtle dance alongside. All are present. All dance with me, now.

Looking up, I see all dancers. Looking down, I see the children's faces of the future returning my gaze. As only a child can dream, I know they are dreaming of what they will soon be, what colors they will express, what regalia they will wear, what dance they will dance. All are present. All dance with me, now.

And like wave flowing to wave, moving to the shore in end-less kindred-joining, we each have our moment, connect with All Present, then connect with the Eternal. The beat has carried Singers, Dancers, and Spirits to the Great Mystery in celebration of the One. All are present. All dance with me, now.

This is Grand Entry.

DANCE YOUR OWN DANCE

As each person participates in the Grand Entry of Life, we celebrate our unique role, our Seventh Direction. Like the dancer who enters the Powwow circle, we need to consciously link our Self with the Sacred Hoop of Life. To truly celebrate the Self, we must dance our own dance.

You may enter Life's Great Circle and still continue to question or doubt your worth. At other times you may try to please everyone, except yourself. This path is the path of failure and depression. How can you dance if you cannot lift up your head? Please, take the time now to recognize the dance steps of your Self.

Ask yourself whose life you are really trying to live. Then ask yourself, "What do I want to do with my life?" These questions must be answered, not by your spouse, parent, or by society, but by you. Only you and your Creator have the answers. To dance a path of Namaji—respect, honor, dignity and pride—you must be able to look up. You must please yourself and your Creator. That is all.

Dance your own dance. Don't mimic the dancer in front of you. That is his dance. Don't copy the dancer behind you. That is her dance. Dance with your affinities, your personal vision, the movements of your Spirit. If you wear moose skin moccasins, then dance with Moose. Learn to dance with others, rather than like others, for your dance must be your own.

I invite you to continue now on your journey and learn how to unfold your own Bimadisiwin[15] and develop your Spiritual Presence. This will be your dance. And like the Grand Entry, your unique dance will begin a Circle of Preparation, for what you do today prepares for your tomorrows.

BIMADISIWIN

Bimadisiwin unites your unique life purpose with the purpose of the Great Spirit who directs the entire universe. This unity can be seen by all in the dance you dance.

Only a person who has experienced this state of consciousness can under-stand the magnitude of this union. When we become one heart and one mind with the Great Spirit, a oneness of purpose evolves. The ecstasy from the union between human spirit and the Great Mystery is far greater than any union in this physical dimension. This agreement of mind and heart puts you in harmony with all who share that consciousness.

Bimadisiwin is a recognition that fate, free will, and purpose play vital roles in your life's direction.

---

[15] Pronounced: be-ma-DEE-ZEE-win and means to live life to the fullest.

Fate is the expression of the Spirit World's intent, desire, and directional input. Think of the coincidences that have taken place during your life. Think of the opportunities that have been offered to you. Think of how one person has made a difference in your life. This is fate.

Free will includes choices and decisions. Life is a series of choices. We are constantly making choices and must live with their consequences. We design our own life each day with our decisions. Do today what you are able, for the most unfortunate and consequential decision/choice we can make is inactivity/indecision.

Purpose is the big idea meant for your life. A life of purpose makes you strong and alive. Purpose is life's yellow highlighter, emphasizing fate and directing your free will.

When all three aspects are in balance, when you open your Self to the possibilities, when you discipline your actions, and when you are excited about what you are becoming—then you have touched the essence of Bimadisiwin.

Bimadisiwin is believing, practicing, and becoming.

Believe in the vision of you.
Practice this vision.
Become your vision.

Bimadisiwin is a conscious decision to become. It is time to think about what you want to be. The dance can not be danced until you envision the dance, rehearse its movements, and understand your part. It is demanding, for every step needs an effort in becoming one with the vision. It takes discipline, hard work, and time. Decide to be an active participant in your life journey. It is rewarding. Embrace the joy your vision brings you, it is yours to hold forever. It is freeing, for it frees your Spirit. It releases you to become as you believe you must.

You looked up from Earth Mother not long ago and thought about the colors you would wear in this life. Now you are here. It is time to wear those colors proudly.

DISCOVER YOUR COLOR

If you ask children what their favorite color is, they usually have a decided opinion. In fact, this is probably one of the first questions they ask each other when forming friendships, for it is a favorite question.

Why? What does color preference have to do with becoming and living a full life?

It is about connection. Children are still very connected to both the Physical and Spiritual Worlds. They eat dirt. They smell flowers. They look to the clouds. They sing. They imagine. They touch Earth Mother frequently. They experiment with Her colors. They see the wonder in the variety of life. They celebrate Her possibilities. They celebrate their possibilities.

It is time to reconnect to this essence of celebration. To learn what your personal dance is, let us start with the most simple step of all. Baby steps. Learn how to dance first as a Tiny Tot, before you attempt to dance the skillful artistic dance of adulthood. Rather than an exercise in humility, let this be an exercise of joy! Give your Self permission to discover the color of your Seventh Direction.

The first thing you will need to do is go out and buy a jumbo box of crayons. The bigger the better. I suggest buying new, rather than borrowing. After all, you deserve a new box of crayons. When was the last time you bought one?

Once you have your box, reserve some time for your Self to experiment with the colors. Color in the same flower outline with all different shades. Color in an old coloring book. Color blank sheets. Color squares or circles. Like the little ones who find beautiful patterns in the cedar paneling, color your walls. Color any thing any way you like. But color!

Now answer these questions. What color do you feel your present shade is? What color makes you feel the best? What color brings you the most peace and joy? What color releases the most inner harmony? What is the predominant color of your Ain-dah-ing? What color have you painted the inner hide of your teepee? Close your eyes. Look deeply into your Spirit. What color do you see? This is the color of your Seventh Direction.

Celebrate this discovery! Wear clothes in this shade! Paint your room with its color! Surround yourself with a hint of its essence. Paint pictures with its presence.

Then discover your paint brush.

Will it be your fingers? If so, finger paint! Will it be your garden? If so, cut a grape vine and chew its end into a soft brush! Will it be your long hair? If so, dip your braid's end into its fine color and paint the color of your Self!

Be creative and enjoy. It is your time to explore the Dance of Life as a Tiny Tot. Give yourself permission to walk through your fear, to stumble, to be uncoordinated, to smile, and to dance! What's the worst thing that can happen?

Perhaps you'll learn a little more about your preferences and your inner Self. This discovery may be the first step in learning your dance and your purpose in life. Allow the child in you to teach you how to connect with the Physical and Spiritual Worlds. You must first open the door before you can enter into the room's warmth and comfort. You must first touch the spray of the waterfall before you can experience the power of its shower. You must first come to know your child inside, before you can become an adult.

Let the child teach you about your creative potential. This is the East Direction, the season of our child. Find the joy and life-giving energy this direction offers. Discover that a life with purpose will sing and dance! When one creates, one returns to youth. Return to your youth. It is the door closest to the power of creation.

VIBRATE WITH EXCITEMENT

Penetrating Earth Mother with body vibration, I quiver as a dancing drum.

Give yourself the gift of time to discover your purpose.

In your silence, in Ain-dah-ing, slow down long enough to know who you are, where you are.

> *Let your heart move to grasp*
> *what is not written,*
> *what is not said,*
> *what is not heard,*
> *what is not read.*
> *And know it is not lost. You are it. You are that Spirit.*

Return to Your Breath

Listen to your drum. In the quiet of Ain-dah-ing, listen to your heart beat steady. Discipline yourself to follow your breath. The Great Spirit awaits on the other side of your breath, for that is its source. Tap your Ain-dah-ing and discover the strength, the view, the power, the peace, the energy, the unlimited potential that awaits your connection. As you learn to follow your breath each day, these gifts of Ain-dah-ing can be lived on the outside hoop of life. Come to realize that each beat, each silence, is as important as the one before and the one to follow. The present is your vital opportunity.

Don't hurry, don't worry, do your best and forget the rest! "Hurry and worry" are in the future. "The rest" is in the past. The present is where one does the best. Allow these possibilities to be grasped by your heart and your spirit. Allow your Self to become the possibility.

Allow Purpose to Float Into Your Consciousness

Clear the waters of distractions and incidental life demands. It is time to allow your purpose to float to the top of your consciousness.

To begin this exercise, give yourself space and time without distractions. Without this gift, it is unlikely you will be able to fully participate in the exercise, for there will be enough internal distractions for you to deal with. Once you have ensured your environment will be clear of outside interference, pour yourself a glass of carbonated water. Be sure it is a clear glass and that you have sufficient light. Then watch the water. What do you see? What percent of the content is air? What percent is water? What are you?

Look into the glass. With your values in mind, follow the tiny, nearly invisible, bubbles as they rise to the surface. Let your thoughts rise and follow the bubbles. As the bubbles pop, let your thoughts pop.

Like the air bubble trapped far beneath the ocean's weight, first settle the sand that imprisons you, discover the open space, and release your purpose to rise to the surface. Then listen to Bubble's language. It's pop will give you rare certainty and welcomed liberation.

Stir your glass, so that you are able to do this exercise over and over until your thoughts become clear[16]. Do this until you are able to get beyond the internal distractions, beyond the shoulds, beyond the fears. Distill your thoughts to the very essence of who you are, what your vision of yourself is.

Which thoughts continue to rise to the surface as a new bubble? Which thoughts will you entertain and which will you dismiss? Entertain the thoughts that reflect your talents and abilities, your joy and your interests. Come to know that the heart is smarter than the mind. Continue to follow the bubbles, and identify the things in life you most enjoy. Joy is the key to this discovery. If you find the joy, you will find your purpose. See the bubbles fulfill their circle of life. With their pop, they return to the surface. Discover your purpose and return to surface of Life with your own joyful pop!

In achieving this, you have allowed purpose to float to your consciousness. This is a significant step towards dancing your dance. Now you are aware of what you truly want and need to become. Congratulations! You have identified your Life's dance!

More than likely you are feeling something new. You may be filled with an energy that you have forgotten exists. Experience the celebration as it begins inside, as you now wait for your moment! This discovery must be celebrated! Cry if you must! Laugh deliriously if you can! Allow tears and laughter to flow in celebration throughout your being. Let all of your Self celebrate! Quiver with its excitement! Feel the internal-moving-joy it brings! Celebrate the dance of your Self! What a gift you have given your Self! This is a gift of Ain-dah-ing.

LET THE QUIVER MOVE YOU

Give yourself the gift of discipline. Let discipline sprout from the quivering energy of discovery.

Tap your inner strength and watch yourself grow strong. Remember, the waterfall was once a trickle. There will always be beginnings, and begin-

---

[16] This exercise is very effective at the foot of a waterfall. Follow the bubbles in the stream, the same way as described above.

nings are seldom easy. The water must wash over jagged rocks, travel through dark caves, and move upward under Earth Mother's weight.

What strength can you tap? Do you know your strengths? Oftentimes we are blind to this side of ourselves. Living has clouded our essence and we forget what we do well. We have buried our talents, understandings, and interests under the 'shoulds' of this world. Make an honest appraisal of your strengths. If you are still unsure of what you do well, I urge you to take an interest and aptitude test. There are many of them available. Go to a library, local school, or look to computer programs to help you with this discovery. No matter your age, identify what your interests are and what your aptitude is. We need to honestly appraise both. Both are necessary ingredients in discovering our true strengths. Learn to identify and applaud what you are good at. Become your own best fan! Celebrate your strengths!

What dark caves must you walk through? What do you fear? What are the things that make you swallow hard or tighten your jaw? What memories still bite you? What situations or people do you avoid, postpone, run away from or aggressively blast through? These are your dark caves. Take the time to write these things down. Become intimate with your fears, for if you pretend they don't exist they are empowered, and then, they rule your life. Learn to walk through your fear. It is okay to be afraid and nervous and scared. You will not break. Each time you walk through your fear you become stronger and fear becomes weaker. Each time you walk through your fear you learn more about yourself. Some of the best learning experiences I have had in life are the ones in which I was afraid. Learn to learn about your fear. For fear is part of your Self. Learn to learn about your Self. Fear can be your teacher, if you acknowledge its presence. Allow your Self to be the student.

What rocks must you cross? What are your challenges? We all have some. No one is exempt. Life would be flat and dull if there were no rocks to cross. We are all handicapped or encumbered with challenging limitations and weaknesses. Find the lesson for your Spirit in your shortcomings. Discover what meaning it offers you. Strong people realize their weakness. Great success is achieved when limitations are understood and compensated. Learn to compensate for what you cannot do. What strengths can you exercise to make up for the difference? Learn to ask for help when help is needed. View life as "we" rather than "me." We are not alone. We are meant to work together as one great system. View your weakness as someone else's strength. That is their uniqueness. Celebrate their uniqueness!

What possibilities await for you? Knowing the colors of your strengths, fears, challenges and joy, what possibilities appear? What hue splashes Sky Father as your Spirit now soars? *As these parts of your Self converge, infinite possibilities emerge.* Your dance can be danced with a variety of steps, a variety of expressions, a variety of emotion. Keep a journal of your strengths, fears, challenges, and possibilities. Add to it when you can. Reflect on this often. Take the time to look over the results of the above discoveries. This is a mirror of your Self. From this reflection, the final dance will appear.

Look to other dancers. Each dancer has a story to tell. Watch them lift their knees high, causing their heart to beat fast. Watch them twirl with excitement as the tempo of life increases. Watch them nearly fall, only to impress us with their intricate footwork. See them sway with the wind, touch Earth Mother tenderly, look out to Sky Father and honor you with their dance. Notice the difficult movements, the sweat of their efforts, their extreme joy, their ultimate transcendence. See how their entire body—their entire Self—empowers the dance. See how the dance empowers the Self.

It is a continuous and circular exchange of energy.

The energy sustains the discipline. The discipline sustains the dance. The dance sustains the energy.

You, too, can connect to this current. Engage! Quiver with the power! Allow the excitement, the vibration of purpose, to lift your own legs, twirl your own spirit, touch your own heart! This energy will be your cocoon of transformation. You will move—then become—the beating of your heart. You are the Drum!

VISUALIZE PAST, PRESENT, AND FUTURE AS ONE

Time is where you are this moment. Present is who you are, what you've become and the bundle of knowledge-sticks you carry. Think of every bit of knowledge and experience you have acquired as a stick. Know that the bundle has value only when you figure out what to do with it. This is wisdom.

In an instant, time also becomes the past.

To design your future, visualize where you want to be, and then build the bridge from your present, to that place. Your vision becomes your destiny, and your bridge becomes your path. Assure your bridge is strong with well-defined plans.

Flow with time, but be present with each moment. Consider the vibration of the hummingbird's wings. Which of its' flutter is flight? Is flight the past fluttering of its wing? Or is flight the next flap of the wing? Come to see that flight is all of this. Transcend and flow with time, yet be present with the moment. Like all of the winged, in order to transcend, we, too, must be in movement. We must vibrate. Truth after truth after truth reveals itself at each fluttering of our spiritual wings. Like the gradual shading of blue to green, we become, we live the transformations. It is as though we are in a cocoon within a cocoon, within a cocoon. The more truths we experience, the more we are set free in colorful flight. Always in movement, the different levels of consciousness we experience lead us to the next level. This is how we come to soar!

During this spiritual metamorphosis, you will remember your past and greet your future. In your transformation, you will give Namaji to both your ancestors and your legacy. You will grow to appreciate your mistakes and your pain because it was the fluttering that kept you in flight. In your flight, you will understand the connectedness, the relationship of all. With this view of All connected, you will truly experience Mitakuye-Oyasin. We are all related. We dance to One Drum.

If I handed you a magic wand right now, what three wishes would you request? Take the time to discover this and write these three wishes down. This list will reflect your values and your "dream-vision." If it doesn't match the earlier exercise of identifying your joy and purpose, discover which exercise was done with the mind rather than the heart. Listen to your heart. Remember, joy is the key to true dance discovery.

Write down your vision, your joy. It is your future. Write down goals and define the steps to achieve them. Like the inch worm, gather up your internal strength, visualize the goal, stretch your boundaries, reach out for the next step, and experience the internal celebration. Do this, inch by inch, and you will go far. Build a bridge to the future. But like the inch worm, recognize that you are that bridge!

CELEBRATE!

Give your Self the gift of celebrating what you have become, what you have worked for. This is your dance!

Experience the satisfying feeling of completion. Like the dancer at Powwow, celebrate your Purpose, even as it is being fulfilled. Celebrate what you may encounter along the way. Do not miss the gifts that touch you and heal you. The smiles of a child, the teaching of an Elder, the sunrise and sunset, the power of a simple word.

When you listen to a song, don't you celebrate the moment of the song, the harmony and beat and melody of that moment? Focus on the instant, positive, vibrations that you are experiencing right now. Twirl with excitement! Step with Namaji! Surf the moment! Engage the energy! Life is to be celebrated and honored. Thank your Self for your strengths, honesty, courage, and discipline. Thank others for their help, love, guidance, and dance. Thank the Creator for your life, spirit, gifts, and purpose! A purposeful life is a good life. And a full life has purpose.

Hear the Elders say, "Come to the good life of Bimadisiwin!" Sing your song! Dance your dance! Know your heart! And release your Spirit! For, it is your Song, your Dance, your Heart, and your Spirit that you celebrate.

In the tender Opening
Of flower in the Spring
I hear my Song!

In the waves' Eternity
I find my Unity.
And I Belong!

In the closing of the night
A morning star shines bright
I find my Way!

In the open cloudless Sky
On Eagle wings I fly
I Dance all day!

SPIRITUAL PRESENCE

Standing on the shore of Lake Michigan, Water washing over my feet, Cedar perfume pleasing my nose, Sun warming my body, and Wind gently moving my hair, it would be impossible to feel spiritually absent. Surrounding our Selves with experiences of nature connects us to the Great Spirit, for it is the *Creator's creation* that fills us.

When I drink water, inside I am more water. When I look at true beauty, inside I am more beautiful. When I hear birds' songs, inside I am more harmonic. I become more of what I fill with. When I fill with the experience of creation, inside I am more of the Creator.

When I fill up with negative thoughts, inside I am more worried and distracted. We cannot escape from our worrisome mind unless we unravel the mental fiber that we have erroneously woven. Take the time to reweave new thought patterns based on the natural harmony of the universe. Spin threads of harmony and reality, rather than discord and delusion. Discover how positive thought patterns spin a soothing steady pulse. Within this mesmerizing experience, you are freed to go beyond the thought process to the place of peace. Here, you will hear the Creator. Go from your head to your heart and live in the present. *It is only here in the present, that a person can experience spirituality.*

Free your mind.

Allow your mind to gravitate toward nature, for it will bring you to the order of all things. Allow your heart to move with the freedom of nature, for like Earth Mother, you will pulse with Ain-dah-ing. Give your Self permission to fly with the Creator, for the spiritual currents will sustain you in the Eternal.

Walk into the water's shore—a river, a lake, an ocean, a sea—and feel the Water Spirits hold you. Allow your Self to experience the spiritual ecstasy of being connected to the Great Mystery. Allow the waters to teach you about yourself. Hear how the women are the keepers of the water, for the waters of their womb ensure procreation. Hear how the men are the supporters of this world, for the water that holds you is held up with the Great Mishomis—

the masculine energy—of Earth Mother. Hear how the oceans unite all people and blend away all human boundaries and separations. Hear how the children of Earth Mother need the same water to live. Hear how the sea brings us back to the sky. Honor all this and more, and you will develop spiritual presence.

You know you have arrived when you are just as happy sitting on a stump in the woods, watching the leaves fall, as you are being served at your favorite elegant restaurant, or sweeping your kitchen floor. This is the mark of Spiritual Presence. It matters not where you are, nor who you are, but rather if you are!

I CELEBRATE

See me, Great Spirit, in my red ribbon ties.
Watch me honor You and be the Me I am inside.
Teach me, Great Spirit, to sing the song of One.
It is the song you sang to me the day I had begun.

My feet touch Mother softly, now, to honor all her gifts.
My eyes touch Father's soft laced clouds, and my Spirit lifts.
Let me touch Your endless Love and give to all I see.
Let me now become and celebrate all that I will be.

See me, Great Spirit, honor Brother Bear.
Watch my Spirit move inside his skin that I now wear.
Teach me, Great Spirit, the meanings all around.
What I see, what I touch, the taste, the smell, and sound.

My feet touch the future, now, and honor what they need.
My eyes touch the past, when all honored life for me.
Let me touch the endless waves where all is truly One.
Let me touch today with love and give back to Everyone.

Celebrate your Grand Entry into this moment. This moment is gone, already. Now celebrate again and again and again. Live your life as though, at every moment, you are waiting to pierce the Circle of Life, the Eternal Beat that calls you to enter. Feel the excitement. Feel the honor you are given as your special moment arrives. Our Creator reserved this moment just for you!

Connect your heart and mind to the Great Mystery. Be Spiritually Present, in the Now. Wonder, as a person born blind, what colors our ancestors in the Spirit World now wear. Wonder what you will wear when you are there! Wonder what Earth's children will wear! Then celebrate this Mystery! Remember, all our relatives have come to celebrate the celebration of Self.

Once you have experienced a personal Grand Entry of Self, when you have given Namaji to yourself and your relatives, when you have held high your uniqueness, and when you come to dance your purpose, you will want to do it again. So, let the energy renew and cause you to dance the dance again. Remember that when one moccasin is down, the other one is up. See how your life becomes an ongoing series of movement and transformation. Like nature, each cycle sustains your dance as one hoop leads to another hoop to another.

Flutter! Sing! Become! Celebrate! Spin! Laugh! Vibrate! Cry! Fly! Transcend! Unite! Dance! Grand Entry is your celebration.

Now look at the footprints you have made in your Grand Entry. The marks you have left on Earth Mother are your unique marks. The path you have made is your path. The dance you have danced is your dance. Pierce the Circle of Life and dance once more. This is your right, your privilege, your honor. This is the Seventh Direction.

Forever, celebrate your Grand Entry again...and again...and again...

HONOR DANCES

*Allow me to honor you, for with your presence
you have honored me.*

Honor dances are conscious, deliberate celebrations of recognizing someone or something for their inherent worth. They are dances of Namaji. They
bestow dignity, honor, respect, and pride upon the honored one. In the
giving of Namaji, Namaji is gifted back to the giver.

Namaji begets Namaji in full circle. Like swirls of paint, sinking and dovetail-
ing into the color of the next, Namaji blends the essence of one into another,
until all become One. In this merging of separate colorful individuals, the
Eternal Reflection of Mitakuye-Oyasin appears, is experienced, and becomes
truth. In our individual Celebrations of each Self, we celebrate our unity as
One. We understand that we are all related. I cannot exist without you, nor
you without me, nor we without them. In the sharing of breath that unites us,
we recognize this connectedness. Inside the Sacred Hoop's endless presence, Namaji weaves its web of Mitakuye-Oyasin.

Namaji is the Weaver.

Namaji spins an internal celebration of Mitakuye-Oyasin, then weaves it into
an even greater desire for Namaji. Those who understand that we are all
related, know that to honor one is to honor all. To disrespect one is to disrespect all. The Honor Dance of Life connects all who are present on the
Sacred Hoop to the Great Mystery.

Just as the sea meets the sky, honor gives form to the other. Without the sea, the horizon would disappear into itself. Without the horizon, the sea would wash away. Each gives the other the contrast of existence[1]. Yet, can you really find a separation of sky and sea? You may sail far into the Great Sea to reach this separation of sky and sea, only to become more absorbed in the unity. To separate one from the other denies their unique relationship.

Likewise, to separate giver and receiver of Namaji would deny the unity of the One. For both are receivers. Both are givers. Both merge into each other on the Eternal Circle. Separation would sever all union and would disconnect our spirits. *Honor gives form to the other and unifies the relationship. To be honored for your uniqueness, honors Mitakuye-Oyasin.*

Honor and unification are ever present on Powwow grounds. There is laughter, smiles, storytelling, celebration, family unity, community bonding, jokes, tears, prayers, and silence. Powwow celebrates life by balancing our mind, emotions, body, and spirit. In dance and song, the unification and honor of our entire Self with All is strong and vibrant.

There is no hostile competition (separation), even in "competition" dances. For when we follow the signs to Powwow, we follow our heart. It is the trail of Mitakuye-Oyasin and Namaji.

Tribal people celebrate and honor one another and Earth Mother. Powwows across the entire continent move with the beat of Namaji. It is as inherent to the essence of Powwows, as water is to the clouds. Powwows continue to be public celebrations because they flow with Mitakuye-Oyasin. Without Mitakuye-Oyasin, there would be no gathering of the people. Without the gathering, there would be no Powwow, no Mitakuye-Oyasin.

To further understand the basis of Native American Honor, you are invited to follow the Sun Trail of First Dance and Elder Dance. Follow this trail of timelessness as you dance the colors of Self, as they splash against the possibilities of Sky Father.

---

[1]   Sky in the Lakota language is referred to as, "I am the difference."

FIRST DANCE

First Dance is just that: an honoring of a child's first dance[2]. It is the first time these dancers wear their regalia to publicly celebrate their uniqueness.

Parents give the Drum group loose tobacco to request an honor song, and all present stand to honor the new dancers[3]. A Great Celebration takes place in the Circle, and within the heart and spirit of all who attend. Joy leaks out like a ripe berry touched gently with our fingertips. For we taste the sweetness of First Dance each time, regardless of our individual experience and age. It becomes our dance, too. Mitakuye-Oyasin: there is no separation of time, space, and spirit. All know the importance of this dance. The parents lead their children to the Circle of the First Dance. Children are not carried. They must learn to walk and make their own path on Life's Circle[4].

Honor the child of the Universe as you now hear the dance of Minnow.

WEE-GITCHIE-NE-ME-E-DIM
(Big Dance)

Minnow held his mother's hand tightly before he let go to enter the big circle. This was his Wee-gitchie-ne-me-e-dim, his Big Dance. And to Minnow, everything was big.

The sights were big. The people in their regalia were like moving colorful trees. The little boy had seen the moccasins and leggings of everyone in the circle by now, but he still wondered what their faces looked like close up. Moving in line to where the Elder spoke, Minnow counted three bustles brush his face as the big dancers passed by him.

The sounds were big, too. The jingling, the voices, the Drum. Minnow wondered if his heart sounded as loud to

---

2   These dancers are often referred to as 'Tiny Tots;' yet, a person's first dance may occur beyond the toddler years.

3   Respect is shown and all hats are removed unless the hat bears an eagle feather.

4   Traditionally, a parent who carried their child was asking the community to do for the child what they were incapable of doing.

Mosquito when she landed on his chest, as the Drum sounded to Minnow's own ears. The Drum was so loud he could feel the beat vibrate right into him. It felt good! It made Minnow excited to dance. Minnow remembered his father's words and thought how powerful Drum must be if it is the Heartbeat of Everything!

Most of all, the Circle was big. So big! He had always envied the older children's fast dancing and would sometimes count (as high as he could) to see how long it would take them to go around the full circle. Minnow wondered how many counts he would need to dance his Wee-gitchie-ne-me-e-dim.

Minnow heard the Elder tell everyone that this dance was very important. The Elder said a lot of other words too, but the words were just sounds to Minnow. Sounds that spoke to Minnow's racing heart about dancing for his first time.

Then the Drum began beating his personal song.

Minnow moved into the group of first-time dancers and was pleased he could see their faces. A boy passed him, smiling all over, jingling loudly as he walked. Minnow noticed the beautiful bustles of another, but when the dancer turned, Minnow could not see his eyes hidden beneath the feathers. Thinking how the headdress must feel, Minnow suddenly felt eyes on him. Turning around, Minnow saw a girl wrapped in her shawl watching him.

But it was time to dance and so with all dancers in line, the group followed the woman at the front. Moving slowly, Minnow and the other dancers became sound. Minnow noticed how the woman lifted her eagle fan to Sky Father and honored the Drum. He had seen many dancers do this before. Minnow knew someday, he too, would lift his own fan. "There must be something out there that they are trying to reach," he thought.

The little boy moved slowly, saw the girl once more, and believed the Eyes of the World were on him. The leaps inside his tummy distracted him from the music. The colorful bustle of the dancer in front of him made him curious about everyone else dancing and Minnow stretched his neck to see what they were wearing. He leaned too far and almost lost his step. He peered shyly around to see if anyone had noticed.

The touch of his yellow and red grass dance regalia, now swishing around his arms and legs, suddenly felt unfamiliar. Minnow thought of the many nights he had practiced dancing in this regalia. How he had begged his mother to put it on again and again! "It hadn't felt strange then. Why does it feel different now?"

The beat of the drum encouraged the little dancers around the big circle, but Minnow still moved cautiously. "This is not like I practiced," Minnow whispered to himself, remembering how beautifully he had danced at home. His forehead scrunched up with worry like he had seen his father's do.

Then Minnow felt a breeze rustle in the roach on his head[5]. The wind felt like a loving whispered breath, as it tickled his neck. Minnow decided to concentrate on Wind and noticed the big pines swaying. Minnow tried to sway like the trees. He smelled familiar cedar breeze and relaxed into the scent of the wind. He heard once again the familiar soothing beat of the Drum.

Then Minnow felt the Drum.

His body moved with the beat. One beat, then another, and another, and another. With child-surrender, the Great Heartbeat slid naturally into Minnow's moment.

---

5   A roach is a warrior's hair piece made from deer tail, porcupine or horsehair with one or two feathers in the center.

Minnow's mind forgot everything around him, while his heart remembered many things he had forgotten.

Living memories carried his steps. Remembering and dancing, Minnow merged into the Great Circle.

As his heart moved with the rhythm of the Drum, Minnow remembered the sound of his Mother's needle tenderly poking through the material to make his regalia. He felt the scarf tied snugly on his head by his Grandma. Whirling with the music that had forever been with him, Minnow remembered and felt the flap of Blue Heron just like it had flown over their boat, fishing with his father.

Then Minnow remembered the water's ripples, the little fish below the water, and he looked down at his own reflection. Minnow saw himself in his regalia.

Minnow *became* the regalia. He realized, the regalia hadn't changed, it was he who had changed!

Minnow now danced with Energy and Spirit. His head, shoulders, and body moved easily and loosely. Minnow stepped tenderly on Earth Mother, as he was taught to do. He looked around, and saw big people alive with the same Energy and Spirit. The colored dancing trees moved alongside him. Minnow saw Coyote move past him. He heard the growl of Brother Mu-kwa[6]. Minnow felt the Winged flap all around him. He touched Earth beneath him.

Deeper into the song, Minnow moved into the Eternal beat. Minnow discovered delight as he opened to Circle's gift of space. He inhaled the Big scents and the Big sounds, hungry for more. Minnow's Wee-gitchie-ne-me-e-dim was completing. Melting into all the Bigness, Minnow flowed like the Great Water. He had danced the Sacred Circle without counting.

---

[6] Pronounced: MA-kwa, and means bear.

Now Minnow was as big as the Sounds. As big as the Smells. As big as the Circle. As big as the Drum. Minnow was Wee-gitchie-ne-me-e-dim. Minnow was the Big Dance.

Ah ho.

CHILDREN MUST MAKE THEIR OWN PATH

It is a marvel to see children's coordination and their awareness mature. From toddlers to teens, the Circle is danced with much learning. To watch the children dance is to watch the hand of the Creator gently guide them in a new direction. Each child will create their own path in life. Each will celebrate or grieve their life choices. Each will learn the teachings of love and hate. Each will return to the Beat.

But it is each child's path, each child's choice. Allow Earth Mother's children to walk on their own, and discover the beauty of memories, of connections, of Oneness. Do not carry them. Let them feel rock sharpness and grass lushness. That is the right of their feet. That is the right of their mind. That is the right of their emotions. That is the right of their Spirit. Let them experience life in balance. Let them experience Life's balance. The joy is in the discovery. Do not take their joy away. Let them empty and fill their own internal buckets.

TWO GIFTS TO GIVE

What must we do for our children? If we let them experience life, what then is left to gift them?

There are only two things that we must give as parents and caregivers. We must give them life, and we must give them love. As simple as their smile, this offering from our heart provides immeasurable sustenance.

To give life requires much more than tending to the obvious biological demands of child birth and the physical needs of childhood. To truly give life to your children means to give them that which will sustain them. Give them food, but only as needed. Give them water, for cleansing, inside and out. Give them shelter from the storms in life, but let them get wet and even cold at times, for it connects them to the physical world. Give them clothing, but let it honor their uniqueness and the world. Give them your touch, for it heals and promotes growth. Give them your time, for it nourishes their spirit. Give them direction and boundaries, for they cannot give that to themselves.

Give your children love, for love gives life. Love must be evident in all that we do for our children. Make it constant.

Love enters into dark places and showers them with beauty and light. It is difficult to watch our children experience Life's ugly side. It is tempting to soften and filter the view. Allow your child to experience the pain of mistakes, the sorrow of regrets, the difficulty of truth. Be there for them, but do not carry them. Do not filter their view with falsehood. Offer them a look into life. It is their right. Recognize when your child needs to identify and experience these truths. Like Mother Buffalo who gives milk until the calf's digestive system is prepared to eat grass, see that there is a time for all of Life's teachings, a time when your child will be ready to chew on life's difficulties. Be the teacher. Guide them through the dark places. Enter these places with your child. In this way you show a love that shines the light inside. The lessons children learn, the understandings they gain, the changes they become, expand their view on life and their internal self. With exposure to the dark, light is more beautifully appreciated and understood.

Love invests itself for itself. Love, although other-conscious, is also self-serving. As we love, we feed our love within. Although two are needed in the exchange, love itself is unchanged, unbroken. Love remembers itself and will urge you toward true loving behaviors. Listen to the voice of love, even when it demands, for love knows what is loving and what is not. Love transcends the experience. True Love perpetuates itself, even in the midst of pain, the greed of self, the fear of tomorrow, and the challenge of today.

Love is open, free, and spontaneous. Gift yourself and your children a meadow of love. Without time constraints, without preoccupation, without past history, love will move you into a wonderful moment. Experience the moment. Love colors the experience with a free flow of energy. Love exists in the now and is evidenced and celebrated with each new moment. Love is the frolicking pony, the fresh breeze of Spring. Gift your child this painted-pony of love.

Love is easy. Although situations may be difficult, love itself is easy. Separating the child from the mistake is like tasting sweet honey without Bee's sting. Love is the balm of mistakes, the bridge that gifts the child into a new moment. Without love, we might give up at the first mistake made. Love is the easy comfort of a mother's arms, a father's hug, parental direction, family support. Like dangling one's legs in a cool lake on a hot day, love is an easy reminder of what really matters and gifts both giver and receiver with comfort and rejuvenation.

Give your children love, for love is life. Love is both the gift as well as the giver.

THE LAKE, THE LIES, THE DREAM

You fell into the lake;
I watched as you got wet.
You lied to me one night.
In truth we finally met.

You sat upon my lap
and I comforted your tears.
You moved right into life
and carried in the years.

The berries that you picked
scratched up your face and arm.
The answer to your dream
is now inside your charm.

I am glad for the lake
and the lie that made you grow.
For your journey and your tears,
and the truth that you now know.

I am glad for your sweetness
and for the dreams you live.
I am glad for *your* life,
and the love that you now give.

What will your children remember? Let it be only two things: love and life.

EARLY CHILDHOOD MEMORIES

Often childhood memories contain both pain and joy. For life contains both. Like Minnow, discover what you need to empty from your memories. Your first dance awaits. Return to your own innocence and you will be ready to dance. The following exercise will help you return to the East, the direction of innocence and childhood.

Think back as far as you are able and write down your earliest childhood memories. Give your Self the time to remember. Return to your silence and allow the memories to return to you. All it will take is the initial first memory. Go to a picture book, if you need help getting started. But go to the silence of your Self to continue once you have begun.

Indian Lake has filled me with many memories of life. Listen to one memory. For it is one I return to often and changes as I grow old.

MEMORY

As a young boy, Moccasin Mike, an Elder from across the lake, taught me much about myself and the woods. As he was very old, he taught me many things. Although he had a wooden peg-leg, he took me to places I could not go myself. Together, we spent many years.

About once a week, I would row us out to the deadhead— the log that was pushed by the winter ice around the lake. Rowing was hard work and slow crossing, as I was young and the oars were heavy. But there was no hurry. Eventually we would reach the log, tie a rope connecting us to it, and fish. Here, we were certain to catch pan fish, the bluegills and perch, that hid around this moving home.

Once at the shoreline of Mike's house, we would then fill a bucket with all the little fish we had thrown in the bottom of the boat. Climbing up the bank that led to his house, fish-smell announced our arrival. Scampering around our feet,

Mike's cats anxiously waved at the air. Emptying the
bucket, another filled.

One day, as we rowed out to the middle of Indian Lake
to complete another circle, I heard a whoosh! A great
gushing sound!

Mike pointed past me and exclaimed his joy, "Ho-wa!"

Feeling the spray of water, I, too, turned to discover the
sound and the source.

I couldn't believe my eyes! Like a tree of water piercing
through the lake's surface, a great geyser grew! Rising to
about eight feet above the lake, and thirty feet away from
our boat, I watched as the sky filled with water. Accepting
the cold spray on my face, arms, and legs, I joined the
sight and sound of Geyser.

"How...?" I asked, trying to move closer to the Geyser, as I
moved to the end of the boat.

"A new spring. The Water Spirits are talking," Mike answered.

The boat tipped slightly as Mike moved to the seat I had
just left. Picking up the oars, he understood. Gliding to
greet the deadhead, I continued to stare as Geyser slowly
became part of the lake, as we became part of the cycle
once more.

This memory has gifted me a lifetime of understandings. Over and over I
have returned to this memory. In the early years, this memory became
knowledge about the world around me. I would swim across the lake, and
recognize the circles of cold water that would suddenly greet my submerged
legs. It was Geyser, now bubbling slowly to the surface. I would remember
Geyser's beginning, knew that Geyser continued to spiral, making unseen
circle-sand paintings on the bottom of the lake.

As life changed, the memory changed. The memory of Geyser returned to teach me about life. I remembered Mike's words and listened. Water Spirits told me to visit my unconscious mind. If I do not, like Geyser, the pressure may also build and blow through a seemingly peaceful exterior. My needs would find a channel. To what extent would I go to be heard? What effects would my burst of unconscious pressure have on those around me? How long would it take for me to return to the pool of peace?

Eventually, the memory of Geyser became a memory of Mike. Namaji for Geyser dovetailed into love for my neighbor. Swimming through the cold circles of water reconnects me to my old friend who now dances in the Spirit World.

Geyser is a lesson and a memory. For memories are often lessons, if we listen to them. What memory do you have that needs to be recognized. What is the lesson for you to learn? What are the Spirits trying to tell you? Open yourself up to the memory and the lessons, and you will complete its hoop.

Consider a deer trail traveled over thousands of years and how it has imprinted the forest with memories of countless deer following their Sun Trails. Like the deer, like me, you have traveled many times over the same mental and emotional paths during your life. You have created your own imprints. How have your paths affected your emotional forest? What were you feeling at the time your specific memories occurred? What common threads run through your recollections?

How do those experiences and emotions affect your life today? Do they give you joy? Or do they haunt you? How do these memories, experiences, and emotions continue to govern your actions? Is it time to run down the path and celebrate freedom? Or is it time to travel a new way? Is it time for a new direction?

More than likely, you have found paths that lead to beautiful places, as well as paths whose roots continue to trip you. Perhaps your memories are of neglect and abuse, or fear and shame. Your memories may be of joy and togetherness, or discovery and fun. Take this time to discover the patterns. Remember we are all of them, the shadows and the lighted places.

The fact that you have identified old patterns is a significant step in healing any emotional scars left behind. The truth does set us free. By remembering, talking about our memories, and raising our awareness of these experiences, we have allowed healing to occur. The attention, affection, recognition and approval that is needed can be given by Self, and can heal. This will begin the reforestation of Self. And like emerald forests, you too, will celebrate new growths, new stages, new treasures of Life.

If some painful imprints of trodden paths continue to negatively affect your life's direction, first attend to your wound by gifting yourself forgiveness and heal with the help of another. Then blaze a new trail through your emotional forest. Redirect your pathway. Make new memories! Determine your life purpose through silent reflection. Unite with All. Experience Life in the Now. Celebrate each new day and your uniqueness. *This re-celebration becomes the new path.* Follow this new trail, over and over, and the old path will fade into the new growth. The old memory will take on a new meaning.

You have the privilege to plant whatever you desire in these quiet open spaces. Plant the seeds of nurturance and celebration. Become rooted in your Self.

NURTURE YOUR CHILD WITHIN

So if you must, heal yourself. Get your box of crayons out and begin to color in your vision of your heart. Let the dark colored memories accentuate the brighter colors of your Self. Trust the shadows to direct you to the light beyond. The hurtful memories will not bite so much, and the good memories will lick your wounds. With healing, you will come to see the great possibilities of life, and your oneness of purpose to the Great Mystery.

Take care of the child within, just as you would your own child. As before, the only two things you must give your child is life and love. Discover ways to nurture yourself, to Honor the child within.

Love

Take the time to love yourself. Enter into your own ugly places and shower healing upon your wounds. Comfort the child that cries. Give attention, affection, recognition, and approval to the child inside. In this way, you will be free to grow and fulfill your life purpose.

Love yourself for love's sake. Let the Hoop of Love permeate all that you do for yourself. Be committed in balancing your life. Offer this good gift to Self and your ability to love others will grow. Spiraling out into a wonderful moment, let your love dovetail into yourself. Make this moment a gift to yourself.

Allow yourself to love the child inside. Softly approach the crying child. Hug your child with love from Self that is pure and free. Comfort your child for having journeyed the silent painful paths. Balm the wounds without regrets, without anger, without shame or blame. Let love be love. With love alone, comfort the child within. Then soak in your presence.

Play

Take time to play! It balances work. Life should be fun, or what is the point? Find the humor, enjoy the world around you, enjoy yourself! What do you really enjoy doing? Do that! What music do you enjoy? Listen to that! Make your own music! What fun places have you gone to? Return to the joy! Who do you enjoy being around? Join them.

Take a walk through the woods, as though you are a child again! Sing and swing! Splash through puddles! Crawl through Earth's caves! Smear mud on your face! Bake and make a giant mess! Lick the frosting off the spoon! Discover the most beautiful stone on the beach. Listen to the sea in the shell. Bury your feet beneath soft warm sand. Wiggle your toes! Look with child's eyes and play! Feel with child's hands and play! Hear with child's ears and play!

This is the wellspring of youth and vitality. Return to the East, for it is the source of knowledge. Find out how fun and fresh life can be!

Protect

Then protect the child within from re-engaging the painful pathways. Discover the nourishment your child is ready for. You must grow psychological teeth in order to chew on the tough issues in life. Do what is best for the child. Do not over-protect, yet do not neglect. Recognize when it is time to deal with issues. Find help if necessary, in order to guide you to this understanding.

With a healthy adult perspective, protect the child within from becoming a victim[7]. Protect the child within from the dangers of abuse. Protect the child within from the tragedy of addictions and denial. Protect the child within from inactivity and despair. Let your child know his/her guardian is always present.

Change

Look into your inner mirror's reflection and see how your regalia changes over the years. Let it change. With easy child-surrender, allow the Great Heart Beat to pulse naturally with all that you do. Let the direction of the Universe lift your unique purpose to the heights of the swaying Pines. Celebrate this unity with all of Earth Mother's children. Return to your child and dance the First Honor Dance of the Great Circle. Return to your own enchantment and join your Heart and Spirit in the Great Beat of Life.

Come to recognize the need to keep the colors of your child eternally vibrant. If you put your colors away forever, your child within is left holding an empty coloring book. Fill up with the East direction when you are in need of creative energy. Honor your child within, become little again, and discover the First Dance.

The First Dance is filled with the child-like awe of so many possibilities. With the rhythm of the Universe, we engage this unlimited potential. Take time to wonder what it is like to be Cloud when it is first touched by the Sunrise, Acorn nourishing its sprout, Chick cracking open its shell, Stone newly washed up on distant shore. *The First Dance of Life is danced in many ways by many of Creator's children.* Find the child within you and touch your own

---

7   Chapter 4 will address the warrior as protector in more detail.

sunrise, nourish your Self, open to a new day and discover new shores on Earth Mother. This is your Big Dance, too.

ELDER DANCE

You are never too young to celebrate life! We are all babes in relation to Eternity. Our Elders are the older children of this world, still nurtured by Earth Mother. They soon will return to her to be cradled once again.

During the honor dances for our Elders, we recognize this truth, and see that they are but a blink of an eye ahead of the young. We honor the path the Elders have traveled, for it is the path of all. The flowing silver hair shines with the hopes and dreams of youth and expresses Mitakuye-Oyasin. The prayers of our Elders are listened to with open hearts, for we understand it is the prayer of our Self.

When an honor dance is given for an Elder, we stand in honor of their full Life Circle. We look forward to shaking their hands when the moment comes that we may pay tribute to them. The moment is given especially to them, and as we listen to the Drum's beat, we hear the unending beat of Eternity. As they dance, past, present, and future become One.

ELDER WISDOM

Wisdom is the natural harvest that comes when an Elder has danced with all of the seasons. Elders have become intimate with Earth Mother. They have massaged Her back so often, that they have memorized Her high peaks and low valleys. They have heard Her songs so many times, that the melody now sings through their veins. They have learned to listen to Her with sharps ears, that now listening is their language.

At an Elder Honor Dance, we give Namaji to our Elders who have given so much to the community.

There are many different processes that lead to Elder Enlightenment. As unique as each of the thousands of rocks and minerals that Earth Mother has born, Elders have reached their individual understanding through similar processes, the forces and pressures of life have carved out their own spiritual vessel. The heat of anger and passion, the eruptions of great emotional experiences, the erosion of useless defenses, the discovery of rare gems, all teach the Elder what it is to be Mishomis. Some Elders have experienced more pain than others in this process. Others have seen tragedies many have never imagined. Tribal tragedy, death, and addictions have carved many memories. Yet, tribal celebrations, birth and marriages have also filled their Medicine Bags. All Elders have their unique experiences. Respect Elders and you respect their path.

Hear this prayer of Elder, as he dances the Sacred Hoop. It is the prayer of timelessness, connection, understanding and wisdom.

FLOWERS-SENT

I wear flowers.

Bright pink and red flowers color my regalia. Beaded flowers, printed flowers. I wear your flowers.

I lift the Sacred Hoop to honor you, my daughter. I look into the red marbled West Sky. Knowing you dance with me, there is no separation. The red bleeds into the clouds and I remember your joy. I dance your joy. With you, I dance.

Daughter, you are Spring. You are Beauty. I dance for you. I wear flowers.

My dance honors the Spirit Dream that visited me when I mourned your passing. I see violets that dance along the trails in my mind. I see daisies that play amidst the woods. I hear roses sing songs into the wind.

In my Spirit Dream, you danced to meet me at the forest's edge. You held a bouquet of flowers in your arms and kissed my cheek. I move to the beat, now, and know you still see the beauty, just as I still feel the flowers you placed into my waiting arms. I see your smile. I hear your words, "I leave, to honor you."

I dance strong into this memory. It moves me around the Sacred Circle. For a long time I could not know how your passing could be a gift, when you alone were the gift. But the flowers you gave me filled me with peace. Your Spirit guided my hands into sewing these tiny flowers on my regalia. I will honor this Vision. I will honor you. I wear your flowers.

The beat is strong. My memory of you is strong. My dancing joins your moment here. I place my foot down on soft Earth Mother and know you have joined her embrace. I move to the good heartbeat of life and know I, too, will soon join the beginning. I celebrate the song. I celebrate the vision. I wear flowers.

I celebrate your gift. I look to the children, sitting close to the circle and I know I must teach them. They see an old man. But inside the flowers on my regalia there is a young spirit that frolics in the Springtime. I must teach them that I am all of this. I am the child, the adolescent, the young man, the old man. I wear flowers.

It is easy to be old. Old is opening up to another way, another door. As my face cracks, my Spirit sees through the wrinkles of time to see beyond, to see the Spirit World, to meet you again. With your flowers, it is easy to be old.

Some think it is hard for me. I cannot run. But in my mind, I see myself running. I cannot jump, but in my heart I can feel myself jumping. I cannot move quickly, but in my Spirit there is no time, no need to go fast. So it is easy for me. I wear flowers.

I wear your gift. I move inside the flowers, sent like a bee, gathering the nectar of life, of Springtime. I sing the

summer song between strawberry and raspberry. It is the
Red Road. I wear flowers.

On the Red Road of Life, I sing your song. I wear flowers.

Unfair Gifts

It is natural to wonder about the seeming "inequities of life." When tragedy
strikes, there may be no answers, meaning may not matter. At first, only the
tragedy matters. That is one mark of a tragedy. It consumes us. It eats at our
spirit. We must honor the pain of the tragedy. We must attend to our wounds,
the anger, the sadness, and the emptiness[8].

As time heals, may you be free to find peace, to move on to the meaning
and even the gift tragedy has left behind. Ask yourself, "What has tragedy to
gift my Spirit?" Ask also, "Why have I left the Spirit World, if not to experience
life?" Perhaps what is tragedy in this world, is opportunity in the Spirit World.

Life continually gives us opportunities to grow and become. For the most
fragile flowers push and grow out of the hardest rock. The most stagnant
pond harbors life for thousands of beings. Great storms bring life where life
has long been dormant.

Why do bad things happen to good people? The answer lies in the question.
For what is good and what is bad? Certainly there are wonderful moments,
as celebrating a birth. Certainly there are tragic moments, as mourning a
death. But even these mountains and valleys are given the overcast of shadows
and the silver lining of clouds. The gifts of life can not be ordered through a
catalog. For the Giver decides what is to be given. The gifts of life come in
packages of all sizes, from givers beyond your knowledge, with fragrances
beyond your senses, with understandings beyond your limits. Enjoy the
gifts you recognize you do have, now. Appreciate the bouquets you are
sent. Discover the gifts that await you in the darkest of hours. Let the vision
of the Creator fill you with flowers and joy. What is emptied, will be filled.

---

[8]   Chapter 7 will help guide you through the grieving process of loss.

Learn to let Life question you. Listen to the whispers. Learn to allow your Self to question life. For in the asking, you may discover the answer. And if not the answer, the gift of peace.

What Are Your Questions?

Whether you are near the North Door of Elder Enlightenment, or the South Door of adolescence[9], listen with the ears of our Elders, sing with the songs of Earth Mother, and massage her with tender love and respect. In the language of our Elders we can discover meaning.

Ask what meaning your life holds for you on your Life Circle.

What matters most to you, right now? Please write that one thing down. What will matter the most to you five minutes from now? Write that down. What will matter the most five hours from now? Please, record this understanding. Continue with the following questions, taking the time to really reflect what you believe. Then write each response down, so that in the end you will have a list of meanings.

What will matter five days from now? What will matter five years from now? What will matter fifty years from now? What will matter five hundred years from now? What will matter five thousand years from now? Take this time to answer each of these questions. As you go further and further out of time, you may discover the timelessness that Elders now glimpse. May you discover meaning.

If you are unable to identify or discover your meaning, then begin by asking and answering the questions which follow. Be honest in your responses. Give yourself enough time to answer with your heart. This book will be here tomorrow, next week. Better that it takes you two years to truly answer these questions than to rush through this exercise and never know yourself.

Why might I have chosen this path? What have I to empty from myself? What have I to fill into myself? What song has my Spirit to sing? Why do I always

---

9   The North Door on the Medicine Wheel represents the time where one reflects and rests in Eternity. It is the last stage in our life cycle. The South Door represents invigorating growth spurts. It is a time when Self expands and grows outward; a time to collect one's identity.

return to the same thought, behavior, decision, situation? Where do I hope to go? How will I get there? What have I missed along the way? What could I give? What is my unique talent? What do I want to leave for this world? How do I want to leave? What can I discover in the Silence? What is my essence? What will I take back to the Spirit World?

There are an infinite number of questions for you to ask, for the questions change as the days move. When you temporarily run out of questions, look to other people for more. They speak with non-words most clearly. Look at their facial expressions, their actions, their attitudes, their body posture. Are they filled with regrets or gratitude? Are they glad of life or sad of life?

Silence yourself. Spiritual Presence will then aid you in discovering your meaning. In silence, universal purpose speaks. In solitude, world connection vibrates. In unifying ecstasy, Self celebration awaits.

Celebrate your life purpose today. For today is all we have. Find something to celebrate today and you will have lived a long and prosperous day.

Please listen to the silent voices of our Elders. Wonder what it is like to be the *Last Cloud* touched by Sunset, dignified Oak offering life to a new seedling. Eagle soaring closer to Ishpeming, and Stone swept into the current to return to the Great Sea. Come to the Dark Door of the West and color your own sunset, nourish others' spirits, soar to the Great Beyond, and journey to exciting places. This is your honor, too. This is your dance.

Elder Language

Hear my Listening
it Brings
your Beginning
my Memory
our Joining

Hear my Listening
it Moves
your Song
my Heart
our Prayer

Hear my Listening
it Speaks
your Teachings
my Understandings
our Experience

Hear my Listening
it Holds
your Dreams
my Vision
our Future

Our Elders have much to teach. Give them the opportunity to teach the young. Give them your presence. Listen to their great rolling words. Hear the meaning of life that has been filtered through their wise eyes[10]. There is much for you to gain as you listen to our Elders. They need to tell you their story. They need to tell you of the Great Circle of Life. This is their time to teach. Slow down enough to allow your time to meet theirs.

---

[10] Our Elders offer tremendous insights into life, aging, and dying. Discover the lessons Elders teach within their conversations, preoccupations, and memories. Listen to their memories. It is the memory of all. Ask them questions. They want to answer.

DANCE FOR THE ELDERS

Many young dancers do not dance for themselves, alone. As they dance they are aware of the Elders who sit on the periphery of the arbor, unable to dance as they once had. As the young dance, the old are honored. The dancers select someone and keep them in mind as they dance the Circle. In this way, they dance for the Elder.

> I dance for you.
> This is your dance.
> May your body move with my steps.
> They celebrate your wisdom.
> May your heart follow my spinning circles.
> I twirl for your life.
> May your spirit feel my steps lightly touch Earth Mother.
> I honor your journey.
> May you join me as I listen to the Drum.
> I am listening to your language.
> I dance for you.
> This is your dance.

A giving dance is the best dance of all.

HONOR IS FOR ALL

All Powwow dances are honor dances. Each individual has a unique and special purpose and that is cause enough to honor and celebrate. There are as many reasons for honor dances as there are species on Earth Mother. Celebrate every expression of Self; their uniqueness gives us our uniqueness. Celebrate each song and dance; they resonate with the One Heartbeat. Celebrate each with Namaji; they are the connection to the Universal Truth.

Each unique dance style celebrates and honors the Self, Others, and Earth Mother. Like the nature of water (liquid, gas and solid), honor these three and honor the One, as the essence of Self, Others and Earth Mother. All are from the Great Spirit. It is Gitchi Manidoo that is ultimately honored, from which all of creation is born.

The specific dances that follow in the subsequent chapters focus on a unique aspect of creation. Yet, the dancers know, the singers know, the spirits know, that All of creation is honored. The very beat of the Drum resonates this connection, as its vibrations ripple outward through the entire dance circle to include the Creator's All. With that Spirit of Oneness, dance the dance of All. Discover your own Sun Trail and, as One, Celebrate Life.

As one, celebrate The Circle.

Mitakuye-Oyasin.

DANCE WITH OTHERS

Nothing in life is accomplished by one.
Everything in life is the result of many.

PART TWO

WARRIOR DANCE

Warriors return to us bleeding
of
wounded bodies
ingrained memories
saddened hearts
grieving spirits

We must honor the warriors
and their
wounded bodies
ingrained memories
saddened hearts
grieving spirits

We must help them heal
their
wounded bodies
ingrained memories
saddened hearts
grieving spirits

Their blood is our blood
and our
wounded bodies
ingrained memories
saddened hearts
grieving spirits

The Warrior's Dance is a powerful recognition of our warriors, both past and present. It is a moment of prominent Namaji for our warrior relatives. The warrior dance lifts the hearts of all present, as warriors are saluted, valued, and acknowledged for their service and bravery. Our veteran warriors, with their service and sacrifice, are respected as the *first* at Powwow, for they have put their own needs and wants as the last.

In songs, like the one at the beginning of this chapter, we become aware of how the warrior's lives have touched death. In dance, we now recognize and respect their spiritual experience of war. As the Drumstick strikes the Drum, it echoes the voice of both the physical and spiritual worlds, speaking both languages fluently. The "crossing over" from this life to the next is observed. With this consciousness of life and death, warriors are honored for their bravery, for their crossing over, for their spiritual emptying and filling.

FLAG SONG

The solemn moment of the Flag Song[1] is one of the few times all bells are silent during the Powwow celebration.

Following Grand Entry, all present remain standing[2]. We honor all warriors who have died. The Flag Song is sung, the Drum continues to beat, and our hearts respectfully join the Spirits of our ancestors. It is a moment of overflowing regard and love as silence then fills the Powwow arbor. We fall silent, and the song is given to the ancestors to dance within the Spirit World. The Flag Song belongs to them.

Families of lost warriors understand the sacredness of this moment; it is for the families as well as for the warriors. It is an opportunity to celebrate the warrior's life, and their spiritual presence, once again. As hearts and minds salute and caress each other, time and space move into nothingness and separation is no more. It is a joining of physical and spiritual in the present. The Sacred Hoop of Eternity is engaged and families are reunited in Spirit once again.

---

[1]   The Flag Song is an Indian anthem.

[2]   The order of Flag Song, Invocation, the Posting of Colors (flags and staffs) and Veteran's Song may vary. The order given in this chapter is common among Anishinaabe people.

Listen to this eternal honor of those who have died in battle. Listen to the rhythm. Its beat sounds with love, as we stand to feel the Spirits of the Warriors dance.

THE WARRIORS' DANCE

We attend.
Our Silence spans Eternity
Their Presence fans the Melody,
And the Warriors dance.

We extend.
Rhythm gifts their trancing start.
Our Love lifts their dancing heart.
Now they dance.

We intend.
Their Spirits twirl, as hearts entwine
Tributes whirl, roll through time.
While they dance.

We ascend.
Their Love is sent and whispers to
A sweet scent and kiss us true.
Feel them dance.

We transcend.
And Love pours out as Joy in Spring
For now they soar on Wind's Great Wing.
And the Warriors dance.

This connection and honor of Spirit Warriors is needed and recognized by tribal people. The non-Indian world also recognizes the need for this connection. Veteran's Day, Memorial Day, Bastille Day, the Fourth of July, ask us to pause. But do we? For many, these days have become a symbol of our vacation rather than our connection to warriors who were willing to sacrifice their lives. In our busy living, have we lost the meaning of these tributes? If we don't stay connected and remember the lessons from the past, are we not doomed to repeat them?

People are in a hurry today. Drivers weave in and out of traffic, rushing to get "there," only to sit at a red light with the same drivers they previously gestured with irritation and passed. In a hurry to go on vacation, we rush to enjoy. Never relaxing, we hurriedly eat, sleep, work, and play. Life becomes one blurred experience, including our intentions and meanings. Today's prized speed and instant gratification comes at a high price—a forfeiture of Self. We forfeit our Self when we are too rushed to remember who we are inside.

Look to the beavers that appear to be constantly busy. The busy beaver knows when to work out in the world and when to rest in his lodge. He has engineered both an entrance and an exit to the woods. He is able to stop his life in order to gain quietude. Where do you get your rest? How do you? When do you? Where are your exits from the busy world?

We must slow down or we will miss all that has meaning. Meaning is revealed only when you pause, when you stop, when you pay attention. Learn the lesson of tribal people. Put your busy-ness on pause, eliminate distractions, and allow the meaning of life and living to return to you. Slow down in order to connect to the meaning of life.

I invite you to take this moment, now, and join your heart with your loved ones who have given their life in battle. Light a candle, say a prayer, sing. Create music from your heart for your warrior to dance to. Give this moment to them. Be still. Silence your bells, silence your life. Stop all movement, all distractions, all busy habits. Visualize, feel, experience your warrior dancing his or her song in the Spirit World.

Allow the meaning of the Flag Song to fill you with gratitude for your warriors. With your silence, give the honor and the dance to the Spirit World. *Be present.* Thank them for their gifts. Give our warriors love once again. Allow Namaji to flow from this world to the Spirit World.

For this is their song. This is their dance. This is their moment.

OPENING PRAYER

With the help of Brother Tree's walking stick and his son's arms, the old man slowly raised from his chair to accept the microphone at the speaker stand. With the Flag Song complete, the Elder momentarily stood tall at East opening. His family had trailed behind him with love and respect, a glimpse of his life's extent. His clothes, old and forever comfortable, layered his age with easy folds of left-over-room, telling a story of the eventual journey back to nothingness. His feet, clad in tennis shoes, loosely rested on the wheelchair's foot support. Feet that once ran and jumped, that once worked hard, now only remembered. The Elder slowly adjusted his favorite cap that covered his white hair and his gnarled fingers felt the two attached feathers. He was ready.

Holding onto the microphone, as though holding onto a flute, old hands would now offer the people his song. Hands that had carried rough Mishomis stones, touched infants' cheeks, covered tearful eyes, now offered his gift.

In his tribal tongue he spoke. His prayer to Gitchi Manidoo moved like water, spilling and flowing from his heart. The microphone's speakers raced to keep up with what he was saying. Echoes of moments filled Sky Father, as great respect and honor filled the Powwow grounds. All stood knowing that this language had nearly died and honored him for giving it his breath so that they could hear its music[3]. Some

---

3   The history of the loss of language will be more fully addressed in Chapter 7. Tribal Community Colleges and Tribal Schools, however, are now becoming very active in gifting the language back to the people. Today's children are learning their language, thus culture and traditions will survive!

dancers and spectators recognized specific words. Others heard the entire message. But like a whisper of one's own breath, all felt the power of the prayer, for it crossed the boundaries of words.

As the Elder spoke, his voice became a soothing great wave of energy. This language, born from deep within, resonated as a spiritual song and filled the arbor with energy. Like a gentle massage, the sounds of the words reached into each one present. His words gathered the prayers together and lifted them to the Great Spirit. Hypnotized with the moment, all stood completely still. Spirit freeing, the people soared with the experience of his prayer.

"Mitakuye-Oyasin," the prayer ended, then silence. The Elder bowed his head and the two feathers followed, also bowing to honor Earth Mother. The honor beats were sounded and words of Migwetch filled the Circle.

I invite you to hear my prayer that I offer to Gitchi Manidoo. May my words cross the boundaries of language and culture and join the melody of your Spirit. Please open your heart and allow my words to take your needs to the Great Spirit. Let this become an Opening Prayer for the Dance of All.

Oh, Great Spirit, Your goodness is all around. In the songs of the birds, I hear Your melody. In the swaying of pines, I feel Your breath. In the opening of clouds, I know You await. Your goodness tastes sweet in the berries I eat. Your warmth is felt in the fire of my home. Your honor is acknowledged in the vast endless seas that stretch the horizon.

Your beauty is everywhere. In the flowers of the fields and woods I smell Your scent. I see Your reflection in glimmering water. I rest in Your tranquillity that gazes from Moose's eye. I touch Your gentleness, wrapped in the fur of our brothers. I experience Your flight within the feathers of the winged. In the creepers' voices I hear Your movement. In the majesty of Mishomis, You are experienced and loved. Gitchi Manidoo, accept my heart full of love and gratitude.

You have given us this Earth Mother. She sustains us. We understand that we do not own Her. She gives us the fruit of Herself and asks only for respect. Help us give Her this respect.

You understand my heart, for You recognize my call as a mother wolf hears her cub. You give me sweet grass to wipe my tears and laughter to fill my Spirit. You give Grandfather Sun for my day dance and Grandmother Moon for my night dance. Migwetch.

Oh, Great Spirit. Send Brother Eagle to fly over head and bring all our prayers to You. Let him circle with Your goodness and remind us of Your presence.

Let us look to him and vision our own flight. Let us transcend to the same heights. Let us experience the same currents and dance with the same Spirit. Help us to become what we are meant to become. Show us the path of our Self. Like the Great Wind Spirits that guide Brother Eagle to his home, bring us to Ain-dah-ing with Your breath of life. In our life-dance, let us honor You. Let us unite with the Great Mystery. Let us Celebrate this great gift. Gitchi Manidoo, we say Gitchi Migwetch for the gifts You send us each day.

Thank You for the Warriors. For they have given their life, their innocence, their needs. Help us fill their needs, direct them to the East Direction, and honor their life. As our shadows all emerge from the same sunrise and sunset, let us never forget our eternal union. May we honor the Warriors just as we treasure the trees that have survived

Great Storms. Help us surround our Warriors with our
present support, as they stand emotionally scarred in the
aftermath of destruction.

Help us erase all human boundaries. We understand that
just as Sky Father knows no limits, Your love is for all. Let
us give this same love and honor to all our brothers and
sisters. Help us manifest Mitakuye-Oyasin in all our words,
thoughts, and deeds.

Let us become the truth. Let us become the dignity. Let us
become One. Let us reflect Your Eternal Love.

Mitakuye-Oyasin.

"POST YOUR COLORS, SIR."

At the closing of the Elder's prayer, the flag bearers are asked to post their
colors. Each veteran who is honored by carrying in a flag is introduced to
the people. Wearing both street clothes and/or personal regalia, the veterans
stand in line to be honored and to honor. The United States flag is presented
and the veteran is introduced. Loud salutes from the drums hit in unac-
cented joy to honor the veteran. The POW and the MIA flags are each
brought forth and the moment is offered to help mend the hoop, to close the
circle. Again the drums are hit, saluting each flag bearer. Flags from visiting
countries are presented. Finally, the Eagle staff is honored. All tribal people
understand the powerful meaning of this flag. It is the symbol of our people.
Great honor beats are sounded for this staff, for our survival and tradition. As
each flag is presented with honor, each now rests in its waiting holder[4].

The Eagle Staff and military flags oversee the Powwow from this honored
position. With their presence, the Spirits of past Warriors participate in the
celebration and weave their dancing into the Powwow with the waving of
the flags and the flutter of the feathers. Their presence resides with dignity.
The Warriors in the Spirit World are honored, here and now. The Eagle Staff

---

[4]   This may be at the center of the circle or in front of the speaker's stand.

must be humbly retired at sunset, for the Eagle is a day bird, and we honor Eagle in this way.

Like the Flag Song that honors the dancing of our warriors, like the posting of colors that honors the participant, the Dance of Life includes both the Dance of Spirits and our unique Celebration. When we dance, we recognize we do not dance alone. The Spirits have crossed over to greet us on this side of the drumbeat. The Spirit World participates in our experience. They must be honored and recognized for their genuine presence. In this way, we respect their needs.

Come to recognize the Spirit World's participation in your life. Honor their dancing. Greet them, as they greet you, with love and honor. Post your own colors, proudly.

VETERAN'S DANCE

Veterans who have survived the battle, are now honored with a dance. All veterans are invited to dance, regalia or not, for all veterans, have shared a common experience.

Veterans were willing to give their life for their country, for their community, for their village, for their family. In memory of this supreme sacrifice, they come together to dance in the Circle. They are as intimate with the Drum's beat as they are with their own pulse. Warriors are keenly aware that the heart beat is vital to surviving the challenges of the human experience.

Follow Standing Tree into this Circle. Experience his dance. Recognize the same beat, the same strong pulse to life. May his dance extend out to greet you.

STANDING TREE

Standing Tree entered the Dance. The Circle opened to his experience and the sun-bronzed veteran yielded to its familiar comfort. As his colors flew, he knew this dance was for him.

Entering the arbor, his heart pulsed strong and he remembered the day he had entered the service. It had been a warm sunny day, like today. A day when the future nearly cracked open the gateway of the present, for many dreams had offered to prepare Standing Tree for war. Entering the dance now, the past, present, and future merged into one view. Standing Tree finally understood his dreams of war.

Outside the Circle his mother stood in honor of her son. Standing Tree moved by her, to the same rhythm as when he had felt her tears kiss his cheek good-bye. "She is proud again," he thought, feeling the warm sun in his hair.

The Drum continued. The singers honored him with an old warrior song. Standing Tree knew the Straight Song[5] had been sung for his ancestors when they had returned from battle[6]. Honor circled once again.

"I feel like I just returned," he thought now and wondered if others who passed by him felt the same.

The beat pulsed on, just as Standing Tree's heart had continued when his body was exhausted with war. Sweat dripped down his cheek and he suddenly remembered Two Feathers' jokes. His friend had always made him laugh until he cried. Two Feathers had even made him smile right up until Two Feather's heart had stopped beating. "But mine still beats," thought this man becoming strong again with the memory of his friend. "Now I dance for you, Brother," his heart murmured to Two Feathers.

---

5 A Straight Song is a traditional song without words. Vowel sounds such as hey, ya, hi, accompany specific tones. A lead singer leads off with the first line and is eventually joined by the group. Attention to pitch and tone is the beauty of the vocals of this type of song. Northern singers use powerful, high falsetto voices.

6 Some modern Powwow footwork and dancing is generally recognized as stemming from the war dance societies of the Oklahoma, Omaha and Pawnee's Grass Dance. Widespread tribal ceremonies of thanks, honor, allegiances and sacred celebration of Earth Mother, including feasting and dancing, can be attributed to all Native People.

The dance took Standing Tree to the hidden places inside himself. A knot of memories ached in his shoulders as he whirled with a bold rhythm. The Drum pulsed on, just as his heartbeat had once endured in battle. Eyes closed, Standing Tree instantly saw what his eyes had once masked. He remembered all that his mind had forgotten. He felt again how his heart had once painfully ached.

Faster, Standing Tree danced on the hard earth. His heart pumped quickly. With its surge, he recalled the fear that had once electrified his body. Alerted, the beat persisted. Faced with death, his heart had chosen life. When other's blood spilled, Standing Tree's had continued to flow inside his body. In the spinning gush of emotion, Standing Tree emptied the fear and anger with which his Spirit had once been filled. Cleansing his Spirit, the drum continued.

The very rhythm that had moved on, when Standing Tree lost part of himself in war, moved into him now. "But now it is the pulse of coming home," smiled Standing Tree. Having danced the entire circle, he passed his mother again and remembered kissing her tears of joy, this time. His eyes once again said, "Boozhoo, Mother." Now, he was able to see the sun in her black hair, making it appear purple like Raven's feathers.

It was love that aided Standing Tree to finally feel the sweet surrender of the beat. Inside ecstasy he danced. With the pulse of belonging, Standing Tree felt a deep healing with his people. For the rest of the song, this man of integrity danced beyond time and joined the Eternal beat. Time did stop, as Standing Tree swayed.

Standing Tree looked around and saw his life reflected in the smiles of children and in the respect of the Elders' eyes. He felt the dignity of his people.

In his wheelchair, Standing Tree lifted his Eagle fan, saluted
the Drum, and honored the Spirits. Standing Tree danced
around the arbor to the last beat of the song. His strong
arms paused on the wheels of his chair, and reached to
Father Sky. With a cry of recognition and a hearty smile he
greeted his friend, Two Feathers.

His Spirit danced like the moon on water and reflected
Namaji to all people. His relatives supported him as he
lifted himself to stand tall. His blood pulsed with the
strength of his roots. He saw the Vision of his Dreams. He
felt the healing of his heart. And in the lifting of his Spirit,
the two White Medicine feathers on his headdress felt the
warmth of the Sun of the Dance.

RITUAL WARRIOR DANCE

Warriors were required to change in preparing for, and during battle. This
change must be acknowledged. Many warriors have learned to tap their
Mash-ka-wisen while risking their lives. They have learned to walk through
their deepest fears. They may have witnessed horrible tragedies that ripped
at their Spirit. In the Warrior Dance, their sacrifices are honored publicly. This
honor elevates them toward the Great Spirit. They can now fill with the Spirit
of love. Closer to the Great Spirit, they are cleansed and healed. Lifted up,
their suffering is acknowledged. Encircled by their tribe, they are not alone
in their experience.

This ritual of preparation, traditional understanding, and community healing
becomes the Warrior's blanket. The tough hide of spiritual principles and
tribal tradition protects the Warrior from the outside elements of war, as they
wear and feel the soft warm lining of comfort close to their heart.

TRIBAL WARRIORS

Like the Native American Dream Catcher that captures the bad dreams of the sleeper, the warrior's community becomes a Great Web to catch his embittered memories. The true spirit of Mitakuye-Oyasin commits to the unity of the tribe. With honor and support from family and friends, veterans come home to this Web of Love. The warrior is cleansed and healed through this shared commitment. Thereby, the community is cleansed and healed.

Old age wisdom understands the necessity of spiritually attending to the warrior, mourning the spirits, and celebrating with Namaji—honor, pride, dignity and respect. As warriors reenact brave deeds in their dance, all veterans' war experiences and insights are brought back to the people. Our living warriors need attending to, the warriors of this world need recognition. They must be able to return home to a web of love.

ALL VETERANS OF WAR

Veterans' reactions to traumatic experiences have sometimes been referred to as "shell-shock." A more contemporary diagnosis of these symptoms is commonly referred to as Post Traumatic Stress Disorder, or PTSD.

Consider the numerous support groups for Vietnam Vets as they try to heal from the horror of their war experience. Consider the veterans of all wars, all over Earth Mother. Think of their sadness, their loss, their grief. What did they return home to?

Imagine the world offering a dance of recognition to our Veterans when they returned from war. What difference would that have made in their lives? In our lives? What spiritual healing would have taken place? What cycles would have been stopped? What new direction would begin?

Now, consider the children—the tiny tots, the adolescents—experiencing the shelling, the hate, the death of war, growing up in this, becoming this, living this. What dance do we offer these children? What spiritual healing takes place within the web of Mitakuye-Oyasin? What is offered to the survivors of trauma?

OTHER SURVIVORS OF TRAUMA

Many survivors of traumatic experiences, such as child abuse, spousal abuse, witnesses of violence and death, are diagnosed with PTSD. There are many warriors of life that need to be recognized for their experiences. Like the veterans, their honor, too, needs to be recognized and saluted.

Just as Veterans are recognized as both brave warriors and victims of war, we must also recognize the other warriors of life that are victims. Victims are people faced with circumstances that violate a part of themselves. Loss is involved. Injury has occurred. Suffering has been endured.

With violence rampant in our society, we do not have to go far to discover victims. They may be your next door neighbor, your family or friend, your co-worker. Perhaps the victim is you.

What sadness stills grips at your heart? What anger must you release? What trauma do you have to dance? Honor the trauma of your Self. If you have been such a victim, please, find someone qualified to hear you, to help you heal and understand your pain. Look to your experience with the soft focus of Ain-dah-ing. See the world, honor the questions, and enter into the dark places. Allow the pain of your trauma to help lead you back into the light of peace and balance.

Dance the Warrior Dance of Self. Heal with your family and community. Wear the blanket of the warrior.

WELCOME THE SURVIVORS HOME

Victims need to be healed publicly, for community support and honor is good medicine. A tide of Namaji is the first washing needed to heal the open wounds of great tragedy. Its current carries survivors into community acceptance. On this shoreline they are able to make footprints anew.

It is time to welcome home the victims of our society. Returned to the safety of peace, of Ain-dah-ing, their transition must be honored. It is up to each individual to acknowledge our warriors' pain and to honor our victims. Like Standing Tree, today's warriors need our strength to help them stand tall once again.

Do you know a victim or warrior? Have you given them your time? Have you committed your Self to their healing? Take the time to lift the fallen beams of daily living and uncover the victims in your life. Their anguish waits to be eased. As we help pick up the heavy and oppressing weight of past pain, we will share in their renewed celebration of life.

Learn to be a good listener. Give victims a chance to talk about their experience. Let them feel the pain. Give them time to heal. Help them remove their thorns. With your presence you honor them. Be present for them.

Recently, a young Wisconsin girl was abducted and taken away from her family and community. As the community prayed for her safe return, a wave of love and concern connected all together as one. Each day of her absence brought the community closer together. This week, with great relief and joy, the entire community celebrated as she was found and returned to her family. Two days ago, the girl and her family led the community in a candle-lit march through her town. The community has welcomed the girl back. They have celebrated her life. Connected to one another, this web of love will be an integral aspect to her healing. Their prayers will lift her spirit and heal her heart.

Honor the warriors and victims in your world. Be active in your community in welcoming them back home. Help in ways you are able. With your time, resources, love, energy and honor, give the victim the chance to be whole again. Discover ways in which you can participate in the dance of renewal.

Let your heart pour out. What can you offer? Empty your bucket, so theirs can refill.

THE WAR FROM WITHOUT

Perhaps the most difficult of life experiences is to be a victim.

Many children grow up today with many issues. As victims of divorce, alcoholism, abuse and neglect, the hand they have been dealt is stacked against them. It is easy for the child to continue the victim role into adulthood, for the patterns have been established. Yet, there are some remarkable people who recognize that the hand they are dealt is the only hand they have. And with that, they play their cards carefully and deliberately. They play their cards right. Suddenly, their life is transformed into a winning hand! They have taken the power back. They recognize that it is their life, their decisions, their future. The present honors the past with the decision to live in the now.

Attention, affection, recognition, and approval can be given by Self. Discovering your purpose in life, engaging Bimadisiwin, and celebrating each day will inevitably give you these Self nurturing tools.

Take this moment to look carefully at the cards you were dealt. Honor the pain. What learning must you acknowledge? How can you play your hand so that you, too, will be victorious? How can your life be redefined so that it transforms into a life of worth and dignity? What can you choose to do for today? How can you move from victim to brave warrior? Reframe your thinking so that <u>you</u> are in control of your own destiny. Allow yesterday to remain in the past. The past IS NOT the present. However, honor and allow the past to guide your decisions today. Make decisions that will create and direct a new future. Discover the joy of living. Relish in the possibilities of tomorrow. Live in the now! Create the best moment of your life! To all you remarkable people, I honor you for choosing to live your life!

Only when victims are no longer victimized, will a new empowered generation of Self be born[7]. It is time to gift the world with Self nurturance and Self respect. Help end the abusive cycle so a new cycle of Namaji can permeate our world. It must first begin with you. Respect your Self.

Like Brother Tree, compensate for your injuries and grow around your wounds. Notice that trees that have endured terrible injuries can flourish with astonishing growth. Like the Pine Tree who sprouts an amazing concentrated area of needles around his injury, concentrate on how you can flourish. It may astound you. Celebrate your healing potential! Celebrate your

---

[7]   Usually, abusers began as victims themselves. Their expectations that others would reciprocate their kindness and respect were not met. From this innocent beginning, the cycle of abuse forms. When others did not respect them, their expectations were crushed. Often the victim became aggressive in reaction to the abuse. Passive-aggressive behavior patterns thereby develop.

miracle growth! Celebrate your purpose! Heal your Self, and your rings of life will someday be counted by others.

Be deliberate in your daily choices. Each day presents itself anew and each day you have the right to choose differently. Give your Self permission to be in charge of your actions. Govern your Self. Be honest in your reflection, be clear with your alternatives, be strong in your decisions.

When war from without, in the form of people, circumstances or society, presents itself, recognize whether or not you need be there. If possible, free yourself from the abuse or injury being inflicted upon you. Choose not to be someone else's doormat, spittoon, or punching bag. Someone once said, "The best way to defend against an attack, is not to be there." You have the right to live a life of Namaji.

Look to the animals. They respect their limits and needs. They naturally choose the path of safety. The Winged fly south when it is too cold, while Brother Bear grows a warm coat and hibernates. Deer find a windfall to escape the fury of the storm. Animals race to leave the burning forest.

Where do you go for shelter? Where do you sleep safely? How hot does your forest need to get before you leave it behind? Discover your safe path so you can flourish. Choose to respect your needs. Choose to respect your Self. Don't hold yourself hostage and terrorize yourself with abusive thoughts. Only in this way can you offer complete Namaji to this world and to your healing.

PREPARE YOUR SELF FOR WAR

Unfortunately, it isn't always possible to change environments and leave warfare behind. Like our ancestors, we may need to confront undesirable situations with dignity and honor. Like our warriors, we must prepare ourselves for the demands of possible war. We must recognize that without adequate preparation, victimization is more likely to occur.

We must acknowledge the warrior side of our being. Come to understand that warriors were not innately aggressive. A warrior is not essentially brutal or insensitive. Warriors are simply normal people who are prepared for war. Through training, they are prepared to do battle if and when war is unavoidable.

It is best to be prepared for battle, even if you never have to engage. Through the following training, you can learn to deflect the arrows that may come your way.

War Shield

Tribal warriors used war shields to defend themselves against the arrows, spears, tomahawks and war clubs of their enemies. They embellished their war shields with symbols to represent their particular strengths. Signatures were painted as Eagle's wings swooped, Mukwa's claws scratched, or Weasel's eyes burned with fury. Earth Mother offered the warrior many symbols for his shield. Connected to her children, She provided this identity. The pictures of warning named the warrior's essence.

The warrior engaged his Mash-ka-wisen and walked through his fear. Developing access to Ain-dah-ing, the place of peace, the warrior experienced calm inside. This calm offered him a soft focused view of Life. Able to see beyond the moment into the eternal essence of himself, he was freed from his fears. Although afraid, he was not controlled by fear. Here, bravery was born. Mash-ka-wisen—inner strength—neutralized the fears. Able to consider options and alternatives, the warrior responded rather than reacted to his environment. In this way, warriors carried both a physical and psychological shield into battle.

Some warriors carry rawhide shields into the dance circle of Powwow. Like the hide that is at first pliable and able to learn what it is to become, the warrior honors his own becoming, his own ability to learn how to be strong. The shield reminds the dancer to ward off attacks that may come his way, as well as become a symbol of internal strength.

Although most people today do not experience physical aggression or attack, many may frequently experience verbal assaults. A shield can be useful for identifying and developing your internal strengths. Take the time now to design your personal war shield. Allow your shield to reflect that part of you that stands out front and takes charge when you are being physically or verbally assaulted or attacked. Let the shield become a symbol of how you will ward off the attacks that may present in your life.

Construct your shield out of any material you desire. If possible, go to Earth Mother for this gift. Find your own rawhide or bark. Give Earth Mother something back in return as you thank the giver. Make your shield about thirty inches in diameter so you will have adequate room to illustrate your protective symbols. Identify the warrior side of you—your strengths, values, and untapped abilities. It is vital to identify your warrior person, for if you ever need to defend yourself or your values, you will have quick conscious access to your strengths and abilities.

Then get out the paint! Choose your war colors[9]. With the guidance of the Spirit World, illustrate the strengths that reside in you. Listen to your dreams and your visions. Choose potent symbols. Lightning bolts may symbolize rapid detection. A black tornado may represent power. Your hand print is your uniqueness. Water may represent your ability to reflect an image back to the sender, as a mirror. A Benaysay[10] cloud may hold your passion. A star may symbolize your worth. A firefly, your ability to respond to the moment. A tree may represent precious values for you to protect. A yellow jacket hornet may speak well to repetitious stinging responses. A falcon may tell of tenacity. What could symbolize your verbal mastery? What could represent your subtle perception? Be sure of your potential and profile. Be certain each symbol has personal meaning, for without meaning it represents nothing. Be balanced in your illustrations. Honor all aspects of your being. Be aware of the Circle of Life of which you are a part and honor the entire circle on your shield.

Then take out your beads, feathers and leather to attach to your shield. They must be items you understand and respect. Do not attach a feather because you think it might look good. Attach a feather because you honor the winged's flight. You enjoy their song. You understand the feather's purpose and its meaning for you. May you only attach that which you honor and hold sacred. May you honor your Sacred Self in this way. May you honor all of life in this way. May each poke of your needle pierce your heart with a deeper understanding of that which you embellish. May you become more as you create your shield. Let this be an experience of celebrating yourself!

---

9   Some shields traditionally contain the four directional colors: yellow, red, white and black, which are also the four race colors and the four peace colors.

10   Pronounced: be-NAY-say and means thunderbird.

The warrior's role is to defend and preserve. Vividly illustrate your shield to fulfill these two needs. Defend who you are to be! Know where you begin and end. Understand that you are what you decide you are, not what someone wants you to be. Defend your values by holding up your internal shield when others would attack or try to coerce you. With your shield of knowledge, you will be prepared to stand firm in who you are and defend your values when attacked. Then keep the shield forever with you. It will preserve all that you have striven for. Let your shield become an internal peace treaty that you honor and hold near your heart.

Eight Departments of the United States government, Commerce, Defense, Energy, Health, Justice, Labor, State, and Veterans have an eagle on their shield. Three eagles clutch arrows. One shield depicts a lightning bolt. The Department of Interior has a buffalo and Sun Trail on its shield. The Presidential Seal portrays Ganu[11]: with arrows clutched in one talon and a branch in the other, military readiness and peace-mindedness are recognized as equal strengths[12]. Yet, I wonder if the people in these Departments still remember, understand, and uphold the intended meaning of the shields? Symbols are meaningless unless the meaning is upheld.

As you finish your war shield, may you always be ready to protect yourself and recognize the value of peace. The shield will only have purpose when you give it meaning. Choose to find its meaning. Discover the freedom that psychological preparation gives you! Be prepared!

Warnings and Natural Defenses

Warriors have long painted their bodies and faces in preparation for battle. Like a wolf raising his fur and barring his teeth, war paint exposes the internal warrior for all to see. As both a warning to the enemy and a representation of the strengths of the warrior, war paint was a meaningful aspect of warfare.

---

[11] Pronounced: ga-NU and means war or death eagle.

[12] It is becoming commonly recognized that much of the Constitution and democratic ideals originally came from the Iroquois Nation's Great Law.

Look deeply into a mirror and ask to see the warrior inside. If you let your warrior paint him/herself, what would you see? How would you feel[13]? Befriend the face of the warrior inside. Try it on. Just as the shell protects the turtle, the warrior exists to protect you. Thank the warrior for his readiness.

Animals and plants have their shields for protection, warnings, and weapons to defend themselves. Rattle snakes give warning before they strike. Antlers, fangs, thorns, claws, venom, coils of muscles, webs, stingers, beaks, poisons, and talons are some of the natural defenses other relatives use to survive.

Just as natural defenses and warnings are necessary for animals to survive, presenting your warrior side is quite natural *if it is appropriate to the situation.* Remember, we too, are animals. What are your warnings? What are your shields? What are your weapons? How will you survive?

Learn to use your shield to warn others that you will not tolerate abuse in any form. Like the rattle snake, assertively communicate your intolerance for disrespect. Be open, honest, direct, calm and specific as you communicate your intentions.

Shield yourself from abuse. Your best defense is your brain. Use it. Always consider your alternatives in any given situation. Always determine the consequences of any decision you are about to make. Deliberately decide strategies for escape if necessary. It is not the survival of the fittest, it is survival of the wisest.

Use your senses as your weapons. Like the bat's sonar, learn to pick up on other's nonverbal communication. If you perceive potential problems, you will not need to raise your shield. Tune in. Approximately eighty percent of what we communicate is nonverbal. People give many clues to what they are thinking and feeling. Watch for warnings. Listen to silent threats. Beware of incongruencies. Avoid falling into the same patterns. Tune in to your surroundings. Do not ignore your sensations. Honor your instincts and intuitions.

Give your warrior side respect and honor. Hope that this side only needs to stand guard and not engage in battle during your life time. But if forced to

---

13 Halloween has traditionally been a culturally accepted time to allow the warrior inside to paint up. Isn't trick or treat really war or peace anyway?

engage, let your warrior step forward and confront the perpetrator that would attack you. May your war cry be heard! Prepare yourself so you are not victimized! Become the warrior!.

THE WAR FROM WITHIN

The most dangerous war is the one in your mind.

It is common to hear someone say, "He or she made me so angry!" Less often do we hear, "*I* made myself so angry!" The war from within is the war that threatens us the most. Unfortunately, it is also the war we recognize the least.

Vulnerable elm trees are tragically destroyed when they become internally infested with disease. They may appear beautiful and strong on the outside for years, even while they are becoming hollow and weak on the inside. This internal affliction leads to death.

External stress, like the bark beetle, detects your vulnerability and, when it enters your person, transforms itself into internal tension. Tension is a disease of Self. It leads to many physical and psychological ailments. If left unattended, tension will chronically affect your life and may lead to the death of your body, obsession of your mind, crippling of your emotions, or weakening of your spirit. Learn to leave what is outside of you (stress) outside. Learn to keep what is inside of you (peace and tranquillity) inside.

Practice deflecting external stresses with your shield. Ask yourself if you will allow them into your person. Slow down! Pausing may give you enough space to think clearly. Remind yourself of your values. Remind yourself of your abilities to deflect the stresses. Remind yourself of your options. Find the humor in a stressful event. Is it really that big of a deal? You do not have to take everything that is outside, inside. You do have a choice! You do not have to make yourself angry, frustrated and afraid! Choose to free yourself from the stresses!

Your most powerful tactic to deflect stress is to stay in the present. Maintain your presence in the present! Respond, rather than react, to what presents itself. Let go of the past. Realize that fear is always in the future. With this understanding you will be able to recognize options and alternatives. You will stay calm even in difficult situations. Be here, not there.

Keep a thin veneer between your inside world and the outside world. Develop a crystal clear sense of boundary. Know where you begin and end and where the outside world begins and ends. Announce and be who you are. Let the world be what it is. Distinguish between what you want and what you need. Needs are born within your Spirit. Wants begin from outside. Differentiate between your internal vision and your external vision. Honor each view with a healthy separation.

Like walking in the rain, realize the droplets of stress do not have to penetrate your being. Let what is outside be allowed to remain there. Let what is inside remain within. Let your skin be a rain coat, keeping your internal Self dry, safe and warm. May stress slip off you as easily as rain off a slicker.

The stressors that escape your shield and penetrate you in the form of tension must be released and returned to your outer world where they came from[14]. Like clouds, empty the contents that weigh you down. Discover an appropriate avenue to relieve your tension. Like the rolling thunderclouds overhead, find a physical way to release your tension. Allow your body to sweat it out, just as it is meant to do. Complete the cycle with release that nurtures Self. Understand cloud release.

INTERNAL WAR FRONTS

We have four war fronts within: the mental, physical, emotional, and spiritual. These war fronts must be recognized so we know what we are fighting.

The mental war front must be won first. Through thorough and honest evaluation, we will achieve intimacy with both our conscious and unconscious mind. This intimacy will determine the effectiveness of the other three war fronts. In this mental war, the conflict is labeled as "indulgence versus discipline." We must understand the vast potential of our minds, both con-

---

14 The tape, "Follow Your Breath" is designed to guide you to accomplish this task. You can acquire this tape through Commune-a-Key Publishing by calling 1-800-983-0600.

structive and destructive. When we see ourselves as capable, we work at proficiency within and without. When we view ourselves as unworthy, we cannot see the possibilities. We must recognize the consequences of our decisions at all times. See with eternal eyes. See how repercussions circle outward. Let each moment be viewed with soft focus. We must become active participants in life, deciding to do what it takes to fulfill our purpose. Discover your joy! Set goals to achieve! Creep out to your vision like an inch worm! Experience the exhilaration of the journey!

Work is beneficial. Discipline your Self to contribute to your own health. The easy way is not always the best way. Exercise discipline first and it will carry over in the other realms. Observe how purposefully birds make nests, how beavers build dams, how squirrels collect nuts. Their focused activities create homes and food for their family. Notice that people who have learned how to discipline themselves are often very successful in other areas. Their self discipline has created a comfortable home within and nurtures their Spirit. Notice also, that those with little self discipline often seek to control their environment and others to compensate for their lack of self-control.

The physical war front revolves around habit formation. The conflicts are labeled as "good habits versus bad habits." To prepare your Self for effective interaction with people and your environment, it is important that new habits of physical endurance and health replace laziness and apathy. The target is believing in the physical vision of who you can be, practicing good habits that lead to this vision, and finally becoming this vision. Your interactions with people reflect how we perceive our physical self. Three keys to winning this internal war are: deliberate choices; self-discipline; and self-celebration. Be deliberate with what you put in your mouth and when you rest your feet. May your sleep be as deep as your living is complete. Be deliberate with what you choose to do with each moment of your life. Discipline yourself by asserting the power of your mind and spirit. Let your mind become the impulse behind doing what you must. Do what is best, not what is easiest.

Then celebrate yourself! Acknowledge your growth, your successes, your trials, your journey! Pay attention and recognize what you have accomplished. Approve of yourself. Give yourself the sweet nectar of self-affection.

Love yourself and celebrate what you have become! Liberated by your own acceptance of who you are, you are free to accept others. This war is being waged daily by countless dieters, overeaters, television addicts, and at health spas. Discover how you can tend to your physical Self today.

The emotional war front is an internal war that seeps its toxins into others. This toxic transference may be seen as the problem, when it is actually only a symptom. The key to controlling one's emotional roller coaster ride is not to focus on the individual ride, but on the conductor of the ride itself—the mind. The combatants in this war are, "reason versus emotion." Listen to your emotions, for they are good indicators of your internal temperature. Cry, shout, laugh, sing. Listen. They speak a language your mind can translate. Honor your emotions. Acknowledge their voice. They tell you about the conflicts that beg to be resolved. In order to find resolution, a calm disposition is needed. Pause and figure out what is really causing the negative emotion. With the self discipline of the mind, you can calm your emotions to be in a better position to confront the real issue.

The next time you find your Self upset, take a time-out and slow down your breathing. Take your pulse. Feel and follow your heart beat. Let your heart guide you to calm waters. Talk your upsetting emotions "down," just as surely as you had talked them "up." Emotions cloud your thinking. When you have used your mind to calm yourself, determine the underlying issue. Consider possible solutions to the problem. Then implement the chosen solution. Do what you can do today. And learn to accept the imperfections of the world.

Finally, it is the spiritual war front that offers the most joyful and the most painful experiences during the life cycle. The conflict can be termed "the Light side versus the Dark side," and our human condition demands a taste of both. To be fully human we must embrace both the agony and the ecstasy in our life. It is common for people to deny their shadow side. It can be frightening. Yet, honoring the potential that resides in your dark side is liberating. A child who recognizes that fire burns, respects its power. As I recognize how I can hurt myself, I become aware of my personal power. If I know there is a bee in the house, I will be careful not to get stung. If I know there is a bee inside me, I will be careful not to sting others. I realize that I do not have to hate the bee. I simply must respect the bee as a part of who I am. Respect the dark side of yourself. But don't neglect the Light side. If you believe you are only the Light, then you may become self-righteous, condescending, and judgmental. You must walk the Red Road and remain in spiritual balance between the two sides[15].

The Red Road is the neutral perspective of life.... for, what is, is. The Red Road is the path of tolerance, acceptance, truth, honesty and humility. Keeping your eye on the horizon, you will be able to distinguish between the important and incidental issues of each day. This Strawberry Road is walked with Namaji, honoring the red blood that carries our life.

The four internal war fronts can be reconciled if we focus on balancing all areas of our life. The Native American Medicine Wheel speaks well to this challenge. Balance your work and your play. Work to become 50% internally focused and 50% externally focused. Keep your awareness 5% in the past, 5% in the future, and 90% in the present. Do all this and your wars will be over. Peace will permeate your being.

> I am the warrior.
> I defend and protect my values.
>
> I am the warrior.
> I ward off the arrows that others would thrust.
>
> I am the warrior.
> I see a new day and its possibilities.
>
> I am the warrior.
> I walk the Red Road that leads to peace.
>
> I am the warrior.
> I make today's decisions, for tomorrow's children.

---

[15] The Red Road is the guiding principle to stay between virtue and evil, and to have a positive focus.

I am the warrior.
Sadness moves into joy.

I am the warrior.
I find the calm and do what is necessary.

I am the warrior.

THE WAR DANCE OF OUR CHILDREN

I counted seventeen ravens as they circled above. Their rehearsal of aerial acrobatic warfare captivated my attention. I watched as they continued their war dance.

On a branch of a dead pine tree, a young eagle watched with nonchalant interest, eating his morning meal. As they approached the eagle, the ravens boasted of their bravery. Closer and closer, the ravens came to Eagle's breakfast table. Harassing the young eagle, the ravens tried to intrude upon his nourishment.

Although the strong Wind Spirits helped to spiral their black feathers into blurs of rolling balls, Ravens did not intimidate Eagle this day. Eagle finished his meal and flew into another important moment.

The tree limb was immediately overtaken by the ravens and the remains of predator's kill was scavenged upon.

There was no aerial combat this day, for the order of nature remained intact. The ravens played their part and kept the natural order clean. Both the eagle and the ravens won this day. Ravens displayed integrity and purpose. Eagle displayed tolerance and generosity.

War is the break down of order. And violence is the extreme outcome of this break down.

Civilization has accelerated the occurrence of war. For with progress and special interest groups the gap of the "haves and the have-nots" continues to widen. Motivated by greed, power and control, nations of warring individuals determine who will get the spoils. Motivated by hunger, poverty, oppression and resentment, groups are fighting back the only way they can. Listen carefully and you will hear oppressed segments of society scream with Ravens' voice. Watch the news and you will see gangs scavenge the ghettos. Look around and you will witness the war dance of our children.

Stop and wonder if gang activity may be an attempt at scavenger survival.

Yet, see the difference. As the eyes of the ravens reflect the natural order and their rightful place on the Hoop of Life, the eyes of our children reflect their circumstance and social neglect. Look into the eyes of our children. What order do they see? Hierarchy or equality? Who determines their food chain? As green trees are sacrificed for green paper in wallets, philosophies like "me" and "mine" dominate the world. When the "me" is prioritized, the "we" is sacrificed. "We" need to become a world family in order to transcend to the heights of both Raven and Eagle—where all are respected as members of the Sacred Hoop.

Raven respects Eagle. Eagle respects Raven. Can we say the same of civilization? Does civilization promote mutual respect? The "me" focus of this world fosters competition and more greed. Are prisons the only future limb we can extend to our children? Can prisons be built and supported fast enough to sustain a forgotten population? What can we share? How can we become united in spirit and *in truth*? What have we to offer our children?

Look to the lesson of Eagle and Ravens. Eagle feasts and returns to Sky Father, then Ravens descend to share this feast. Feasting is integral in the natural order. Wolves share a kill. Deer graze together. Geese feed in flocks. Bees and ants share storage mounds. Humans have feasted after hunts for thousands of years.

We must learn from the natural order and prepare and offer a feast for our children. All of the children. We must make this our priority. Although many organizations understand we must feed our children and distribute foods worldwide, come to see that our children need other nourishment, as well.

Children thirst for our love, time, and touch. They hunger for both wide opportunities and narrow limits. They become malnourished when they grow without values. They may starve from a lack of meaning. This is the food of the Heart. This is the food for the Spirit. This is the food we must share.

Come to see that there is an abundance of all of this! Just as food goes to waste each day, much of what could be offered to our children's mental, emotional and spiritual diet is also thrown away. There is no need to be greedy when love, time, touch, opportunities, limits, values and meaning are bountiful. When we give of these things, the rewards multiply and strengthen society. More seeds are planted, more fruits are harvested, more health pervades.

What nourishment can you offer from your high treetop view? Give freely to the children of the world. Make a concerted effort to offer sustenance to Earth's children you encounter each day. Like Ravens, people are searching for internal nourishment. May we come to truly understand the food chain that we spearhead. Like Brother Eagle, may we offer the gift of nourishment to others.

HONOR YOUR ENEMIES

Porcupine quills have a screw-like barb. If your dog has ever been quilled, you have seen the pain the barbs inflict. Yet, the porcupine is known to be the key to survival if you are ever lost in the woods. Porcupines are slow enough that you can actually club them to death. Their slow pace gives your dogs painful quills and gifts you with life-giving food. Although well defended, the porcupine will sacrifice its life to you if needed. Enemies are often that way. We may fear them and detest them, for they give us pain. Yet remember the porcupine, for your enemy may also give you something you need.

Honor your enemies, for they teach you about your Self. Look to your enemies. What danger do they pose? What values do they threaten? Honor your enemy for reminding you of your cherished values. Defend your values as you would defend a child.

Do not be surprised when you look into the eyes of your enemy, if you see your own reflection. Ask yourself what it is in the enemy that you detest or fear. Why does this enemy bother you so much? How are you alike? What do you dislike in your enemy that you don't like about yourself? Then ask, how are you different? Questions like these are difficult to ask. However, if you are willing to look, you may discover wars within yourself that need to be resolved and celebrated. Honor your enemy for the truth they help you gain!

Like a sharp pebble on a sandy beach, allow your enemy to remind you to walk carefully, look around, and pause to see the beauty of the sea.

FALLEN EAGLE FEATHER

*The actual Fallen Eagle Feather Ceremony that takes place during Powwow is sacred.
As all sacred ceremonies are to remain protected, revealing the ritual is forbidden.
No pictures are taken. No recording is allowed. Following this tradition, certain aspects of the
ceremony will not be revealed. What will be shared is public knowledge and teaching.*

Occasionally during Powwow, an eagle feather will drop off a dancer's costume. When this happens, everything stops. According to an old story, a tribesman noticed that his enemy had dropped an eagle feather during battle. The warriors, understanding the importance of the sacred feather, waited to see what their enemy would do. Prepared to ambush, they waited for the enemy to return. That night the enemy group returned to look for the feather[16]. The small group was captured, blindfolded, and taken to the village. They thought their fate was inevitable. But instead, the Chief had a feast and gave gifts to the captives. Since the warriors had honored the Spirits of taken warriors and had risked their lives in stopping an entire war to retrieve the meaningful feather, they were spared and held in honor. In recognition of this pause in war, Powwow is also stopped to honor the fallen eagle feather. Powwow honors the spirits of fallen warriors whenever an eagle feather is dropped. Namaji prevails.

---

[16] The feather embodies a life taken in battle.

Traditionally, only wounded veterans are allowed to dance and retrieve the spirit of the feather. Four veterans dance around the feather, representing the Four Directions. First, the Creator and the Spirit of the fallen warrior are respected. Then, the dancers enact specific battle feats. Finally, the honored veteran whose strength in Spirit matches the fallen warrior, picks up the feather with his left hand and, facing the East, raises the feather to honor the Spirit World.

Tobacco is offered and the person who dropped the feather gives thanks to the Veterans. The feather will now be cared for. The Spirit of the fallen warrior is honored. The Spirit World is recognized. All is elevated.

Honor your enemy's life. Native American warriors have long understood this honor. In combat, their enemy's spirit is revealed. War is often just two people fighting for their beliefs, their values, their people. Forced by circumstances, they join together in the dance of life and death. Both want to live. Both honor life. Warriors understand that if they must take a life, they must honor the spirit of the fallen warrior. They must honor the sacred within.

SPIRITUAL JOURNEY

Warriors are on a sacred journey. Their journey is difficult, for it includes great love and great loss. With love as the beginning and loss as the return, a majestic emptying and filling of spirit takes place.

Let us accompany the warriors on their spiritual journey as they return home to us. With the support of the community, may their bodies, minds, emotions, and spirits heal. May they grieve their loss, realize their purpose, and transcend with spiritual understanding. May the spirit of Mitakuye-Oyasin soften their path to help them heal, renew creative potential, and find meaning.

Let us honor and support our returning heroes. With their bravery, they have embraced our fears. With their fear, they have embraced our lives. With their lives, they have embraced our society.

We give a big Gitchi Migwetch[17] to you, the Warriors of this world! You are the arrow of our spirit, for you carry our dreams to the edge of the world. You touch the sunset with your shadows and the sunrise with your open spaces. With our hearts, we touch you with our love!

---

[17] Pronounced: GI-chi ME-gwich and means big thank you.

RECONCILIATION DANCE

I offer you my hand, each other we will gain.
I offer you my heart, it waits to share your pain.
I offer you my mind, to understand your past.
I offer you my spirit, to dance with yours at last.

Just as wars erupt from threatening change, reconciliations emerge when we reconnect to our beginning truth. The resulting return to order is a celebration of relief and joy. The Reconciliation Dance circles the Sacred Hoop of Life with a sense of rightness and completeness. Those who both offer and accept peace are gifted with meaning, purpose, and a higher state of consciousness.

I invite you now to listen to the words of history. Listen to the dance of reconciliation. Feel the movement inside yourself. Listen to the peace within.

TRIBAL STORY OF WAR AND PEACE

Tribal people lived peacefully for thousands of years. The world in which they lived made sense. Namaji was predominant across the continent. Earth Mother's cycles were left undisturbed. She was not conquered. Ownership did not exist. Caring was the way of life.

Many tribes hunted, fished, and riced together. They shared buffalo meat and woodland game with their neighboring brothers and sisters. They learned to share in this way from the animals. Like hundreds of other tribes, the Dakota, the Ojibwe, and the Iroquois were simply custodians of adjacent lands.

It was only after the Europeans immigrated to this continent that war broke out intertribally. The threatening change, European "ownership" of land and domination of Earth Mother, clashed with natural harmony. Native American displacement and all its consequences resulted.

Tribal warriors fought only to protect and preserve their way of life. They fought for their right to exist. They died so that their customs, ways, and traditions would prevail. They shed their blood so that their bloodline would continue to dance the circle. They died so their spirits could live.

They did not fight for land. Indians did not (and still do not) "own" land. Indians only have one possession, their Self: body, mind, emotions and spirit. It was this possession that they fought for.

Thousands of original Americans battled the circumstance of European invasion and died with dignity. As we honor them, let us always remember the truth of the events. It is the people of this land that experienced the events. Let us remember the people! The present must not close its eyes to the terrible truth of the past. History and her students must acknowledge the suffering of the warriors of Turtle Island[1]. As Earth Mother's children we must taste the salt of her tears, we must continue to honor the truth that is remembered in her powerful rocks.

Mishomis stones are the rocks beneath your feet, the mountains of your view, the support of the vast oceans. Mishomis is the energy and consciousness of the rocks and minerals of this world. The rocks hold the memories of Earth Mother.

Hold the stones and you will hold the hand of reconciliation. For the rocks —Mishomis—remember what actually took place on this continent. Their presence did not waver when blood and tears were shed. Mishomis has seen it all. They remained certain even when changes separated families and all was uncertain. Mishomis remembers it all. They heard the stories of

---

[1]   Turtle Island refers to the earth of North America. In the Ojibwe creation story this land rests on a turtle's back.

sadness and gladness as they contained the fires of many people, moving, relocating, wanting to live. Mishomis has heard it all. They felt the lessening of the hoof beats as the buffalo were slaughtered. They felt more of Sun's heat as the shadowed wings, which once graced the mountainsides, suddenly disappeared. Mishomis has felt it all.

Go and let Mishomis find you. Walk the length of the beach and let the stone call your name in the quiet of your spirit. Then hold the stone and discover the stories that it has carried. Hold the Mishomis and hold the pain of others. Share in their stories. Feel their experience. Hold Mishomis and your hold history in the palm of your hand.

The first step in becoming worthy children of this land is honoring past events[2]. We become Earth Mother's children when we acknowledge the story of her forests, her plains, her mountain tops, her shores. Earth Mother links us to the past, future, and present with her lessons, memories, and truths. Let us reconcile ourselves to all of this and find a new sense of rightful order to this world!

This umbilical cord of truth is rooted in Earth Mother's trees. Listen to the cycle of birth, death and rebirth. Just as the pine trees sway in the wind, hear Native American Elders whisper the stories of their struggle to survive. Learn from dignified Elders who nourish the hope of their children. See how tribal people sprout from this same ground as did their ancestors for 70,000 years. Follow your own roots and discover when you were planted here. You are here for a reason. Your history must be acknowledged and understood. There is meaning tangled within your roots. There is nourishment for your own Spirit. Honor this story of yourself. Sing the song of One as our branches reach out to Sky Father together. Let us join hands and connect with our neighbors and form an interlacing arbor of love. May our forests of Mitakuye-Oyasin remember the first trees and welcome the new. May the shade of our connections provide comfort for all who live here.

Within the interlacing of Mitakuye-Oyasin, may we grow with understanding of one another. May we learn of each other's beginnings. May knowledge

---

2   Chapter 7 will focus more on the "reorganization" of Indian people.

flow through our veins. May knowledge gift us wisdom. What do you know about the history of this land? What do you know of the neighbor which grows beside you? Listen. Listen to Four Winds. They speak truth.

Our ancestors' stories blow across Earth Mother's plains. Five hundred original languages ride her currents and circle this Earth Mother. The old age wisdom of her people continues to rise and fall with the drifting of our hearts. See how a soft breeze touches a child on a swing and fills her world with imagination. Understand that an Elder braves the gale to learn of life and is honored by the insights of the storms. The Wind Spirits carry our ancestor's stories, their lessons, their truths into the hearts of all who would turn to face its energy. May the lessons of our ancestors find you empty, so they can fill you with their power.

Yesterday's truth can be seen from Earth Mother's mountain tops. Climb to the heights and view both the high and low places. Do not be afraid of looking at its entirety. Honor the battles of the past, the suffering, the sadness. Let yesterday's view gift you with a clear perspective for today. See the truth as the clouds create shadows and the rivers move swiftly. The dark shadows of past tragedies stress the sunlight in today's efforts. Although the river can never be the same, it will always move with the power of the Water Spirits. With the Water Spirits, cleanse the earth of past hurts and pains. Honor the same view that was seen by our ancestors. Feel their deep and timeless Namaji for their Mother. See with ancestral eyes. Feel with ancestral hearts.

Warriors' spirits silently walk alongside us on Earth Mother's shores. Gift them your recognition. Honor their trail as you walk with your sisters and brothers through the same sands. With Earth Mother, we must honor the past. She awaits to accept our gifts of remembrance. Reconcile with yesterday's conflicts by acknowledging your relationship with today's enemies and allies. And then may your footsteps melt into other's experience in the future.

Unlike political history that may be written by the biased historian, Native American stories are told by the participants and are remembered in rocks, trees, waters, and shores. The stories have been meticulously memorized and retold, and their truth lives on. It is time to hear the sad story of tribal people as it was memorized and retold[3]. As one's word is sacred, so are the stories. Let us hear the songs of the warriors.

Hear the story of the shores of Lake Superior. From her high cliffs, see her view. Among her trees, listen to her songs. With her winds, feel her lesson. On her shore, touch her past. Find the spiritual truth in the words. Discover the lesson for today. Connect with the warriors of yesterday. Their battles await your recognition. With Namaji, connect to the spirits that abide in this great land. Connect to your sisters and brothers. Connect to the total experience of this Earth Mother.

Reconcile with the past, and you will discover wings for the future.

REMEMBER THE PAST

Over three hundred years ago, the battle for hunting territory became fierce as settlers pushed the Iroquois westward, from upper New York State, into the Ojibwe lands of northern Wisconsin and Canada. This resulted in further displacement, as the Ojibwe moved into Sioux territory in Minnesota. After thousands of years of harmony, the established balance of hunting, gathering, and fishing was disturbed. Intertribal friction resulted in a grave attempt to protect the tribal need for food and clothing. Panic brought intertribal wars that were fought not for greed, but for survival. This experience was replicated across the continent as Europeans immigrated to this land.

The Ojibwe, Iroquois, and Sioux were among the countless victims of this circumstance. Listen to a story of two of these nations. Told and retold, I invite you to hear my experience of these warriors' pain. Listen and hear the silent threat. May it open your heart to the truth. Touch now, the memory of the red rocks that beautify the shore of Lake Superior and reconcile with the past.

---

3   Of approximately 10,000 cultures throughout history, only 106 had a written language. Does that make the other 9,894 cultures inferior because oral tradition was the means of language transfer? Consider the Iliad. Most scholars agree that it is a great literary work. Yet, it began as a story that was memorized and retold. Only later was it written down by Homer.

BLOOD STONES

So it was decided.

The powerful Iroquois would send a war party into Ojibwe hunting territory. The women and children watched their warriors as they followed the setting sun and honored them with their tears. With somber hearts, the men cut silent ripples as they canoed along the sparkling shore of Lake Superior to reach Bau-a-tig[4].

With a sea of sadness between them and home, the Iroquois warriors sang songs to fill the emptiness of the journey. Deep with the war they were about to make, their war songs followed the currents of the wide river. They did not realize that an Ojibwe chief and his people watched carefully from the opposite shore, filled with the peace they wished to keep.

Seeing only the survival of their tribe, the Iroquois warriors were blind to the hundred eyes that watched their silent paddling. Hearing only their future celebration, they were deaf to the hundred ears that heard their spirited war songs. Feeling only life in their beating chests, they ignored a clan mother's dreams of death.

With a fateful paddle, the warriors coasted to the shore that would soon bear their name[5]. On the land they hoped to live, they began the dance for war.

While their ceremonial drums filled the forest, the Ojibwe chief sent for two medicine men. "Go and shadow the movements of our enemy. We must know their minds so we can understand our hearts."

As invisible spirits, the Ojibwe medicine men crossed the river and observed the Iroquois' camp. At dawn an otter

---

[4]   Bau-a-tig is now called Sault Saint Marie. It was a campground for the Ojibwe tribe.

[5]   It is now known as Iroquois Point.

whistled and a beaver flapped its tail in warning. Emerging as shadows from the woods, the medicine men returned to their camp. Just as silently, they approached their chief who waited by the camp fire to hear of their vision.

The first one squatted near the dying embers and spoke. "The forest spirits have told us many things." Warming his hands close to the embers, he continued. "The Iroquois warriors will dance for four days and four nights."

The Ojibwe chief did not look up and continued to stare into the tiny red fire memory.

"They are like plants without rain," whispered the other man. "They have no strength left with which to fight."

The second medicine man gathered sand into his fist and threw it on the dying fire. "Like lightning, we must strike! Or it will be our children who will hear the thunder of their clubs!"

So it was decided.

Before the great silence of the fifth rising sun, the Ojibwe warriors encircled the sleeping Iroquois. With uniform silence, they knew their own survival rested on this strike. With one mind and one heart the Ojibwe warriors quickly attacked. Barely beyond their dreamless sleep, all but two Iroquois braves were killed.

The two spared braves were sent back as a warning, while their slain brother's heads were severed and placed along the beach that extended for half a mile on the great lake. The warrior's blood dripped onto the rocks, staining some of them permanently. This day and the spirits of these warriors became a memory.

So it was decided.

The red rocks would tell this story to all who would listen.

This is a story of the red rocks. A story of unprepared warriors. A story of brother fighting against brother in order to survive. Ultimately, this is the story of reconciliation, for the spirits of the slain warriors were, and still are, respected.

To this day, no houses have been built on this shoreline. Trees do not grow there. Ojibwe children do not play amongst the rocks. This stretch of beach, where the red rocks reach the shoreline, remains sacred. Here, fallen warriors are honored. Here, the past remains in the present. Here, the future remembers the past. Here, the present learns for the future. This is Iroquois Point.

May your heart reconcile with the spirits of your enemies. May you forgive them their offenses. May you gift them with Namaji.

PEACE EXCHANGE

Strawberry Island in northern Wisconsin, was another battle ground where warriors from the Ojibwe and Dakota Sioux nations fell during hand to hand combat. Like the story of the Blood Stones, victims became warriors as brother fought against brother. There was no victor in this North American War for Survival, as thousands of years of peace were lost. Located on the Lac du Flambeau band of Lake Superior Chippewa Reserve, Strawberry Island is a sacred island. The remains of fallen warriors from both nations rest there, while their spirits dance eternally with Namaji.

In the summer of 1995, the Ojibwe and the Dakota Sioux nations met on the Lacdu Flambeau reservation to mend the Sacred Hoop of nations in the proper way. The healing was a week long event of feasting, story-telling, and dancing. The purpose of the gathering was the exchange of peace. The feasting was delicious, the dancing was invigorating, the sharing was uplifting. We shook each other's hands in good will and our minds joined as one. We laughed at endless jokes and our hearts encircled as one. We danced to the same eternal beat and our bodies became as one. We prayed for our ancestors and our spirits mingled as one. With the strength of these two peaceful nations, the sacred status of the island was upheld for all to witness.

A DANCE OF RECONCILIATION

You honor me.
I honor you.
We honor those who died.

The strong drum sings.
The clear song brings.
Dance lifts our people's pride.

The past is now.
The now is new.
New is the Eastern Door.

We dance to heal.
We heal to feel.
We join for ever more.

The Reconciliation Dance is an honor dance. The guest drum plays his best song so the echo of the strong beat will touch all those present. The reconciliation dance is a momentous event. With the dance, the reconnection of people is publicly witnessed. All present stand in recognition of this occasion.

The head dancers of the hosting nation lead the honored guests[6] into the dance circle. The accepting visitors follow them with dignity and honor. Circling the drum together, the Hoop is mended while many feet touch Earth Mother in unison. Dancing to the same beat, all hearts are healed. Honoring the past, present, and future—spirits unite. Where once the people of these nations fought, now they dance in peace.

The Circle is danced. The spirits are remembered. The healing takes place. The future is new. With the drum still beating, the honored dancers form a line to greet each participant. People swarm to shake their hands and say Boozhoo. The moment of reception and reconciliation grows as each person takes their place in the line after they have greeted the last person waiting to honor them. In this way, I greet you, you greet me, we greet all

---

6   The representatives of the visiting nation are often descendants of the original chiefs.

present. This moment of reconciliation is for everyone. All persons are honored for being present. All accept and give greetings of the heart. All connect. All experience Mitakuye-Oyasin.

The reconciliation dance becomes a growing, pulsing snake, where brother declares peace with brother. Once all greetings have been exchanged, the snake moves back into the dance, circling the One Great Beat of Life. Mitakuye-Oyasin is revealed.

The Circle opens.
Peace has won.
The Circle closes.
All are One.

PEACE PIPE

The highlight of the Strawberry Island Peace Ceremony came when Archie Mosay, the medicine man of the Ojibwe Midewinin Lodge[7], gave the Dakota delegation a hand carved sacred pipe. This Elder offered it with Namaji and instructed the Dakotas to use the pipe frequently.

The peace pipe must not remain a decorated reminder of things past.

As he held the pipe up in honor of the Spirits, the Elder instructed the people to use it honorably. The pipe must be experienced by all people of the Dakota nation to honor this day of reconciliation. It must be used in sweat lodge ceremonies, on occasions of births, marriages, deaths, as nations visit with each other, and with vision quests[8]. The sacred peace pipe is not just for the big events in life, it is for All of life. For as our breath mingles with the spirits of the past, present and future, the breath of Mitakuye-Oyasin is shared. With this sharing of the One Breath of Life, reconciliation in all aspects of life is possible. The smoking of the sacred pipe makes the invisible— visible. The smoke becomes the visionary instrument, illuminating the mingling.

---

7   Pronounced: Mi-DAY-win and refers to the Ojibwe Grand Medicine Society which is a sacred and closed lodge. Ceremonies and rites within the Mida are not to be shared.

8   Vision quests are Native American ceremonies where the participant abstains from food, light, etc. in order to obtain a spiritual vision to guide his free will in directing his purpose. Sometimes conducted in pits, mountain tops, or near a waterfall.

With this, the pipe of peace was accepted by the original Dakota Chief's grandson.

It can be difficult to put down the shield of the warrior and lift high the pipe of peace. It was the children of the Ojibwe Lac du Flambeau reservation that pursued this peace offering event. We need to return to the trusting of youth to offer our enemies the hand of reconciliation.

Unfortunately, we become comfortable behind our walls of protection. We come to know life without the view beyond. Asking ourselves to put down our shield and pick up the peace pipe is asking ourselves to open up to potential risk. As we release our trusted reliance, we open the door to the winds of change. Change is uncomfortable. Oftentimes it is demanding. To offer the hand of peace, is to offer a vulnerable part of ourselves. It is letting go of life as we know it. Yet we must hold visible our peace pipe in order to allow others to enter the new order. The new order is peace. It is the joining of separations, the mending of hoops, the sense of rightness in the world.

If we refuse to reconcile ourselves to our past, we refuse our present life. For life asks us to come to peace with the situations, people, and experiences we were given. Life asks us to resolve past wars. Unfinished business, unresolved issues, uncomfortable feelings need to be worked through and released.

As the peace pipe is held up and offered to the Four Directions: East, South, West and North, the one who holds it offers his peace and mends the hoop. Like the peace pipe, life asks us to extend peace to all of life, not just the big events. To extend peace, we must first experience peace. Come and experience peace in the little and big things of life. Come and listen to the eternal beat of connection. Find the order in your life and offer the hand of reconciliation. Then you can celebrate the dance of peace.

STRATEGIES FOR PEACE

To mend our separations from others (who are spiritually an extension of ourselves) we must resolve our own inner turmoil. We must develop internal peace. Some of our bitter experiences prevent peace from permeating our being.

Guilt—Remorse,
Disappointment—Regret,
Shame—Blame
Anger—Resentment

RELEASE THE SHACKLES OF GUILT

Guilt is a self-inflicted venomous infection we impose upon ourselves. It is no more than being angry with ourselves for something we did or did not do. We experience guilt when we beat ourselves with the club of anger.

With internal anger and pain, we become our own victim and deny self-nurturing. We turn our backs on ourselves and look for validation from external sources. People who feel guilty when they say "no" are living for the external world rather than their internal world. Their guilt is causing a denial of self.

Guilt in its extreme form is debilitating. It can drive a person to compulsive behavior patterns, such as constantly apologizing, frequent hand washing, buying others' forgiveness with gifts or affection, and continuous blaming of others through finger pointing and put-downs. In these ways, a person tries symbolically to cleanse him/herself of former wrongs. What really needs to take place is an internal self-cleansing, self-forgiveness, and self-reflection. Guilt of self, needs Self to free its grip. Only Self can free Self.

There is no need to beat yourself with your war club. You can stop guilt by simply allowing yourself to be who you are. Since guilt lives in the past and future, we can put this debilitating club down by living in the present.

Remorse is re-lived guilt. Just as guilt is a biting feeling, the word remorse means to bite again and again. Why have a pit bull in your stomach? Forgive yourself for your humanism! Don't hold yourself hostage and terrorize yourself with abusive thoughts. Release yourself from both the victim and the perpetrator role. Accept your shortcomings and defects and ask Creator to remove these conditions. Strive for improved competence, rather than perfection. Perfectionism is simply not possible! There's only one thing you'll ever do perfectly, and that is to die. You'll do that just fine! Until that moment do your best and forget the rest!

Revisit your values. Re-define what is most important to you and be faithful to yourself. Do not allow the "shoulds" of others to force their way into your value system. Living to fulfill "shoulds," shackles the person with eternal obligation to others. To unlock the shackles we must find the key to self-nurturance. Remember, we have only two obligations: to our Self, and to our Creator. You are obliged to give your Self: attention, affection, recognition, and approval. Internal, positive, self-dialogue must be practiced.

Take this moment to pause and actually verbalize what your internal Self needs to hear. Look deep inside and find something positive. What are your strengths? Focus on that and give yourself the attention, affection, recognition and approval you need. With these affirmations, build your nest of comfort and security. Learn to be your own best fan! Allow your internal world to be as vibrant and alive as the forests and the valleys! Learn from the birds. Preen your own beautiful feathers. Learn from the snake. Shed your 'shoulds.' Do not expect others to preen or shed them for you.

LET GO OF DISAPPOINTMENT AND REGRET

Everyone becomes disappointed from time to time. Often we become disappointed in Self, others and our Creator in response to difficult life situations. Disappointment is natural. But it is not healthy to hold onto disappointment, studying its every detail, wishing for something else, for we lose out on the rest of what life offers us. Acceptance must be practiced. We cannot change other people and circumstances. Courage must be tapped when internal self-change is required.

If you expect, you may be disappointed. Therefore, expect less and live more!

Disappointed people tend to miss the fun in life, for they focus on what they don't have and their disappointment. They cannot see beyond their sadness. Their illusionary control of life has failed and it leaves them feeling helpless. Discover that life is best when you do not try to control it. What fun would life be anyway, if you wrote all the scripts and played all the parts? Allow life to be life... a menagerie of possibilities and surprises, where you are an actor and not the writer or director. That is the Creator's role.

If I offered you the book of your entire life, including the future, would you read it? If you chose to read it, what would there be left to live? Give yourself permission to live your life, one day at a time. Canoe your own waters of experiences and embrace the surprises, maneuver the changes in directions, engage in the thrill of the glorious ride!

Self-pity has never been attractive and tends to drive other people away, causing the cycle to grow. Find the positive! Focus on that! What do you have? What can you give? What song can you sing? Discover the courage to step out of the role of regret. Regret is re-lived (remembered) disappointment. You always have a choice as to how you feel, what you see, where you go, when you live. Will it be the past or the present? You must decide.

Look for the spiritual beauty inside each moment, the love inside the hate, the answers inside the questions, the freedom inside the Self. In the present, discover the ability to free yourself from disappointment.

Forgiveness is letting go of all hopes for a better yesterday. Allow forgiveness to rush over your disappointment of self and others. Wash away your regret. With this clean feeling inside, you are free to move on with your life in the present. Forgiveness moves you out of the past to reveal the possibilities of the future.

DEFLECT SHAME AND BLAME

Shame and blame, unlike guilt, are externally rather than internally induced. However, both can be internally accepted. People may try to shame or blame you, but it is you who decides whether to accept their validity. Shame and blame are not violations of your internal value system, like guilt. They are others' judgmental finger pointing, based on their rule book. When people give you feedback in an open, honest, direct, calm, and specific manner, shame and blame are not the issues. When people tell you (verbally or subtly) that you're inadequate, insufficient, or not worthwhile shame and blame are the issues.

These shame based messages may leave you feeling as if you are a bad person. This feeling can permeate your being. Pushing your self esteem down around your knees, your head may droop and your focus may blur. The empty space from your head to your knees may fill with fear, depression, and anxiety.

Don't give other people the power to deflate you! Go back to your war shield and ward off their verbal (and nonverbal) arrows and let them know you are not on Earth Mother to fulfill their expectations of you. By raising high your own internal peace shield, you let them know you are your own keeper and you choose to fulfill your own self-established expectations of yourself.

ANSWER YOUR ANGER

Anger is such a volatile emotion! It can paralyze, injure, and kill!

Do not allow anger to stop you from becoming as you must. Use anger to motivate internal changes and to consider new options. Listen to its voice. It screams for an answer. So look for one. Anger demands your attention. So give it yours. It needs release. So find appropriate outlets for your anger to discharge.

Do not allow anger to hurt. Do not allow anger to be in control of you. You are in control of your Self. Like a child's tantrum, anger can be unpredictable and irrational. Give your Self time between the event and the response. Within this gift of time, discover options to your dilemma. Do not feed your anger the fuel of hate and negative self-talk. It can quickly get out of hand. Give your anger your attention and time. Allow it to dissipate.

Recognize that anger can hurt others and Self. We must live with the consequences of our actions. Choose to keep your Self safe. Guide your anger to a place of internal peace. Give anger the right to be soothed away. If you fuel your anger, distrust grows out of its flames of hate.

As anger begets distrust, distrust begets resentments. And, resentments will chew you up alive.

Resentment is re-lived anger. Again, choose to live in the moment, to what is occurring now, rather than what happened then. As a warrior, be prepared and alert. Recognize that life is not always a battle. Do not allow resentment to prevent you from experiencing the peaceful moment. Resentment eats up the inside as you replay over and over the wrongs done to you. Give it up! It is over! A new moment awaits for your attention. Someone or something may have taken from you before, but don't allow them to take from you again and again and again.

Instead, give your Self the gift of release and redirection. Release the tension from anger through some physical activity. Redirect the energy from a negative focus to a positive focus. Take a walk. It will gift you a space of time, exercise your body, and give you an opportunity to see beyond the initial impact to the lesson hidden within.

PEACEMAKERS

The great peacemakers of this world value and express certain child-like qualities. They have learned to return to the East direction in order to renew themselves and others. Let us become like children and offer peace to our brothers and sisters.

Peacemakers are courageous. They experience fear, yet they refuse to let fear rule them. Peacemakers are not afraid to fall. They are willing to take the risk. Only in this way do they learn how to take someone else's hand and walk side by side.

Peacemakers are creative. Without life's blinders, they are able to discover problem solving techniques. They are open to others' ideas. They are inclusive rather than exclusive. They are We, rather than me. They are the colors of the spectrum, finding new shades of other ideas and needs. Peacemakers give life to others, where others would take life for self. Open, free, and experimental, peacemakers honor the Creator with many possibilities and action.

Peacemakers are trusting. They believe in the providence of all—that inside each adversity, there is a seed of opportunity. They trust in the basic decency of others and others reflect that expectation back to them. They have discovered that hope is the other side of despair, that generosity is the other side of greed, that life is the other side of death. Trusting the people to illustrate these truths, peacemakers offer dignity to all.

Peacemakers are joyous. Full of smiles and good will, their days naturally fill with happiness. They experience enormous joy in living every day. The sunrise is more beautiful. The music more moving. The blueberries more sweet. Daily stress is relieved with their abundant medicine of laughter. Peacemakers enter a room and others relax for their self-contentment and joy of living is contagious.

Peacemakers are flexible. They do not limit themselves, nor do they limit others. They are as fluid as the river, moving with time. Eternally open to all possibilities, peacemakers are able to stretch and see light where others would see only darkness. Peacemakers live and let live.

Peacemakers are optimistic. From a sea full of problems, they find solutions. They honor the trail ahead, and know that a path of least resistance does exist. Peacemakers focus on the positive. Choices become adventures. Hurdles become challenges. Setbacks become learning experiences. Peacemakers know that worry casts a big shadow on small concerns. So they stay out of the future, and are present with each moment.

Peacemakers are present. They experience each moment, like children experiencing the first snowfall. They live for now. They honor each moment. They become more fully themselves in each instant of their life.

Behold the strength of a fragile flower, as she pushes her way out from a Mishomis rock. See how Robin cracks his blue egg shell to emerge and fly the dance of life. Watch the mighty oak arise from a core of internal existence. Like our sisters and brothers, reflect the East direction. Discover solutions to impenetrable problems, emerge from your shield of safety to join in the dance of life, and offer shade to others by nourishing Self and fulfilling your purpose.

SEVEN GENERATIONS

Native American wisdom teaches that every decision must be considered within the context of the next seven generations. Learn to reflect on your daily decisions. Ask yourself how your decision and behavior will affect these seven generations to come. Practice this way of thinking. Ask yourself, "What effect will my decision have on children born two hundred years from now?" Their inheritance is our responsibility.

It begins with you. If you allow your anger to hurt others, how will this hurt affect the future generations? Consider the cycles of abuse. They begin before the aggressor and continue beyond the victim. If you offer help to your enemies, how will that affect the future? Will it help plant a seed of self-nurturance? If you heal your Self, how will your healing affect the generations to come? What health will they experience because of your willingness to work through your pain? Practice living for the future, by living today the best you can. The future looks out from Earth Mother and awaits your actions. The future depends on the decisions you make today.

Stop and consider what tremendous effects such awareness would have if practiced on a world-wide scale. What would families be like if nothing was done to hurt the children of the seventh generation? What healing would take place? What joy would be experienced? What monumental changes would occur?

Right now, if policies and laws were made with the seventh generation in mind, everyone would immediately benefit. All generations—our children, our grandchildren, our great grandchildren and their great grandchildren—would be certain to have an abundance of life to enjoy. This vision of seven generations would protect our Earth Mother from harm. Her children would be safe. Her skies clean. Her waters pure. All would be as it was five hundred years ago, here on Turtle Island.

We must offer peace to the future. We must become active participants in today's world, expressing our concern for the seventh generation. We must add one more voice to the chorus, for the children *are* our future. All decisions must nurture the children. Call your legislator. Become a peacemaker. Put pressure on special interest groups, whose only interest lies in the "me" rather than in the "We." May we, as children of this Earth, give as much as we take. May we take the time now to offer peace for tomorrow. May we honor Earth Mother in this way!

Lack of action results in an insidious collection of turmoil. Collective guilt and collective oppression develops when we allow self-interest to govern the people. This collective guilt and oppression weighs heavily and ends up paralyzing people from future action. It is time to break the cycle of inactivity.

Make a stand. Commit to the Seventh Generation. Communicate to others your pledge for world peace and world health. It all begins with you.

Communicate this commitment through your unique talents or gifts. If you sing, sing of the seventh generation. If you speak, speak of the seventh generation. If you write, write for the seven generation. If you influence, influence for the seventh generation. If you teach, teach for the seventh generation. If you give, give for the seventh generation. If you do business, do it for the seventh generation. If you make laws, make them for the seventh generation. What is your strength? How can you promote this offering of peace?

Take this moment and consider what you can do to offer peace. How can we reconcile today with tomorrow? How can we utilize our unique strengths so that the world will be held in the hands of peacemakers? These are the questions. You are the answer.

WAHBEGONI GEEZIS

(Flowering Moon)

In the soft light of Grandmother Moon a little girl was born. She entered the world without crying. She opened her eyes to life without tears. With a head full of black silky hair and eyes as dark as the night, her beauty grew with each passing moon. She was named Wahbegoni Geezis— Flowering Moon— for her gentle spirit had blossomed with the moon and offered beauty to all she met. To her, all things were possible.

Wahbegoni Geezis grew into a beautiful young woman. Her days were filled with laughter, while her nights were filled with sweet dreams. One day as she was picking berries, she met a young man from the neighboring tribe with whom her people were at war. Yet, the young man, White Feather, was honest and brave. He was good. The two met secretly until all of the berries of the forest had dropped and seeded. By the time the ferns began to turn gold, they had fallen in love.

"I want you for my wife," whispered the brave one day as he touched her cheek gently. "Please ask your people that this may be so."

Flowering Moon did not know what to do, for although she had come to love him deeply, she also loved her people. That night, when Grandmother Moon filled the sky, Wahbegoni Geezis looked up high into the golden face with tears trailing down her cheeks. As the moon moved over the water, she knew what she would do.

The next day Flowering Moon stood in front of her father as he worked on his bow. "I want to marry White Feather, Father. He is from the neighboring village."

Putting the bow down he looked into his daughter's eyes. "You know that is not possible," he said gently. "Our people have been at war for a long time. We cannot allow it, Wahbegoni Geezis. There are many fine young braves here in our village."

Flowering Moon expected this answer, but decided to try again. "Father, I want to marry White Feather."

"Wahbegoni Geezis, this is not possible," he repeated.

Still, Flowering Moon did not give up. That night she sat beneath the light of Grandmother Moon and asked the Spirit World what she should do.

The next day, Flowering Moon went to meet White Feather in secret. "I asked my father for permission, White Feather. He will not allow it. Perhaps if your father agrees, he may change his mind. Now it is up to your father to grant this marriage."

The next day White Feather went to his father and said, "Father, I want to have Wahbegoni Geezis from the neighboring village as my wife."

The chief did not answer and simply walked away.

White Feather knew that he too must try until his father approved. The next day White Feather persisted. "Father, please, say you will honor such a marriage."

Instead his father looked up with unwavering eyes and walked away once again.

White Feather was so angry that he left his village. Upon entering the village of Wahbegoni Geezis, White Feather was captured and taken to her father's lodge.

"Why do you hold me as though I mean harm? I love Wahbegoni Geezis. Did she not ask for permission so that we could be wed?"

"That is true," the concerned man said, "but it cannot be. I will return with Wahbegoni Geezis. She will apologize for her mistake. Then you will leave this village and never see her again."

Flowering Moon's father looked all over the village, but he could not find his daughter. No one had seen her. He did not know that Flowering Moon had also left. He did not know that she had entered the village of White Feather. He did not know that she, too, had been taken by White Feather's father.

"My father holds White Feather just as your ropes now bind me," she told the chief. The chief was silent. He looked for a long time at this young woman.

"You are a foolish young girl. But you are beautiful and brave. I will arrange your exchange for my son the next moon," spoke the chief.

A message was sent to Flowering Moon's village and it was decided. At the next moon, the two neighboring tribes would meet between their villages with the young hostages. As agreed, the two would be returned to their people safely and nothing more would come of it.

The night was clear and Grandmother Moon lit up the sky with a gentle glow. As the two tribes approached each other, Flowering Moon and White Feather connected through the distance of their people's conflicts. The moment came when both Flowering Moon and White Feather were released to return to their people. Running to the center of their people, White Feather and Flowering Moon embraced.

"Look at Grandmother Moon!" Wahbegoni Geezis cried to both tribes. "She shines down on both of our people!"

Wahbegoni Geezis' words were as clear as the night and silence entered the hearts of the two chiefs.

The two fathers walked slowly to the center where their children stood close to one another. "Why can't you offer the same light to each other?" White Feather asked them, with the wisdom of all ages.

Under the smile of Grandmother Moon, and with the love of two young people, a hand was offered, another accepted, and peace was made.

Remember when you extend your hand in greeting, another hand will reach out to touch yours. May you offer peace and celebrate with all! May you remember the lessons in the rocks, the story in the streams, the truth in the trees! Open your circle of life to include more of life. Look up and see that the same sun shines on all. The same moon lights our paths. Offer your heart and heal with the spirit of reconciliation.

TWO STEP DANCE

She met him, now different.
He found her, now more.

It was time for the Two Step!

Minutes before, they had each gone their own way, to talk with friends. Now, he searched the Powwow grounds to find her long braid and gold shawl, for his night had waited for this special dance. She scanned the colorful crowd to find his coyote skin regalia, but other sights of Powwow crowded her view.

The night air was crisp, the sky clear, the earth firm as hundreds of colorful dancers rushed to find their own partner and to dance with love and celebration. The strong drum played and the excited partners began to form a line.

Anxious to find each other, both wondered if the dance would start without them. Yet, even across the arbor, they moved with incredible synchronicity. Breathing the same breath of life, their silent love pulled them toward each other. Like two rivers reaching for the same sea, inevitably they merged in a wave of gratitude and love.

And the current of love found its source.

Their eyes met and their arms embraced and their smiles welcomed one another. Under the green boughs of the Powwow arbor, the couple reunited. Instinctively, she began to straighten his coyote skin, smoothing the red cloth that hung from his waist. Her fingers cared intimately for the man at her side. Reaching for her hand, he silently touched her heart. His tender touch kissed her familiar delight, flooding her with him.

And in that moment, they stopped. The world entered timelessness. There was nothing beyond the circle of their love. They pushed back the invisible curtain of time and hid behind it, in another world, a lover's world.

But the vibration of the drum beat penetrated their private circle and reminded them of the dance. And like a great tide, they rushed out to join with the ocean of dancers. Under the stars and within the circle of Powwow, they ran to catch the growing line of eager partners. The soft grass yielded to their soft steps. Earth Mother massaged them, as they massaged Her. As two, they would begin this dance of lovers: he on the left, she on the right.

He heard the rhythm. She heard the song. He thought of nothing. She thought of everything. He moved with joy. She moved with awe. He felt solid Earth. She felt open Sky. His spirit circled her and her heart circled him.

With separate beats, they began the dance of the Two Step. Then with one common beat, their weight surrendered into Earth Mother. With the other as their love, their bodies lifted with a subtle certainty and their spirits entered Sky Father. With two steps they announced their connection to both Earth and Spirit.

He held her left hand securely with his right. Their hands understood each other, like shores that understand the sea.

Their union felt right, felt remembered, felt good. Allowing the beat to swing their arms, their joined hands created a moving circle. Pulsing with the strong beat, their individual life Circles intersected into one.

Together, they followed and danced the path of others. Looking to the lead dancers, they would learn how they would dance tonight. One by one, the partners in front turned, each couple forming a complete circle. Like a great whirlwind, each twirl caused the line to move with greater energy. Soon the wave of twirls reached this couple. He turned her. She turned him. She laughed with delight. He caught her laughter and made it his own. The circling wave moved down the long line of couples until, at last, everyone experienced their moment to twirl in love.

The couple watched ahead, yet were keenly aware of each other. Their hands held; their circling arms continued to pulse, in synch with their steps, with the beat of the drum. With this loop of love, their energy was strengthened by those ahead and was given to those who followed.

Laughter and good feelings echoed all around. The arbor was full of partners, celebrating each other, celebrating life. Lovers found each other and renewed their love. Even the children found partners and practiced this love dance. Both old and young celebrated in the dance of two.

The head woman dancer turned and danced backwards. Holding her hand, the head male dancer continued to look forward to lead their trail. Like the crest of a wave, this pattern traveled through all who joined in the line.

The woman's golden shawl swayed as she turned to follow the wave of dancers. "I trust you with my life," the woman thought to her partner.

"I will be alert," his heart mirrored back.

The drum continued to beat. The spirits of the singers, dancers, and onlookers got caught in the current of love. Everyone was present in the two steps of life.

"With one step, we take. With another, we give," her thoughts spoke to his heart.

"With one step, we honor. With another, we are honored," he thought as he felt Coyote's skin honoring this dance.

"With one step, we plan for the future. With another, we remember the lessons of the past," she understood in that moment.

"With one step, we live. With another, we will live again," his spirit heard.

Ahead, the dancers separated. The head male dancer turned left and danced along the outside of the men's line. Reaching the end, this lead dancer turned inward to close the circle of men. At the same time, the head woman dancer led the women right, creating another circle. She also turned back toward the beginning and both lines met at the center, dancers passing dancers.

Separating, he followed the men and she followed the women. Each welcomed their dance individually. She felt the winds on her face. He reveled in the path before him. She recognized the present movement. He remembered his past. Greeting others as the lines passed each other, they acknowledged the separate worlds. Celebrating their unique paths, each became more.

Yet, passing so many other faces, she again searched for his hypnotic eyes. Hearing others' laughter, he listened for her sweet music.

And like rain showering a dry and thirsty world, their love rushed out to fill each other's opening. She met him, now

different. He found her, now more. Together they joined
their hands in love, anew.

The drum pulsed and the line circled the song. Each
woman reached to hold the hand of the man behind. Each
man reached to hold the hand of the woman in front. The
circle was now complete. Lost in the Oneness, everyone
raced inward towards the center, to meet the beat of the
drum—to honor the beat of their hearts.

And in that moment her love spilled. Eternally drawn to
her sweet essence, his spirit tasted her exquisite nectar.
In their love flight, their hearts embraced while their spirits
soared. Amidst the flight of All, the web of life vibrated with
love, again.

THE STEPS TO THE DANCE OF LOVE

Come and rediscover the steps of your heart. In your dance, you will come
to honor yourself first. This internal recognition will enable you to journey
beyond Self. Free to walk in the now, you will find a path that leads to a
forest of remarkable sweetness. It will lead you to love. For as you are able
to look to burgeoning life, you will discover it is laden with love. Follow the
directions of your heart and pick the fruit of love. Honor its thorns of protection, as you allow its essence to fall into your hands. Be gentle with its fullness. Like raspberry sweetness, taste its flavor. Accept its seeds as well as
its juice. Then, having loved and been loved, remember and thank its Giver.
Plant your own seeds and allow love to flourish for the other to experience.

RELATIONSHIPS

The Two Step Dance is about love relationships. It is about you and me: the
We. It is about our heart. The Two Step Dance is for couples, for Life is
designed in twos.

Consider the dualitys of life. There is soft and hard. Open and closed. In and out, beginnings and endings. Emptying and filling. Dark and light. Female and male. Each part needs the other for completion.

We sing so we can dance. We meditate so we can pray. We listen so we can speak. We give so we can take. We die so we can live. We feel pain in order to recognize joy.

Our own existence demonstrates these two sides. Just as there is life and death, our body's symmetry declares this truth to two ears. Our left and right brain hemispheres fill a unique purpose. Our eyes merge two images into one. We look at life puzzles to discover the missing pieces. Human nature yearns for answers to the questions.

All dualitys in life are connected.

Twilight connects the night to the day. Hard becomes soft, collapsing into its *purpose.* A communicating tunnel connects the right and left sides of our brains. The moment we empty, we are able to fill. In the space of silent meditation, we are connected to the voice of our Creator. Just as the male gifts the identity of female through his seed, the female gifts the life of male through birth. The question offers the answer and the answer accepts the question. You are the connection between life and death.

To connect with others, we must learn how to truly become and celebrate Self: to listen, be present, to give, to accept, to communicate, and to live. These are the secrets to a flourishing relationship.

People naturally yearn for connection. We need other people to fulfill our purpose in the universe. Like the seeds of the fields, we are born into a world of others. Our roots entwine. We grow side by side. We love the same light. We connect and two seeds become one. The natural harmony of the world needs these connections. This guarantees our survival.

Relationship implies connection.

Our life on Earth Mother requires that we connect with others. This is the key to living a full life. We must commit ourselves to the Two Step Dance of Life.

express herself. He could give more. She could receive more. In this way each would teach the other of balance. Each would move more toward the center.

Our Life purpose embraces all of who we are, not just some of who we are. If you only express your strengths, you deny the opportunity to strengthen your weaknesses. As your purpose can be viewed with your soft focus, so can your tendencies be understood in this light. Let the discovery of who you are to become, challenge and strengthen who you are right now. Accept the challenge. Let purpose direct your free will into disciplining that which needs balancing. Balancing your internal tendencies allows your genuine purpose to be fulfilled.

Insecurity, control, selfishness and dependency issues need to be confronted. The antidote is practicing the opposite of each. If you are insecure, become secure by validating who you are and what you are competent at. If you are controlling, practice letting go. If you are selfish, practice giving. If you are dependent, practice independence. Balance all aspects of your being: physically, emotionally, mentally and spiritually and these tendencies will also balance out. Health is balance and balance is health.

We must honor our journey to the secret places of Self. Acknowledge the feldspar and mica that speckle the granite of Self. Upon our multifaceted Self, our monument of Purpose can be built. Recall that your purpose is the big idea for your life. It includes believing, practicing, and becoming the vision of who you are meant to be and what you are meant to do. Awareness of complete Self gives us the insight to fulfill this purpose in life. It is upon our own discipline, strength, and self-endurance that, alone, we can stand tall in this purpose.

Honor Your Purpose

Ask how you can honor Self and at the same time, compensate and strengthen your weaknesses. Ask how you can become more fully you. Ask how you can build your greatest Self. Just as we doubt, we can believe. Just as we take, we can give. Just as we miss opportunities, we can discover purpose. Just as we fail, we can succeed. Just as we cry, we can laugh. Just as we deny, we can embrace. Just as we hesitate, we can decide.

Too often, people are in a hurry to find a partner. Unable or unwilling to first tend to Self, they unconsciously (or consciously) look for another who exemplifies the side of Self that has been neglected or denied. Rushing to find someone who has courage, they never become strong. Rushing to find someone who is spontaneous, they never learn how to relax their control. Rushing to find someone with answers, they never ask their own questions. Rushing to find love, they miss the greatest love of all—the love of Self.

Discover your place in the universe. Your Grand Entry must be honored. Return to your mountain of joy and view your range of possibilities. Visualize your purpose. Engage your Mash-ka-wisen, (inner strength) embrace your Bimadisiwin (the good life) and become your Self. Celebrate your Self. Look at your Self before you look at another. Love your entire Self, before you attempt to love another.

For, ultimately, you wake up alone.
You dream your own dreams.
You think your own thoughts.
You die your own death.

FINDING YOUR MATE

When you have become intimate with your Self, you are ready to become intimate with another. You may choose to appeal to the Spirit World, asking fate to bring your spiritual-partner to you. Once you are fully prepared to participate in a relationship of such intimacy, you may make an earnest request to the Creator.

In your own moment, ask the Creator to allow fate to merge with your free will[2]. Ask the Spirits to bring your mate to you. Remember that a question which already has the answers is not a question. So keep your request pure. Do not specify the person's color, weight, height, age, features or personality traits. Do not specify when or how you will meet. Do not specify at all. Hear this prayer.

---

[2] Refer to *Listen to the Drum: Blackwolf Shares his Medicine* for a more detailed discussion of fate, free will and purpose.

Gitchi Manidoo, as your hand paints the marbled sunset and scatters sparkles onto the white snow blanket, please, paint my life with your colors and patterns, surprise me with Love's sparkling beauty.

Gitchi Manidoo, as your breath moves the Four Winds and connects me to Your timelessness, may your breath swift two paths together. Together, may we draw nearer to You.

Patiently, I will wait.
Honoring in Your Wisdom, I will rest.
In the present, I will live.

Until then, I will look to the water-colored sky and the precious sparkling view. I will move on with Life, to be always with You.

Gitchi Migwetch.

Once your request is made, let go of it like a balloon on a string. Let it ascend to the hands of the Spirit World. That is where fate begins. Ask the Spirit World to provide what you need and you will find, that in the answering, you will want that as well.

You will know when it happens. Like knowing cinnamon before the taste, you will recognize the person. Like remembering the smell of a rose, your lonely winter will melt away. Like gathering wood for the heat it will bring, your heart will know the joy this person will offer. Life certainty comes from the Spirit World, for here, the past, present, and future are one. With no division, your connection to fate opens the curtain where you have both already been. It is remembering. It is knowing. It is celebrating. It is love.

Like the dancers of the Two Step, allow the currents of synchronicity to guide you together. Let the Spirit World be the breath you both breathe. Invite the Creator to create your love.

When you find your partner gift them with this same heart-felt life. Offer the peace of relaxation. Allow your fingers to massage away the tension with the warmth of your internal calm. Share your liberated energy. Become as vibrant as the dancing flames; be the partner who experiences the joy of leaping into each new moment. Explore the possibilities of two people joined in love. Fan the flames of your love, with your breath, your commitment, your attention, and your desire. Let the flames of love consume you. May your partner fill you with their essence, as well. May you exchange the heat of true love, catching on fire with hunger for one another's presence.

BE PRESENT

Awareness is the glue that bonds your free will to the fate of the Spirit World.

Remain present. Fate plays out its role in the now. If you are attached to the past, you may miss her passing. If you look forward only to the future, you may not recognize his presence. Become aware of all that is happening to you right now. With or without a partner, your life must be experienced fully, in the present. Focusing on your request simply means you have not let go of your question; therefore, your question was no question at all. It was a demand. You may think you have the answer, but you don't even know the question! The Spirit World will present the person when and if it is appropriate.

Be present with yourself. If you have come to understand your Self, your spirit will recognize the hand of the Creator. Your heart will beat to tell you that fate has arrived. Having transcended insecurity, control, dependency and selfishness, you will tune into what is important for you. This awareness is in the present and will allow you to experience the joy of pure love. You'll know when you know.

Remember that life can only be experienced in the present.

Together, you and your partner must remain in the present. A relationship that is not lived in the present is waiting for something else to happen, or trying to return to something that it cannot. A healthy relationship is lived in the present, for you will find that each moment is the most important moment. A healthy relationship is the result of each living moment.

The Spirit World speaks to your heart. In the present, your heart communicates with certainty or doubt. In little ways, practice listening to yourself. In your silence, listen to what you need. Offer yourself the silence of Self. It is here, in the space of nothing, that the Great Spirit whispers. Go from your head to your heart, the furthest distance in the Universe. Happiness begins with the beating of your own life. Listen to your heart.

GIVE AND ACCEPT

Remember that Bimadisiwin includes fate, purpose, and free will. It is not just the hand of fate and the direction of purpose. Bimadisiwin also challenges your free will, for you are a free agent.

Bimadisiwin must be engaged in a relationship. Fate may bring you children, yet free will helps achieve your purpose for them. Do the best you can for your children (free will) and their lives will also follow the Spirit World's direction (purpose). This will complete the hoop and fate will again guide them to their destination in life.

Your full life (with or without another) demands your active participation. Life is a series of choices, decisions, options, and alternatives. Live your life wisely. You will carry the actions and choices you make today, for the rest of your life and to the next seven generations. So be careful what you put in your personal knapsack. It will follow your journey and its contents will move along with you into the future. Be aware of the delicate balance that is needed in a healthy relationship. If you disregard this essential aspect to your full life, passivity may open the door to invaders of many faces.

Become aware that your internal balance awaits to complement another who is also internally balanced. This awareness will remove distractions and allow you to see the gifts of the Spirit World more clearly.

Allow your free will to recognize or reject a giver-taker partner. Don't settle for a taker. They'll suck you dry and leave you a shell of a person. Don't settle for a giver or you'll be flooded with niceties; there's only one thing worse than not enough of something, and that's too much!

In a healthy relationship, each partner gives freely and takes freely. Each empties and fills their love bucket, each keeps the love waters flowing. As you relate with your spiritual mate, you will also relate with his/her balance.

Your destiny is designed to fill and empty. Just as you recognize your mate, they will recognize you. The dance of separation and connection, of filling and emptying, of giving and receiving, will begin. Enjoy the dance. Participate in the dance. Connect and separate. Give and take. Fill and empty. For that is the way of the Sacred Hoop.

THE GIFT

A long time ago, when the seas were the only place the animals lived, a few trees stood tall to see the world.

While the sea-animals were learning how to swim, breathe, and crawl, Grandfather Sun peered down upon the trees and said, "It is time for you to learn to spread your own canopy from one shore to the next. Soon the sea-animals will leave the water to live with you on Earth Mother. You must prepare a home for your brothers and sisters."

The trees all whispered amongst themselves upset with this demand. "We are rooted here. We do not have legs to move across the land! How can we fill in the spaces from shore to shore? We can not make this journey!"

The Four Winds heard this discussion and raced to tell Grandfather Sun these words. That night, knowing the trees would need to be taught, Grandfather Sun told the Four Winds what they must do.

The next morning the winds grew strong and shook the entire earth! Green trees swayed in their spots! Branches were torn from their trunks! Yet, the trees remained rooted, refusing to leave their home.

Finally, the winds lessened. Opening their eyes, the trees saw the separation. Parts of them were scattered all around the world.

Little circles of themselves were now far away and looked longingly over at the trees they were once part of. Wanting to return to the height of the branches, the little nuts cried, "Help us! We miss the heights! We miss the leaves! We miss the views! Help us to return to you!"

The trees were sad. In their refusal to change, they had lost part of themselves in the Great Storm. Holding a council, the trees again talked amongst themselves.

"I wish there was something we could do for them. We cannot offer them the heights, for we still do not have legs to gather them," said one tree.

"We can not offer them the view, for they are so small," said another.

"There is nothing that we can do." With their broken branches, their hearts hurt.

One tree looked at the acorns strewn about. "Look. They are cold. We can at least offer our leaves to comfort them."

So it was decided. The trees would ask the Four Winds to circle around them. Understanding their request, the Four Winds gathered up all their might, blowing and whipping the remaining branches, shaking free each green leaf, until finally, all were gifts to the little ones below.

The acorns were comforted. That night, with the warm, soft, green blankets on top of them, the acorns snuggled into Earth Mother to sleep.

When the acorns awoke, they noticed they had grown their own tender leaves that now peeked out of Earth Mother to reach out to Sky Father.

Hearing their squealing joy, one tree awoke.

"Look! The little ones are growing!" he yelled, waking the rest. The trees shook with their own joy as their trunks rushed with internal excitement! And, popping out of their own branches, were new, sprouting leaves!.

Grandfather Sun noticed all that took place and smiled.

It wasn't long before all the trees in the land had grown leaves to replace the ones they had given. The seeds scattered across the land, and grew up to fill in the empty spaces. As seasons passed, the young trees grew stronger and taller, until they, too, saw with the same heights as their brothers and sisters. Soon, the sea-animals crawled onto land and found a thick forest home.

Grandfather Sun, proud of the trees' offering, knew what he must do. Splashing his own gold and red hues onto the trees he said, "Because of your generosity, I offer you this gift of beauty. Let my gift remind you of yours."

So each year when Grandfather Sun moves into the Autumn Sky, the colors are given, the leaves are offered, and a good home is prepared for all the animals.

COMMUNICATE

Build the foundation of a healthy relationship upon trust. Build your walls of friendship and your roof of common interests and aspirations. Decorate your relationship with companionship, love, and lust. Not just love. Not just lust. A sweet-sour flavor is delicious[3]!

Allow communication to bring its fresh air into the chambers of your heart. Promote a healthy relationship by communicating honestly, openly, directly,

---

[3]   Not sexual deviance or sexual abuse, but an expression of our animal nature. Be who and what you are.

calmly, and specifically to your partner. Do this in all areas of your union. Share the feelings and thoughts that pertain to your interests, aspirations, companionship, love, and lust. In this way, you will keep your love alive.

Learn to listen as intently as you speak. Listening is an art. Hear the words and non-words of your partner. Honor him/her by recognizing their need to speak. They may speak with the language of nonverbals. Be aware of what their body is saying. What does his tight jaw really mean? Why does she look away? Is that sadness or gladness in his eyes? Why is her posture suddenly different? Encourage your partner to communicate his/her needs and desires directly.

Do not expect your partner to hear your internal world. It is up to you to share your secrets. Express your pain as well as your joy. Ask your partner to listen to you, as you listen to him/her. Practice this. Make a deliberate decision to communicate more effectively.

Open your Self to your partner. Just as the flap on the teepee goes both ways, let your partner look in, as you look out. Be present with what is happening now, inside and outside, and reveal this perception to your mate.

First, breathe deeply, connect to yourself and the Spirit World. Be aware of what is happening inside and outside you, be honest with your Self, as well as with your partner. Dare to experience both the pain and the joy of honesty. In the emptying and filling, you will grow.

Be direct in your communication. Do not run from unpleasant situations, nor push them away. Give yourself permission to reveal your heart. Let your partner see and hear your heart and thoughts.

Be specific. Know what it is you value and express it. Give your partner the gift of understanding.

Be calm in your communication. When anger or hurt overwhelms you, give yourself the gift of time to respond rather than react. Return to Ain-dah-ing and return to calm. In this way, you will communicate more effectively, without regrets.

Like the Talking Circle, as each member is honored to hold the feather, may you gift each other the time to communicate. Honor each other by listening. Just as the feather lifts the prayers of the council, may your concerns be elevated in importance, May your relationship grow with renewed understanding and respect. May you, too, come to one mind.

LIVE <u>YOUR</u> LIFE!

Remember that you must walk your unique path. Travel alone from time to time, for in your separateness you will bring a fresh heart and a new mind to your partnership. Enjoy the life you live. It is yours to enjoy! It is yours to declare!

May both you and your partner be balanced: spiritually, mentally, physically, emotionally, at work and play; 50% inner world focused, 50% outer world focused (people, places and things), 90% mentally in the present, 5% in the past and 5% in the future. May you each have an intimate, functional relationship with Self. A healthy relationship relies on healthy individuals who are balanced within. Able to journey the Sacred Hoop of one's life, the two intersect as One.

Strive to maintain an <u>interdependent</u> relationship between the two of you, rather than a <u>codependent</u> or <u>independent</u> relationship[4]. The Two Step danced with codependent dancers would result in the dancers toppling, tripping, leaning and falling onto one another. There would be no dance. Two independent dancers would result in chaos, each going his or her own direction, without any awareness of the dancers around them. Again, there would be no dance. The dance becomes a dance only when there is an order and awareness of all dancers. The Two Step relies on a unity in which each separate vision matters.

Realize that passive and aggressive tendencies develop from codependent and independent relationships. Whereas extreme passivity may result in

---

[4]   Without this awareness, people tend to become like one of their parents and marry the likeness of the other. Or they fill a codependent or an independent profile. The codependent relinquishes his own identity and ends up in a secondary profile. The independent person distances himself within the relationship, and is psychologically and emotionally unavailable.

suicide, extreme aggression may be expressed through homicide[5]. Through this ultimate example, come to recognize that one extreme is as unhealthy as the other.

Assertiveness is at the center of these two extremes. Assertive communication implies openness, honesty, directness, and calmness. It is specific to the issue. Be assertive in your relationship. It will promote good, healthy growth for both you and your partner.

INTERDEPENDENCE

Walk the path of interdependence. It is the Red Road of balance. Psychologically and emotionally, stand in your own center. Realize that you do not need a partner to feel or be whole. Do not seek a relationship to bring you feelings of sufficiency or adequacy. Self-esteem must come from Self. Seek a relationship for companionship, for it is healthy, human nature to want a sense of belonging, closeness, intimacy, caring, sharing, and connectedness.

Exchange your ideas with your partner, share your emotions, explore your spiritual essence and exchange the gift of physical touch. Have fun together. Learn together. Cry in each other's presence. Explore the big questions in life, together. Massage one another. Cuddle and enjoy each other's company.

Interdependence is an open system. This system allows each person to enter and leave, to be together and alone. Pursue your personal interests and actualize your unique aspirations. Encourage this same freedom in your partner. But always return to the closeness of the unit and embrace the relationship.

Return in order to belong once again.

In a healthy relationship, you are free to live your own life. You do not sacrifice your aspirations, interests, and desires for your partner. Access and exit the relationship to pursue personal destiny, freely and openly. Live your own life and allow your partner to live theirs, too.

---

5   In relationships where suicide and homicide are threatened, control and manipulation of the partner is usually the reason. These are extreme examples of codependent and independent relationships. This way of communication has become an habitual way of relating to one another. The threat is the ultimate control in this form of communication.

Do not dictate your life circumstance to another, nor allow another to dictate to you. In this way, no one is allowed to live their life as a free and healthy spirit. How sad to be controlled under the mask of love by your partner!

Respect your partner. Offer Namaji to the relationship. May you be free to engage your Bimadisiwin, but may you also recognize that part of your destiny is already at home. Be responsible and accountable to your partner. Gift them your time and commitment. Be there. Understand that a relationship requires togetherness. In this unity, offer dignity, pride, respect and honor to the one you love.

Live and let live. Share and exchange. Enjoy and love. That is the nature of a healthy relationship.

LOVE IS...

Love is freeing.

If you're not free within a relationship, you are in bondage. And bondage is abuse in its truest form.

Do not try to find someone to change, or fix under the guise that love conquers all. Love does not change people. People change themselves, only when they are ready to change. Don't marry an alcoholic and expect him/her to stop drinking. Don't begin a relationship with an over-eater and expect him/her to lose weight.

Love is not a change agent. Love is love.

Love is graciously giving and taking, emptying and filling, connecting and separating. It is a free flow of energies that connect two separate loops. Like a figure eight, your separate life-circles connect and complement one another in a common union and bond.

Experience the joy of a relationship that complements each partner. Let his song become your dance. Let her laughter become your story. Let his giving become your lesson. Let her tears become your understanding. Allow the gifts of your partner to touch you. Honor the companionship and you will be honored.

What's a bird - without his song,
Or drum - without a beat?
What's a shaker - without a rattle,
Or a circle - without complete?
What's a bell - without a tinker,
Or whistle - without a shrill?
What's love - without expression,
Or forever - without until?

Love mirrors nature's cycles. It dances the dance of connecting and separating. Love is an expression of the Creator, for in the midst of love we experience the Great Mystery. It is the song, the view, the dance, the very beat of Life!

Express your love. Gift your partner with the song of your heart. Find ways to give what will honor your mate. Share your view of life, from the mountaintop peaks to the depths of your spirit. Dance with your partner in the many dances that life offers. Realize that sometimes you must dance together and sometimes alone. Connect to the very beat of your partner's existence and honor the life within. In this way, your expression of love will bloom.

For love is that pink wild rose that lives on the edge of the forest, nurtured with good sunlight and shade. Its' petals are the many faces of love: the smile, the frown, the surprise, the disappointment, the joy, the agony, the contentment. All are the expressions of life, and all must be experienced. All must be shared to close the loop of love.

Just as the raspberry thorns protect the berries' sweet juices, the thorns of love protect us from abuse by setting limits and boundaries. The bud, which contains the essence and spirit of the rose, draws its life from the Creator's vibrations. Honor the essence of the Creator in your partner. Light and dark, the rose's shades express the hues of ourselves. Soft but hearty, strong but fragile, love is truly the expression of life. Life is love. And love is life. Ah ho!

The serenity prayer tells the story of love. Hear the voice of my spirit as I add to this prayer:

> God (we all pray to the same Creator),
>
> Grant me the serenity to accept the things I cannot
> change (people, places and things).
>
> The courage to change the things I can
> (myself),
>
> And the wisdom to know the difference
> (where both of these begin and end).

These are the guidelines to love.

THE PATHS OF RELATIONSHIP: SEPARATE AND TOGETHER

Beginning under the same tree of life, there are many paths that lead outward. Celebrate the path you choose. Veer off to discover new worlds. Journeying sometimes alone, sometimes together, enjoy your purpose as it unfolds.

Come to see that separate paths are necessary and good.

Discover that your life does not have to be held under the close supervision and scrutiny of your partner. And vise versa. In fact, exercise your aloneness. You must remember who you are. Return to your own space and discover your uniqueness again and again. Allow your interests to grow. Fulfill your aspirations. Meet new people. Encourage the same of your partner.

Then come together. Share your experience. A relationship grows because of what you bring to it. Become teachers for each other. Allow your paths to connect and see that it is necessary and good.

Commit to companionship. Twirl together in work and play. Trust each other and guide each other. Experience and explore both the Spirit World and Earth Mother together. Recognize the two beats of life and honor their meaning.

Then celebrate your togetherness with others on the hoop of Life! See how your two hoops intersect the Hoop of All. See how together, you are stronger and can do more for your community. Together, participate in healing the world. Together, discover the joy your community offers. Reach out in front and behind you to join the hands of other members in the Sacred Circle. Together, honor the one beat of life.

LESSONS FROM NATURE

Watch the birds. They speak and teach of love relationships well. See how many birds build their nests and feed their chicks together. Recognize that both the male and female incubate their eggs. Both play a vital role in the raising of the future generation.

What is your role in your relationship? Take time to write down what you expect of yourself as well as your partner. Ask your partner to do the same. Then come together and share your individual lists. Listen to each other. Compromise. Discuss. Look for alternatives. Come to one mind. Model this way of living for your children. Let them learn from you, how two or more come to one decision. Learn to balance and share in the responsibilities of life.

Observe that there is no head goose. Flying in a 'V' formation, the lead goose takes this position temporarily. Soon another takes over. By doing this, they prevent head winds from fraying their feathers[6].

---

6   The traditional tribal family had no authoritarian head of family, so there was no need for competition, which sours relationships. Power struggles did not occur because each knew their role and accepted their purpose. With a focus on "we" rather than "me," cooperation moved the family circle.

Recognize that you and your partner can exchange roles. Do not allow daily, routine demands to fray your feathers. Do not allow unbalanced responsibilities to threaten your relationship. Do not lock onto one particular responsibility for the rest of your life together.

Listen to your mate's verbal and nonverbal language and offer relief and acceptance to one another. Exchange roles to appreciate what the other has done for you. Talk about the expectations you have for each other. Be honest in your appraisal. Be open in your dialogue. Be loving in your response. In this way, your relationship will travel far and wide to view many new spaces in the heart.

Watch the many animals that help groom one another. How can you help your partner be clear of the stresses that fill his/her life? If you have a free hand and your partner has asked for your assistance, help in the grooming. Tell them what you see, for you can see parts to them that are out of their vision. Offer them honesty. Share this gift.

CELEBRATE THE SEASONS OF LOVE!

Celebrate the love you are given! Give yourself to the other! Offer your best! Empty and fill! Connect and separate! Then connect again!

Honor the seasons of your love!

In the spring of your love an abundance of growth occupies the view of your spirit. The explosion of exotic flowers and sweet scents are celebrated! Life is wondrous! Great excitement with each other and the possibilities of all to come fill the heart! Honor this and see that it is good. This is the season of joy. Nurture the tender, budding relationship and experience the explosion within.

In the summer of your love, you become each other's best friend. Sharing the world around you, you offer companionship. There is healthy growth and the beautiful procreation of the two made one! Honor this and see that it is good. This is the season of growth. Give to each other that which will help one another develop. Discover ways to channel the energy of two. Be separate and together. Balance your togetherness, determine your expectations, and enjoy the growing familiarity.

In the autumn of your love, the crisp air of the Spirit World quietly rustles your growth as you separate from past attachments. You delight in the colors of each other! Respecting the essence of your mate, you understand his heart as you know your own. Honor this and see that it is good. This is the season of knowing and anticipating each other's thoughts as though they were your own. Relax in the comfort, but surprise each other with new gifts that honor.

In the winter of your love, your hearts are silent, but, oh, so full! Like a bird sunning, sitting atop a snow covered branch, your spirits are content. Nestling in each other's warmth, it is a time of quiet understanding. It is a time of mature love, a time to give without being asked. Honor this and see that it is good. This is the season of silence. Listening to each other with one's spirit is now possible. Prepare to separate for a time. Honor the journey you have shared.

Discover that these seasons are timeless. Each taking its place on the Sacred Hoop of Life, there is no beginning or end. Without division, each season is accessible to you whenever you choose. Go to the East Direction to experience Spring infatuation. Go to the South to engage love's Summer winds. Travel to the West to connect to love's Autumn's colors. Enter the North to experience the white blanket of love.

Choose to return to each season to renew and reflect. Honor the seasons of your love. Experience the gifts of each. Then may the sun paint your vibrant love. May the winds drift it to empty spaces. Resting beneath your shaded growth, may you gift this love to others. And may love sprout anew!

MIGWETCH!

Has your path joined with another? Are you committed to your personal internal balance? Are you committed to your relationship? Have you thanked the Spirit World for delivering this person to you?

Take the time to answer these questions. In the privacy of your personal time and space, give your attention freely to these important matters of the heart.

Then find a meaningful way to thank your Creator for gifting you the people in your life. Gratitude is a message to the giver from the heart of the receiver. From your heart, offer your thanks. And in your thanking, pause to reflect upon your life. Consider the fate of your meeting. Discover the purpose of your relationship. Look at the choices your free will offers. In your thanking, open your spirit and slowly savor the flavor of love. Allow this occasion to become a moment of meaning.

Thank the Creator by offering your joy to someone else. Splash the colors of your love onto someone in need. May your love spread to fill the empty spaces.

Then trust yourself to fulfill your purpose. Believe, practice, and become who you are meant to be. Trust your partner to be who they are intended to be. Trust this journey that the universe offers. Trust the supreme intelligence that steer the stars and guides your heart.

Then listen to your heart.
Listen to the silence.
Listen to the song.
Celebrate the Music!
And join in the Two Step of Life!

Merge with your partner to dance the good song. Honor each other's movements and discover the journey alone you must take. Then may you come together to share what you have learned and become. Enjoy your dance! It is the dance of flaming hearts!

GRIEVING DANCE

*Our Spirit dances the circle to discover death
is the survival of our Spirit.*

In my dream-vision, I saw spiritual arms reach, as loss contracted this grieving spirit into internal spasms of agony. Yet, the dancer's feet remained grounded to Earth Mother, connected to this world. The dance moved a contorted, disjointed spirit through each moment, as grief rode the vibrations of the beautiful music that honored humanity. Through this dancing circle, a gradual healing took place. This is the grieving dance of the spirit.

Loss is a spiritual journey. It is where we become acquainted with our sadness. Here, we look out from within our heart, becoming both the griever and the grief. Here, our spirit wanders, searching for the other. Here, our mind returns again and again. Within the grieving experience, our human condition touches the eternal circle of life and death. For grief carves depth into our spirit, so meaning can enter to fill our emptiness.

Honor yourself when you experience grief. Honor others when you mourn. Honor all, for your spirit must dance beyond the veil of life.

FULL CIRCLE
(Part One)

Long Shadow preceded her steps.

It was time for Sun on Her Back to be released from the grieving. Her family followed as she walked into the winter circle. Two summers ago Sun on Her Back felt differently. Then, her mind had been misted with a great nothingness. Now empty, she was ready to fill again.

Looking only at the snow-packed earth before her, she painfully recalled finding him on the great rock under the cliff. She had withered up when she had seen his blood. Sun on Her Back had moved further inside herself as she had approached his still body. And the mind-mist entered, then. The mind-mist had taken her, had changed her, had claimed her.

Now, beginning this dance, prepared to let go of the mind-mist, Sun on Her Back remembered it once more. How many times had she seen this thing? How many times had she remembered kneeling next to him? Screaming, wailing, then weakening. Holding his head in her arms, she had felt his weight one last time. Sun on Her Back had frantically touched his broken body, his soft dark hair—trying to make him whole with her intent. Rocking him into her, she had smelled his scent, smelled his blood, smelled his death.

Until the sun passed nearly straight overhead, Sun on Her Back had knelt. Until her knees were raw from the rock that claimed her love, she had stayed. Until she absorbed the very last of his energy, Sun on Her Back had held her husband.

In the mind-mist of confusion, she had thought that the longer she stayed by Long Shadow, the longer she would have him, and would remain connected. The longer this would not be real. Here, next to him, she could keep the rest of her life from beginning.

For a long time she had remained there on the massive gray rock. Clouds drifted in and out. Trees swayed without notice. Forest shifted with sounds, not heard. Inside her deepest self, Sun on Her Back was entirely still. Stunned, she did not know what to do, how to do what she must. How to leave his still body. How to journey back. How to meet her people, changed. How to let go of him. To leave him meant to leave everything.

The cool air encircled her broken spirit and Sun on Her Back had stood up. Backing away slowly, she groped for her old life. Hesitating on the edge of rock and grass, she had reached out to him with her eyes. Suddenly life-tired, her thoughts became entangled. She moved away until her memory replaced the sight.

Each step back to camp had ingrained the mind-mist even deeper. Each step had taken her further away. Each step made his death more real. Each step led her on a journey where questions tried to replace him, to become her companion. Why? How?

When Sun on Her Back reached her home and when her people understood this thing that had happened, only then did she give up. Surrendering, she laid down on Earth Mother and cried. With pain seeping from every part of her, this woman cried into the bosom of her Mother. Tears mixed into the cool rich soil, and her pain entered Earth Mother.

And she was gone.

And for a long time Sun on Her Back stayed away. Away from other people. Away from her family. Away from herself. Away from Earth Mother.

Sun on Her Back was gone.

PERSONAL LOSS AND GRIEF

LOSS

To define loss is to insult the griever, for there are no limits to the losses experienced in life. You lose parts of yourself as the circle of life continues. Yesterday, today, and tomorrow are grieved. You lose youth and possibilities. Abilities and attitudes are lost. Life-styles, life-partners, life-ideals are grieved. Loved ones are lost. Your body loses its hair and skin to tell you that loss is part of the human experience. You even lose, when you gain, for good fortune replaces poverty's innocence. It is natural to lose. To win is to lose, as to live is to die.

Loss touches the griever intimately.

No one can really know what it is like to be you and to lose what you have lost. Your relationship with a lost person or experience is unique to you. Your grief is also unique. No one can enter that place of grief. Do not expect them to enter. Do not ask them to enter. Do not wish them to enter. For it is meant for you, alone. Alone, you must experience the grief and ultimately say good-bye.

Although others cannot enter, they may grieve alongside you. Loss can be the great storm that brings all clouds together. Connecting with each other's unique spiritual condition, let your tears join others. Just as each cloud empties its own contents, realize your tears and experience are your own. For loss is turning your medicine bag inside out[1]. Your collection of identities must be grieved, as loss permanently renames the contents of your medicine bag.

An Indian's most prized and valued belonging is his medicine bag; come to honor all that is you and all that is me. Do not expect your grief to be mine. Nor mine to be yours. Honor the other's solitary experience. Honor the other's medicine bag, for it holds the essence of both.

Every day, someone, somewhere experiences the Eternal Circle of Loss. Come to see that when it is your turn to ride the waves of this sea of tears,

---

[1]   Chapter 1 refers to the medicine bag that collects our personal identity and adorns the regalia of dancers. For further elaboration on Medicine Bag, refer to *Listen to the Drum: Blackwolf Shares his Medicine.*

you are not alone. All of life participates in this circle, for the vast sea contains the tears of all: past, present, and future. Timelessly, with your tears, connect to the hearts of all who have grieved.

Like Sun on Her Back, enter the sea of tears to grieve. Here, you will join others. Here, you will experience the depth of Mitakuye-Oyasin.

I
lie to
hold my
heart close
and I cannot
cry.....for my
self or for
him.

I
try to
leave the
sacred circle
and mind-mist
hides my raw
heart. Then
I drift.

I
cry to
quiet my
pain and life
lifts my Spirit.
I return to the
eternal love
circle.

Stars brighten the night path, and the light of the Spirit World awaits to shine upon your journey of loss. Star People[2] are forever present to light up the sky. The spirits of all are present, as you dance your steps of grief. Come to see that all await to help ease your loneliness. You are not alone, even when you must grieve alone.

Just as star people have five points, you have five senses. Walk in cadence with the star people with your five points: your two feet, your two hands and your head. Hold high your dignity as you experience your loss.

EXPERIENCE THE GRIEF

Like a snake's venom that travels the veins, loss permeates every aspect of our lives. Temporary or ongoing, our response will decide the effect. We can allow loss to stop us or we can choose the antivenin—the serum to neutralize its pain by accepting the grief. Released from the paralyzing effects of grief, we can choose to live again. May you partake of this serum in order to release yourself from the fangs of loss.

Those who attempt to deny or limit the experience of grief will suffer the long term consequences of its poison. Like a snake bite, the longer we deny the reality of grief, the more damage to Self we inflict.

FULL CIRCLE
(Part Two)

Sun on Her Back now danced. With her family following
her steps, she knew she was not alone. Her sister, brothers
and parents all shared in her release. They were always
there beside her and their presence supported what she
must do. The strong beat of her people mixed with the
cold air of winter. Dressed in warm furs, the dancers
became part of the snow scene that surrounded the dance
circle. The crisp air lifted her essence and carried it to the

---

[2]   Star People refer to the belief of the Anishinaabe people that our ancestors reside in the stars after they die, and watch and guide their children below.

places she knew she must go one last time. To the memories. The memories of her mind, body, heart and spirit. The memory of her journey must be complete.

Feeling her people's strong presence behind her, Sun on Her Back remembered the long days of great sadness. That first summer had vanished without memory-making, for there was only one deep memory. Wrapped in summer's safe warmth, life was only sad.

But then, life moved forward. Even without Long Shadow, the leaves changed color. Even without him, the geese began to fly. Without her husband, the nights became cold. Autumn's barren forest had announced how different life really was and the deep hollowness of Owl's hoot reminded Sun on Her Back that she was alone. Life pushed off the safe blanket of sadness and left emptiness.

The dancers circled. With the connection of their feet, Earth Mother opened to her children as She did that first day of mourning. Sun on Her Back's heart met the frozen earth. Her grief was big and penetrated, burned, from her eyes. The hard drum beat carried easily through the cold air and entered the woods around the circle. It announced this releasing to her brothers and sisters. The cold wind touched Sun on Her Back's wet cheeks and reminded her of the desperate moments. Like a rock helplessly sinking to the bottom of a cold, dark lake, she remembered trying to claw her way back up. But there had been no way up. Nothing to hold on to. There had been no way to reach the surface. The death of her husband had become a great weight, the rock that held her down. Down and deep. Down and deep, she had separated from everyone and everything.

Her cloud-breath led her around the circle, around the good strong beat of life. She pulled the warm otter fir up around her neck and remembered. The first winter, the first endless winter memory, was as cold, as hard, as brittle, as the sheet that had covered the frozen lake. It had been only instinct that had kept Sun on Her Back fed and warm. Nothing had mattered that first winter. Like dead leaves tumbling over the wind swept ice-lake, nothing had entered. Nothing warm. Nothing good. It had all been a great cold nothing.

Then, from the nothingness, emerged something. A simple thing that finally mattered. Dancing into the East Wind, Sun on Her back touched her medicine bag and felt the curled shape. "Migwetch," her breath whispered visibly, within the sacred dance circle.

Sun on Her Back remembered that day. That first new day. She had been gathering water at the receding iced-lake. Spring had carried the singers, crawlers, and creepers back to the woods. Yet even the new life that had flitted about could not reach to where Sun on Her Back had gone. The mind-mist had settled in. She now expected to feel empty. She expected life to be empty. She expected nothing more.

Sun on Her Back had walked over to the birch tree whose trunk curved out rather than straight up. Always her favorite tree as a child, she would often climb its branches to overlook the small lake in front of her. The now frail woman sat down with her back against its trunk, the sun warming the ground, the ground warming her.

To escape life. To stop life. To forget life.

Without thought, she picked up some birch bark trapped in a few remaining granules of ice-snow. And its unique shape coaxed her mind open.

She noticed how the bark, about the length of her hand, had curled into a tight spiraled scroll. And suddenly, Sun on Her Back became curious about something outside herself.

"But how did this happen?" she began to wonder, turning it over and over in her hand.

Grasping the cylinder shape, she felt its toughness. She pried open the edge and looked in. There were two parts to the bark, she noticed. The outside that she held in her hand was a golden brown. While its backside, within the tight curl, remained beautifully white. The next layer had served as the outside of the tree. The inner most bark was the color of the tree itself—somewhat gray, torn, somewhat weathered.

Sun on Her Back tried to pull the birch scroll apart, but stopped. She knew that if she unwound it, it would surely break. No longer whole, it would quickly crumble. As it was, it remained an odd reminder of the tree it was once part of, protected in its callused rolled up shape, separated, from the world around it.

"There is no way to unwind what time has done to it," she realized. Slowly, like the melting lake before her, Sun on Her Back began to open.

Sun on Her Back closed her eyes to the day-sun that caressed her eyelids. Feeling the good warmth, still holding the birch bark, she imagined the scene.

"Something—some injury—must have torn at the bark," she thought. With a soft eye, she caught a glimpse of the moment. Perhaps the stress of growth, perhaps a storm. Severed horizontally, both above and below, one vertical edge had ripped and had begun to whither up, to curl in on itself.

"Still, one edge must have remained in tact," she thought now as she felt the scroll in her hand.

Sun on Her Back wondered how long it had taken before the entire curled bark loosened itself from the tree. How many days did it take before the weight of separation pulled on the edge that remained attached? When was it certain that this bark would fall? What had caused it to finally tear away from its life source? Was it the curling that tore it? Was it the weight? Or was it both?

A crow cawed.

Sun on Her Back began to shake, suddenly wet and cold. Memories of Long Shadow broke through her thinning emptiness. Suddenly, she saw him chasing her through the field, his caring eyes, his strong hands, the way he'd thrown his head back and laughed. It was all so near. So near her once again. Flooding her. Washing her.

Her heart seemed to break as a tremendous ache raced through her entire being. Forgotten tears found new release. Her back began to ache against the hard tree and Sun on Her Back instantly saw her days curling up on life. With great grief, she saw Long Shadow's death once more. She realized that she had turned inward and twisted with pain. Heavy with grief, she had finally separated from Earth Mother and Sky Father.

How hard and tight would her spiraled seclusion make her? What would happen if she never released herself from the inward direction she was moving? Would she, too, break apart if someone or something tried to peer inside her?

Like the great Earth movement, she cried. From deep within her abdomen she wept. Grief shaking free, without time separation, Sun on Her Back cried for Love.

Cried for herself.

Connecting to her loss completely, she allowed each tear to fall and be honored.

Then a silent calm entered and peace filled the carved emptiness.

Feeling her wet face, Sun on Her Back noticed a new fern pushing out of the soft earth. She heard the soft sounds of birds in grass. She felt the warm breeze from the South. Standing, allowing the sun to touch her completely, she saw the intent of the Spirit World. Brother Birch had lost part of himself to offer her this gift. Sun on Her Back put tobacco down, then carefully placed the spiraled birch bark in her medicine bag.

"You will remind me to chose life," she promised the birch bark inside her medicine bag. With her head high, her mind clear, her heart open, and her spirit proud, Sun on Her Back honored Brother Birch as she danced the Sacred Circle.

Released from the weight of her pain, Summer winds had healed her. Even as the leaves dropped, it was now time for Sun on Her Back to look at life once again. The drum pulsed strong and fast. The woman danced with new energy.

"It is time to live again," she thought. "It is time to give."

With the sun now at her back, the dance ended. The young woman turned to look at her people. Greeting her new life, a Long Shadow briefly touched her and left. The circle was complete. Sun on Her Back was released.

Loss is painful. Allow yourself to feel the pain. Allow your heart to cry and your emotions to spill. A single tear drop carries all the love in the world. Allow your mind to remember. A single memory honors all. Allow your body to cry and shake, for the memories are in your muscles. Let your muscles remember. We must remember it all before we can let it go. Feel the loss. Experience the grief.

Then, like Sun on Her Back, allow your spirit to find the meaning and celebrate the past, present, and future.

Hear the wailing of your heart, as your spirit wanders the world of pain. In the experience of grief, come to understand yourself more fully. View your hidden places. Touch love's tender bruise. For just as grieving is a necessary part of life, you must experience the all of life in order to be fully alive. Although it is a part we wish to avoid, like lightning, see that the strike of loss nourishes our future growth. You will honor the one beat as you come to understand the necessary role of loss.

Come to see that all loss must be acknowledged, experienced, and reconciled. Loss must be experienced in order to be free to ascend again.

COME TO EARTH MOTHER

No matter your loss, your mother waits to embrace you.

Earth Mother will dry your tears. Her open arms wait to accept your pain. Her whispers yearn to heal you. Her green branches will lift your aches. Her bosom will hold you in silence. Her view will uplift your spirit. Her valleys will hold your sadness. She gathers your tears to fill Her oceans. Her beaches caress you. Naturally, She heals. Naturally, She cares. Naturally, She waits for you to return to Her lap of comfort. Naturally, you will find your essence within Her touch.

Loss disconnects us. Go to Earth Mother to reconnect. The vibrations of nature will heal you, will soothe you, will listen to you. No matter your position in life, no matter your degree of loss, Earth Mother wants you to come to Her. She waits patiently. She will not leave you. She will not neglect you. You can neither be inadequate, nor above Her. She is your mother. You are Her child. She awaits you.

Go to nature and find the healing powers where you are alone. Do not distract yourself from your pain. See that brother and sister tree have waited for many years, waiting to hear of your pain. Go to Sister Cedar or Brother Pine and tell of your loss. Go to the mountains and listen as your cry is heard by all. Go to the oceans and let Her water wash your pain away. Go to the open fields and connect with eternity. Go to the Wind Spirits, the Water Spirits, and Mishomis. All of Earth Mother waits to heal you.

Wind Spirits

The Wind Spirits come from the Four Directions. East, South, West, and North speak their own language of healing. Listen to their whispers as they touch you with their power.

From the East, feel the soft breeze of new birth. Your pain opens the door to a new you. Neither bad nor good, it simply is. You are now different, new. You cannot be the same. Let the new breeze of the East flood you with morning energy. Let the fresh air breath you. Let the Creator create you. Allow the power of the East direction to fill you with the winds of nurturance and new beginnings. Let your prayers ride their strength and carry your message to the Creator. The Great Mystery will honor you with peace and creativity. This is East Wind, where currents bring rejuvenation and open you with the sweet grass.

From the South, allow the winds of change to enter your opened Self. As the seagull cries to the wind, so the talking Wind Spirits come for your wailing. Wail into their warm comfort. Let your self grow with their summer winds. Become strong again as they touch you with tender approval. This is the time to grow in a new direction. Tap your own nurturance. Send your prayers on the winged. May bird songs sing your spirit, may their journey honor your path, may their freedom of flight gift you with ascendance. This is South Wind, where currents touch the sacred tobacco fields.

From the West, experience the tempest of self discovery. Powerful and unpredictable, accept the direction of your new life. Allow its currents of life to create wonder within your deepest self. Accept the storms, for tribulations beget wisdom. Endure sudden loss, for as we empty, we will also fill. Send your prayers into timelessness. Let your understanding become an answer for another spirit who now searches in pain. This is West Wind, where currents touch the cleansing sage.

The North Winds wait to cover you with their white blanket of eternal peace. As the sharpest ear belongs to the wind, let your spirit sing the song of loss. Let your heart feel the sense of loss. Let your mind and body remember it all. Then let the sharp wind cut your pain into tiny pieces. Allow your pain to scatter and connect you to all directions, all people, all pain, all joy. Discover the meaning in the North Wind's power. In the crisp winter air, see and feel your breath before you. Listen to the Creator as you are breathed. Accept the message of the Spirit World. This is North Wind, where currents brush Sister Cedar's healing hair.

Water Spirits

Learn of the mystery of life.

Water Spirits teach us the mysteries of the Creator. See how frozen water is hard and masculine. See how liquid water is soft and feminine. See how water in the form of vapor transcends the Earth into spirit. All in one, one in all, all forms of water support the other.

The Water Spirits are the most powerful of all. Water cuts rivers through mountains, sculpts the deepest Canyons, rearranges entire landscapes. Let Cousin Water cut through your pain. Let the Water Spirits sculpt your new self. Let water's movement, move you. Let the waterfall wash away your negative energy and fill you with positive energy. Let water cleanse you, fill you, heal you, direct you.

Talk with the brooks as they babble of their journey.
Talk with the waterfall who has a thunder voice, but hears your faintest whisper.

Listen to the sea who bids you to hear your own silence.
Listen to the ocean who teaches you of the rhythm of the universe.

Connect to the thawing lake. It understands your pain.

Mishomis

If you are experiencing a loss, I invite you to participate in the following exercise. Experience the mourning in total. All of you. Not just your body, your mind, your emotions, or your spirit. Give your entire being permission to remember the past, experience the now, and open to the future. Allow healing to take place[3].

Find your Mishomis. Walk along a beach. Do not be in a hurry to pick up any stone. Experience Mishomis finding. It will want to fit in the palm of your hand, so you can take it home. You will know the stone when you see it, for it will speak to your heart. Mishomis will find you.

Mishomis is the invisible energy visible as rock beneath our feet. In the Ojibwe language, Mishomis means Grandfather and is the male spirit energy which has amassed for thousands of years. Grandfather's energy and consciousness has ridden the glaciers and contained the campfires of many Indian villages. Mishomis has seen all, heard all, and understands all. Mishomis has experienced all, and therefore can understand your experience. The spirit of Mishomis knows your heart, your fears, your pain, and will help you find yourself. Go now and allow your Grandfather to find you, for he will become your eyes to the Spirit World. When you return, cradle him in the cup of your hand. Listen to the words of prayer that will open you to the experience of Mishomis healing. Tell your Mishomis your words of loss.

> Grandfather, I hurt.
>
> With my heart, I shake with grief and shock of what has happened. With my mind, I remember what I have lost. I see all of it. I remember all of it. With my body, I feel the memory of the loss. The tension, the disbelief, the hurt. My spirit roams and wails for what is no longer mine. My loss has made me hard. I need to give you this hardness, this pain. I need to become open again.
>
> You are the container for my pain. You have waited for me and this moment for thousands of years. I am now ready

---

3   If you are currently being treated for an emotional or psychological disorder, or if your personal history suggests that you may need psychotherapeutic assistance, the authors recommend that you seek professional guidance before, during and after reading this exercise.

to let go. Thank you for waiting. Into your patient depths, I pour all my pain. All my regrets. All my sadness.

Thank you for taking my pain. Thank you for holding the weight that I can no longer carry. It is yours.

Take your time as you surrender your hurt to Grandfather. Be complete in your giving. When you have fully emptied yourself, go to a stream, a lake, a brook, or any water source and call on the aid of the Water Spirits. Ask the Water Spirits to wash the pain out of your Mishomis. Feel the water cleansing your Grandfather. Then hold your Mishomis up to Nee-ba-gee-sis[4] and ask her to permeate Mishomis with Sahgeen[5]—love and respect.

In the letting go, you release the negative energy that stifles your Self. In your grieving, you have carved out a greater opening that now waits to fill.

MY LOSS / YOUR LOSS

The effects of loss deeply touch those within its world. The mind-mist of loss takes the griever down and deep inside. In the journey, the griever changes forever. Injured with pain and loneliness, unseen wounds bleed for a long time. Come to understand that the scars of loss may not completely heal for seven generations to come.

Your experience of loss affects all those within your world. Those who are touched affect others in their world. This pattern is passed on, sometimes diluted with time, sometimes accentuated with time, to those who follow.

Look to a field of high grass. In the growing season, each spear supports the other as they grow strong towards Grandfather Sun. Yet, in the autumn, one spear topples onto another, until all lay down for winter sleep. What will be the affect of your loss experience? Will you grow stronger with support, or will you topple others with your grief?

---

[4]   Pronounced: NEE-ba-GEE-sis and is the Ojibwe word for Grandmother and refers to Grandmother Moon.

[5]   Pronounced: San-GEEN and means love and respect.

COMMUNICATE

Grief needs to be expressed. Not accepted. Not given. Just expressed. Express your grief. Acknowledge its weight. Allow others in your world to hear your pain. Let them support you with their presence. Communicate your human condition through your words and non-words. Be who you are at each moment. If you are grieving, be yourself and allow others to see your grief. Gift them the vision of your innermost Self.

Listen to another's pain, as willingly as you welcome their joy experience. Give them the gift of Namaji and be present for them. In honoring their pain, you honor all. Support them with your listening.

Take this opportunity to look at your life. What losses have you not expressed? What losses have you not communicated with another? Who, in your world, can you share these with? Take this moment and honor the losses in your life.

BE PRESENT

People tend to avoid the griever. Uncomfortable with the griever's uncertainty about life, deep sadness, encounter with death, and changed Self, we turn away when we are needed the most.

Look at the times when, perhaps, you have turned away. What were you avoiding? Most likely it was your own uncertainty, your own sadness, your own changes, your own mortality. In order to be comfortable with the uncomfortable, you need to confront your life issues. Take this time to look at the veil of life.

Aught Coyhis, a seventy-three year old Mohican, shares his view with you. Sixty years ago, he drowned in the Red River, yet was resuscitated. His near-death experience gifted him with the view of the other side of the veil. For sixty years he has never feared death. Without this fear, he has been able to live fully ever since.

How do you view death? How do you view life? Take the time to answer these two questions. They are the most important questions you will ever face.

Consider the meanings, the inevitable changes you must go through as you live. Consider how you may need others to be there for you. Look deeply into your Self and your existence, and face the questions that we all must someday face. In so doing, you will be gifting yourself, as well as another.

Be there for another.

Your physical presence reassures the griever that life is still a familiar scene. The griever needs your presence more than your words. Your presence gives a sense of order to a world that has been turned upside down. Your presence offers peace and comfort. Your presence connects the griever to the world. Connection is needed more than ever.

TOUCH

Then give the gift of touch. Touch understands and is understood. Touch is the harmonic healing the grieving spirit craves. A gentle touch on the back, the shoulder, the head, the hand tells the receiver more than what can be expressed. Hands held can quickly heal and bind together more than months of psychotherapy. Touch is the great gift of Self that offers immediate renewal and certain connection for both the receiver and giver.

Allow yourself to heal, to touch. Simple. Momentary. Revealing. Touch brings a unity of spirit to ease the pain. Give yourself permission to touch someone dear to you. As babies, our physical bodies would die without it. As adults, our hearts and spirits may break without it. Touch is not a luxury; it is a necessity.

Give or receive the gift of a massage. The painful memories are stored in your muscles. Touch them. Honor them. Release them. Heal them. Honor your body. It is as important a part of who you are as is your spirit. Remember, we live in two worlds.

THE CIRCLE OF GRIEF

Then experience the peace that follows. It will close the circle.

Look up! See how Eagle rides the invisible. Up and down, coasting, then back up and down again. With deliberate intent, she maneuvers her wings in order to catch the next current, rising to a new height. Leveling and riding a straight course, she gains new sights. Then, accepting the inevitable downward drift, she surrenders to each experience. Invisibly changing and unpredictable, the air currents carry Eagle to the places she must go. Eagle understands the dance of life and accepts the downward as naturally as she accepts the upward. Eagle is as dignified in her descent as she is in her upward flight. With her eye forever on the horizon, Eagle accepts the view. Eagle understands the dance.

Just as air currents go up and down, we must follow the currents of life in order to transcend to greater heights. Like Eagle's flight, the circle of life changes unpredictably. We, too, must learn to ride life's currents with grace and fortitude. Like the currents, life experiences are sometimes higher, sometimes lower. On the Sacred Hoop, sometimes our spirits are lifted, sometimes depressed. Sometimes we are young, with great energy. Sometimes we are old, with quiet reflection. Sometimes we are connected, sometimes separated. Sometimes we are rising with exciting transcendence to ride effortlessly on the Red Road of life. And sometimes we are overwhelmed by the downward drift of despair. We journey with great sadness and loneliness, into the places within.

For Life's challenge is not in the ascent. Life's challenge is in the descent. Grieving is about experiencing the fall. Once in grief, we can never be the same. Grief quietly changes us just as a quiet stream cuts through the solid bed rock.

Grieving is about loss. And life is loss. Life is separation and closing. The only thing constant in life is change. We all experience life. We will all grieve. We will all change.

I invite you to participate in your spirit's grieving dance. It is not a dance simply for others. It is a dance for all, for we all participate in Life. And life includes grief. Without grief there would be no bucket to fill. Grief carves caverns to open us to new journeys. Grief is the journey of the underworld. It is time to get on your belly and make your way through narrow places. Embrace your "flying foxes," your cave bats, along the way. Use your spiritual sonar to see your way through.

THE MEANING OF LOSS

Once we experience the pain fully, we are free to open to its meaning. We are ready to catch another rising current. From this opening of our spiritual wings, we are able to move onto the soft breeze of joy.

Listen to the questions that have been asked throughout time. For what nourishment can be found in the hollowing-out of tormenting grief? What solace can emerge from painful stabs to our hearts? What comfort can we discover in the thick blanket of mourning? How can we climb to greater heights if all we see is the downward despair of the moment? Listen, now to hear the answers that ride the winds of the Four Directions.

Life's meanings circle Earth Mother. Our ancestors, like you, have reached up, out of their despair to catch the answers during their time of need. Released back into the Four Directions, life's meanings circle again, ready to provide teachings to those who listen. I invite you to reach out to Sky Father and find your answers. Do this and then release them back into the Four Directions, for another time, another place, another spirit.

Come to see that your ancestors dealt with great loss, as will your descendants. Eventually, inevitably, completely, all experience grief. For as they have lived, they have also lost. As we live, we will also lose.

Look to the questions, now. Even if you are presently riding the currents of stability, consider the possibilities of the grieving experience—now. Acknowledge the path of grief, for surely, the dance awaits your steps.

Pause and be aware of all that you are. See that you include your losses as well as your gains. See that you are both the celebration and the grief. See that you have access to both the questions and the answers. Honor life's directions. Understand each momentary significance.

THE HEALING POWER OF PUBLIC AND PRIVATE MOURNING

Today, many people experience the public mourning that takes place immediately following a death. This is right. This is good. Even so, some cultures are more free than others in opening to the deep anguish of losing someone dear. Do not restrict yourself in your mourning. Do not allow culture's norms to dictate to you what is the best way to mourn. Mourn as you must. Listen to your body, your heart, your mind and your spirit. Your entire Self will tell you how to mourn, when to mourn, how long to mourn. Listen to your Self and mourn privately and publicly, thoroughly and honestly. Yield to this experience.

Native American tradition recognizes the fact that grief does not know time. Thousands of years have taught tribal people that mourning does not end when the burial is over. Or after three months have past. Or six months. Or one year. Tribal tradition recognizes the fact that each person mourns in his or her own unique way, in his or her own unique time. There is no time limit placed on the griever.

Unfortunately, today's world places a high premium on happiness, happiness at all costs. Be happy. Be happy. If someone has not "pulled out" of mourning by a designated length of time, it is considered unhealthy. Tribal people understand that the dance of life includes times of happiness, as well as times of sadness. It is okay not to be happy. Unhappiness is a necessary part of life. It is okay to grieve. Grieving is vital to living fully.

Tribal people understand that just as the immediate mourning was shared by the community, the circle must be completed in ceremony. Like Sun on Her Back, the family is released from mourning in a public dance, for all must share in the completion of the circle.

THE DANCE

The griever will know when it is time to dance again. Like Spring awakening the frozen ground, the Spirit World will nudge the grieving Spirit back into life. Listen for your Spirit's awakening.

The Grieving Dance is similar to other honor dances. All stand in honor of the person's life circle. The drum plays an honor song to open the path of the grievers. The griever, in very simple dress, dances between the head dancers, who are his wings. The beat is solemn. Family members dance, following the person who is to be released. The focus, however, is different. The moment is different. The dancer is different. Bimadisiwin—to live life to the fullest—is in the hearts of all. The person, now to be released from grieving, comes to honor the role of fate, purpose, and free will. It is time to honor the Circle of Life, once again.

Fate is the silent hand of the Creator who connects and separates. What is, is. Tobacco has been offered in preparation for this dance and the Spirit World is acknowledged, thanked and honored. The dancers honor fate as they dance the circle.

The dancer may smudge with sage at the Sacred Fire to cleanse in preparation for this ceremony[6]. Then, he or she is ready to accept the role of purpose. Purpose is life's meaning that is accepted, if not yet understood. Purpose has been fulfilled or is being fulfilled as the griever moves on with his or her life. With this cleansing, the dancer is free to fill up.

A dancer may then smudge with sweet grass, ready to fill with the Spirit World's gifts. The dancer realizes that receiving only occurs in the giving. Free will must be engaged. Free will is the beat of our own heart. It is the active participation in life, the giving of oneself to life. The dancer is committed to making life decisions, recognizing options, and determining choices. The released person now chooses to live fully. To fill up with Bimadisiwin. To fill up with the good life.

In the public declaration of this dance, the family members are free to move on. Cedar may be burned to carry the prayers to the Spirit World. Prayers are offered and the mourner is released to live a purposeful life. It is a declaration of emotion, of mind, of body, and spirit. The dance, like the prayers lifted

---

[6] This refers to the sacred act whereby the participant releases (through burning) the spiritual essence of the sage and wafts the smoke over himself. Becoming one with the Spirit World through the gifts of this world is the purpose. This act is done with Namaji and with sacred intent. Sage symbolizes cleansing; sweet grass symbolizes filling up with the Spirit World; cedar symbolizes the sending of prayers; tobacco symbolizes gratitude and opening the door to the Spirit World.

out to Sky Father, encompass their entire being. The weight of the loss is lifted. The present is finally free from the burdens of the past. The knot is untangled.

YOUR SPIRIT DANCE

Do not be ashamed if you mourn or for what you mourn. You have the right to be sad. Accept loss and grief for what they are, a part of life. Allow yourself and others the right to empty their bucket fully, so that they can then be filled. Allow yourself and others to heal in their own way, in their own time.

There is no time limit on our sadness, just as there is no time limit for a rose to bloom. When the weather is right, the soil nourishing, the sun shining, the rose will bloom. Not before. Allow yourself to bloom in your own time, when your conditions are right. Do not force your bud to open before its time. The beauty will be lost, the aroma short lived, the opening premature. Time is a healing factor. Give yourself time.

Support one another in the healing process. Then when it is right, release yourself and your loved ones from mourning. If a cultural ceremony is not possible, design your own ceremony. Do what is right for you. Burn a candle. Sing a song. Look at pictures. Take a hike through the woods. Walk along the beach. With your loved ones, experience the mourning. With your loved ones, announce your new life.

Then when the candle has burned out, the song has ended, the pictures are finished, the path has opened, publicly release yourself from grieving.

Celebrate the new you! With a feast, thank the people who have nourished you along this spiritual journey. Celebrate their presence! Celebrate life! In this way you honor your past. Honor the Future. Live in the now. Commit yourself to Bimadisiwin and live a good life. Take good memories with you upon your return to the Spirit World.

Even as Moon

Passes behind treetops,
I fill in Her circle.

I connect Her contour   My heart remembers
                                 She is complete.

Your heart remembers   your whole Self
                                 even as You

Pass behind the pain.
You will be complete again.

COLLECTIVE LOSS AND GRIEF

Personally and collectively, loss touches all. The tree that loses a limb bleeds for a time, heals and then sprouts new growth. Collectively, we must also bleed, heal, and live. As the water reflects the changes of the shoreline, see that the future will reflect our collective loss.

See how Earth Mother yields to her losses. The fire that has destroyed the forest, prepares the ground for new growth. Forest succession occurs because Earth Mother knows how to heal. She yields to what is and does not expect the old to instantly reappear. She allows time and the Four Directions to heal her wounds. New seeds arrive on the East, South, West and North winds. Her soil enriches with time. New growth replaces the old, until eventually the forest returns, but different.

Consider how the effects of loss reach beyond you. Family-loss, cultural-loss, and world-loss are realities that need to be recognized and experienced, before a collective healing can take place.

FAMILY LOSS

Families lose one another. If one family member experiences loss, the entire family experiences the reverberation of loss. As life takes the familiar, the cherished, away, the family must grieve. Losses from cyclical abuse, tragedies, sicknesses, and great change are some of the losses that families must endure.

A family's loss is felt seven times over. The cycles of mourning and depression affect those for seven generations to come. Families need to be cared for as a unique entity, just as we tend to our personal self. The family unit experiences loss in its own unique way.

Ask yourself how your family has dealt with loss. Was it limited to the initial acknowledgment of grief? Are there buried pains? Does your heart still ache? Have you and your family acknowledged the power of your loss? Has your family been released from the grief?

Communicate with one another. Acknowledge the loss that affects your family. Only by opening the infection, can you clean your wounds and heal. Get help if your wounds are raw. Qualified professionals can help your family heal. Please see that without this collective healing, the family will not be functional. In order to be released, the family needs to go through the steps of grieving. If someone in your family is angry, then allow anger. If your family is sad, cry together. If someone cannot forget, then allow them to remember the loss completely. If your family is prepared to let go and embrace Bimadisiwin, they can be released from mourning. It is right. It is natural. It is part of the eternal circle of separation and connection. Each person's grief must be acknowledged and honored. Then collectively, you can mourn and heal together.

CULTURAL LOSS

Collective cultural loss is passed from generation to generation. It is inherited.

Groups of people have been abused and victimized throughout time. Conquered indigenous people have experienced great pain. Exploited, used, abused, victimized, massacred; cultural roots have been ripped up, identity stripped away, beliefs, practices, and celebrations denied. The inevitable grief has severely affected the generations to follow[7].

---

7   This has been identified within the Native American community as Ethnostress—the loss and grief experienced by conquered people.

The American public is only now beginning to recognize the atrocities that tribal people have gone through (and still endure) since the first Europeans arrived. Covered with false blankets of political and religious justification, Americans of all ancestries are beginning to open their eyes to the truth. For all circles must close in truth.

The outside world has long recognized the true roots of the Western Hemisphere. From afar, it is easy to see that the indigenous people who lived with their brothers and sisters on Turtle Island gave this land her history. Their stories are deeply embedded in her mountains, follow her valley's tributaries, hide her forests' secrets, and blow across her plains. Without competing for Earth Mother's spaces, the rest of the world is able to acknowledge this visible truth.

Non-Indians can take the first step in healing the cultural loss of our tribal people. Acknowledge the collective dignity of Earth Mother's children, and honor the suffering they have endured. Become unified in a public attendance of this cultural loss and grief. Recognize the original "Americans" for their unique and honored connection to this land.

roots journey deep
seasons have circled
a people she keeps
who laugh and cry
hope and sigh
live and die
within her
arms
of
c
l
a
y

Honor the tremendous loss of tribal people. Imagine their wars, their victimization, their loss, their grief. Have you ever considered what it would be like to have your God, your land, your language[8], stripped away? Take time, now, to consider the magnitude of such loss.

Honor the loss of others by giving your time and attention to this very real experience. Think how this experience would change your life. How would you protect your children from experiencing this grief? Could you protect them? Could you?

Tribal people were stripped of their identity[9]. They were carved deep with the pain of multiple losses. To lose in this way, multiplies the grief, multiplies the time, it will take to heal completely.

Yet, life gifts us with a powerful instinct for self preservation. Many tribal cultures survived the horrors because they tapped their Mash-ka-wisen, their inner strength, and nurtured their identity. Although the traditions, ceremonies, language and customs went underground for a time, the sacred core remained the same. Although brave men, women and children died, their spirits still live, their dignity prevailed. Although there has been tremendous grief, today there is a renewal of joy—a celebration of life across this continent, an intertribal mending of the Web.

THE FLUTE

Automatically, the flute carrier's right hand reached up and over to touch the buckskin case hanging from his shoulder. "It is time to hear her song," Half Moon thought, "for I have waited a long time to hear her notes."

---

8 Language gives people their validity (consciousness) as a nation. Loss of language denies people their complete heritage and validity. Language gifts the people their distinction.

9 The inability to translate native words into English promoted even greater exploitation. Since European words had multiple meanings (abstract language), tribal people were manipulated through the conqueror's definition-selection. Thus, European conquerors were not accountable for what they agreed to. As the Native American word came from a concrete language, their word only had one meaning and therefore was a contract of truth. Innocently, Native people expected the word of another to be as honorable as theirs. Treaties were deliberately made, knowing full-well that the covert meaning would not be recognized by the Native Americans who signed them. Consequently, the "reorganization" of tribal people in the 1800's translated into relocation and extermination. This dishonest beginning is, has and still affects seven generations as an inherited collected loss.

The weathered case rhythmically struck his upper thigh as
he walked towards the soldier's drum, in front of the dance
arbor. The familiar movement caused him to smile. The
flute had become as much a part of Half Moon as his own
hair. It had adorned him.

Thinking of their journeys, he looked once more to where
she was dancing. Her long black hair was pulled away
from her face, as she stared off into the distance. Half
Moon wondered what her thoughts were. He had seen that
expression many moons ago.

The first time, she was standing in the Big Water. So
serious. Beyond the sand beach, behind her view, great
pines crisscrossed each other. Some remained standing,
tops ripped off, others had twisted, many caught against
one another as though wailing into each other's arms. The
storm had ripped through just before Half Moon journeyed
to this woman's homeland, and had claimed much from
her people, much from their woods.

As she looked out to the horizon, she could not see the
tragedy. She was absorbed with the constant waves
rushing to the shore. Swaying slightly with each tide, her
skirt soaked up further and further.

Water Crest was the name she was gifted that day[10]. Half
Moon thought of his own gift. His dreams had beckoned
him to journey here to find the song. Instead, Half Moon
found a people in great pain. Some had died. Others were
hurt. The village was destroyed. Half Moon quickly forgot
about his dream and instead began to help this people heal.

But soon, Half Moon began to dream again about the song.
Each night the dream would become clearer, taking him

---

[10] Native American names were often given or received during naming ceremonies, however, others
received numerous names throughout their life. Warriors often received names that spoke of their
character and bravery.

further. On the night of the half moon, a light dusting of clouds softened Nee-ba-gee'-sis, inviting him to the fire.

The young man sat across from Autumn Wind, the medicine man from a different band of Ojibwe, who had come down from Canada to help heal the devastation. Looking only into the fire, both men were silent. The young man thought his dreams. The Elder contemplated the fire.

Half Moon wanted to speak, but mind gathering words sunk like soft wet sand. The more he held on to the words, the more slippery they became. And finally, understanding, the young man let his heart speak.

"Autumn Wind, I have heard you know and hold the old ways."

"Yes. This is true." The old man spoke. The Elder remembered fleeing as a young boy, escaping to the bush of Canada. Then, he had thought the old ways foolish.

"I have had dreams." Half Moon pulled out tobacco from his medicine bag and walked over to the Elder. Squatting next to him he offered his gift. "I have heard songs in my dreams. I have felt smooth wood. I have tasted cedar." Half Moon looked deeply into the hypnotic fire.

The healer looked up at the young man next to him. The Elder understood the fire that consumed this man. Knowing this, the old man said nothing.

"I believe I am to be a flute carrier." Half Moon continued. "How will I know if I am to be honored in such a way?"

The old man smiled, for he knew the question well.

Pointing to Nee-ba-gee'-sis, the medicine man finally spoke, "Who tells Grandmother Moon to cause the tides? Go to Sister Cedar, Half Moon, to discover for yourself." And getting up, the old man left the fire.

Half Moon spent a late summer day wandering the cedar swamps, searching for an answer. He searched tirelessly, sinking into the soft moss valleys amidst massive roots. Sister Cedar's roots lifted out of the ground like huge haunches. With ankles aching, he hoped to find a sign. Tired from tripping on gnarled roots and downed branches, Half Moon sat on the green moss cushion. Looking up from under Sister Cedar's arms, he spotted a beautiful piece of cedar. Putting tobacco down, he carried off the wood.

Sitting at his fire on the cool summer's evening, he peeled away strings of cedar bark. Smoke curled up from his new fire and Half Moon thought long about his first carving, afraid to injure cedar's beauty, reluctant to make a mistake. In twilight morning, when Earth began to take on her color, Half Moon began carving, the knife strong and certain.

By the time his fire again became his light, his wrists ached with new feeling and cedar shavings clung to him and covered the ground, Half Moon had fallen into the rhythm of the knife.

Half Moon worked alone near the edge of the woods. His hands became as strong as his hair was long. Hungry for movement and people, he only paused to watch leaves race the wind. But thirsty for flute, he carved racing leaves and cutting winds. Finally, with the flute complete, Half Moon began creating songs to cedar-sing. Beginning as mysteries, the songs were strangely familiar. Cedar's music played him, even as he played her.

The day he met Water Crest he had been playing the finished flute. She was in the Big Water, one of the last warm days of Autumn. He was on the shore, offering her songs to the Water Spirits. She had looked up, from deep within her thought, to follow the beautiful sound of the flute.

He did not know that they would meet again at the fire.
That night when the forest spoke in the darkness and
secrets begged to be shared, Half Moon sat against a cedar
tree, playing the flute, in the shadows of the people's fire.
Lost in the beauty of her sound and his emotions, he
played the haunting forest melodies for this people.

With his eyes closed, Water Crest joined the fire and sat
next to him. His ears heard only the sound of the flute,
riding the familiar waves, taking him far away. For the
people's sadness and the children's sleep, the flute sang.

With the last long note, his eyes opened to find a woman
wrapped in her blanket. Continuing to stare into the fire she
whispered, "Boozhoo." Softly, like a breeze through the
pines, her voice touched him.

"You make beautiful song." Water Crest reached out of her
blanket to pick up some cedar lace on the ground. She
pulled it apart and smelled the sweet scent. "I heard you at
the Big Water. Where is your home?"

Water Crest's blanket fell off one shoulder and he saw her
scarred skin. Half Moon picked up the blanket's edge and
offered it to her reaching hand. "I come from the band
further west by the Great River."

Water Crest nodded. "Did you hear the thunderers and see
the great lightning?"

Half Moon thought of the great pines snapped in two and
the oak trees twisted like coiled snakes. "No. I have only
heard the stories. Did you get hurt?" Half Moon asked,
questioning her scars.

Water Crest shifted under her red and gray blanket and
wrapped it around her tight. Raising her shoulders, all that
was visible was her head. "No. The twister did not hurt me."

Water Crest looked into the fire and knew she would tell
him her story, for his music had opened her wound. "My
spirit was broken from alcohol[11]. The Medicine Man told
me I must find the old tribal ways. He sent me to
Grandmother Willow to tell her how I was violated."

Her voice grew soft. Each word came in its own time. "I
told her of the mission church. My hair was cut. My hands
were hit, if I spoke with them." Her voice cracked. "I was
beaten." Water Crest stopped. The crackling fire filled the
silence and told Half Moon more than her words. "My friend
died trying to escape. He froze trying to get back home."

"I told Grandmother Willow that I thought it was bad to be
Indian." Water Crest cried softly into her blanket.

"I told her all this, then returned. I saw the Medicine Man,
Autumn Wind, again. He told me to go to Grandfather. 'Walk
in the big lake,' he told me. 'Listen with the ear of the wolf
and look with eye of the hawk. Look and he will be there
for you,' he said. 'Grandfather will come from the bottom of
the Big Lake to find you, to take your pain.' He told me to
give Mishomis my pain and then give him back to the Big
Waters where he must return."

Water Crest looked at Half Moon with dark eyes. "That is
what I was doing, when you saw me today." Half Moon
listened that night to the stories of Water Crest, to the
death, the abuse, the sadness, the loss, the hopelessness.

The rest of that Autumn, Half Moon played to soften the
destruction. At night, he played to remind Water Crest of
her new path. At daybreak, he played to help the people
heal. Cedar belonged to this people, his flute was their

---

[11] Alcohol has been the Indian's major downfall and it continues to take an insidious toll on the people.
It is said alcohol eats our spirit and leaves it vacant. I have seen this look in myself before I got sober
and I have seen this in others. We call this 'fish eyes.' The Ojibwe people were originally introduced
to alcohol by the French trappers early in the invasion of the lands. The trappers were binge drinkers
and also were abusive to people, places and things. This learned pattern of drinking remains today.

song. When the trees were finally bare, Half Moon reluctantly left to rejoin his own people. He journeyed back with the flute to tell them of this people's pain.

Seasons passed and the Sacred Hoop joined Half Moon and Water Crest once more. Both had gone to Sun Dance[12]. Water Crest had gone to heal, dancing for four days. Half Moon had gone to offer his music.

Half Moon recognized her at once, for she danced with a deliberate step. She looked out to Sky Father with dignity. Seeing her again, he saw her as she was. Like the cedar he once held in his hands, she separated—then joined— herself into two worlds.

With her arms pierced to drag buffalo skulls, he watched her flesh rip, her tears fall, her spirit descend. Her flesh was all she had to offer the Creator. Half Moon remembered his own carving of Sister Cedar.

Half Moon at last understood the Circle. Water Crest was the music his spirit needed to hear. *She* was the answer to his vision. Half Moon had journeyed many moons to discover this meaning and purpose, spirit and song. Water Crest was the flute, the sweet melody of healing. So with tobacco in hand, Half Moon offered Namaji to the drum group and asked for her song.

Ah ho.

WORLD LOSS

World loss is a profound moving circle and includes the passing of peace-makers and the erosion of peace. It is time to mourn for our world. In our grief, may we reveal our release, honor all, and celebrate the future.

---

[12] Sun Dance is a Native American ceremony where dancers pray and fast for four days while dancing in the sun from dawn to dusk. Prayers and ceremonial rituals support themselves, their families and their tribes.

Mourn the Peacemakers

As I write, my world has changed. Peacemakers, both renowned and unknown, have died. One was assassinated at a peace rally. Another left this world within his own peace. Even as Earth Mother welcomes them home to her, both passings have emptied another home, have emptied another heart, have stopped another's world.

My world has stopped, my heart has emptied.

One was an old man. One was a young boy. One led in view of all, the other quietly... One, on the crest of life, was to do great things. The other, on a tide rushing to shore, had already begun. Full of open smiles, one had given. With a solemn face, another had accepted. One had touched my personal world, while the other extended my collective view. One reminded me that Earth Mother needs healing now, and the other taught me of patience and tolerance. One moved me into shaking grief, as another carried me to the door of hope. One will forever remain a picture of the East, the other a portrait of the North. Both peacemakers' passing has left me empty. In their honor I must fill again.

Mourned by family and friends, I see their spirit in their relatives and their hearts in world responses. The faces reveal the same grief, the same dis- belief, the same devotion to one so great. How is the heart of the world healed when the great peacemakers of the world are taken? How can such a loss be justified? Understood?

As the peacemakers leave us, we must grieve their passing. We must honor their life, their giving.

My young friend must be remembered. With this prayer, I honor his essence. May his Spirit go to the Four Directions to heal the world. May his father's dream that he would be a community healer, live again. Please, do not let a young boy's passing end the dream. Become the dreamer. Borrow the dream.

Become the dreamer.
Borrow the dream.

Please.

Listen to the rhythm
Of his good heart,
His strong heart.

Hear it beat of honor
Of his joy,
Of your joy.

Feel his Spirit soaring
May you heal,
May we heal.

Please.

Become the dreamer.
Borrow the dream.

Mourn for Peace

You have seen it. You have heard it. You may have witnessed it. On the news, in the headlines, great political and social unrest captures the world's attention. But does it capture your heart?

We have become callused to the repetitive pain that our world rubs against. And in so doing, have distanced our hearts from today's reality. As we listen to the news, we allow our minds to look at bodies lying in their own blood, yet inside we feel as monotone as the voice that describes the scene.

But stop.
Search your heart.

Was there a time—a split second—when you felt the sharp edge of the victim's pain? At that moment, did you imagine yourself in that life, in that place, in that despair? Were you then, in that sliver of time, the mother, the sister, the brother, the son of the one lying there? Were those your tears? Was that your world? Have you ever allowed your heart to view what your mind has seen so many times?

The world needs to learn to grieve again. We have become so full of distractions that often we do not even recognize our own pain or the world's pain. We live with our minds, instead of our hearts. We live with our minds, instead of our bodies. We live with our minds, instead of our spirits. We have disconnected ourselves from our very world. We move and do, from place to place, mentally. Thinking, planning, wishing, regretting... without touching, feeling, listening, or praying.

Lost world peace must be grieved. Lost values must be mourned. We must learn to mourn together. Like Sun on Her Back, we need to open up to life, experience the pain, look at the injuries with our heart. We need to stay connected to Earth Mother and Sky Father. Only through a balanced interaction with life, can we truly connect to all.

EARTH MOTHER'S LOSSES

The wounds, suffering and ruin of our Earth Mother are also experienced from season to season. Her trees are cut, her soil ripped open, her waters polluted and her skies thickened.

Before we can heal her, we must mourn her. In the same way that we mourn personal loss and social unrest, we must grieve for our Earth Mother. With our entire self, we must honor her losses and feel her pain. Only then will we be free to heal her wounds.

See the pollution, the clear cutting, the atomic tests. Mourn Earth Mother's wounds and her losses. Mourn her species forever gone. The ecosystems forever changed.

Then put tobacco down as a peace offering. May your Spirit dance the grieving dance for our environment. Let it change you into a new way of thinking. Let Brother Eagle raise your consciousness to do what you can to change your world. See that your purpose is connected to Earth Mother. Do nothing to interfere with who She must be. Recycle. Educate. Practice Namaji for our Earth.

RELEASED FROM MOURNING: LIFE CELEBRATION CONTINUES

Life circles continue to be celebrated after death, for even death cannot stop the moving circle. Death is the survival of our spirit.

Do not be ashamed to continue to live and love! In doing so, we honor Life itself. Commit to being balanced. Work to be physically, emotionally, spiritually, and mentally alive! This formula will assist you in your journey to a new life!

Celebrate the Spirit of another! Celebrate your Spirit! Celebrate the Great Mystery! Consider the truth that we must lose in life, in order to be free to transcend to greater heights. Mourn, then release yourself. It is time to fill the emptiness the pain has carved. It is time to sing the songs of life, and dance the songs of another life to come.

Namaji is the healing balm for world, cultural, and personal loss.

Fill up with Namaji. With dignity, honor, respect, and pride, link your Seventh Direction to the moving circle. Practice this in all aspects of your world. Apply the healing balm of Namaji. If you do not have Namaji for the world, you do not have Namaji for your Self. Namaji is both singular and plural in its beginning and end. Like tracing the Sacred Hoop, one touch leads to the other. Recognize and feel your connectedness to the World.

Your loss is my loss. My loss is yours. We are all related. Chief Seattle proclaims we are part of the Web of Life. What I do to you, I do to myself. What you give me, you give to the Universe. What the universe gives, she gives to us. What I feel, you feel. What you become, I become. You are not alone nor am I. You are forever with me, and I am forever with you. What we do to Earth Mother, we do to ourselves. We are brothers and sisters on the Web of life. Mitakuye-Oyasin.

INDIAN MEMORIAL ON DEATH

Author Unknown

"Do not stand at my
grave and weep:
I am not there. I do not sleep.
I am a thousand winds that blow.
I am the diamond glints on snow.
I am the sunlight on ripened grain.
I am the gentle autumn's rain.
When you awaken
in the morning's hush,
I am the swift uplifting rush of
quiet birds in circled flight.
I am the soft stars
that shine at night.
Do not stand at my grave and cry:
I am not there. I did not die."

GIVE AWAYS AND BLANKET DANCES

Here, where giving is the way, my gifts ask to be received.

Earth Mother's fullness becomes radiant just before she gives herself to winter. All shades of greens, reds, yellows, golds and browns paint the landscape. When grasses and flowers still reach for the sun, and lakes sparkle blue, the highlights of Earth Mother are revealed.

Her beauty is accented by the contrasts of hues. Her gifts open our eyes to what previously had not been visible. Appreciating the life all around us, our spirits sing her praises. Suddenly, Earth Mother has become full!

Likewise, in beautiful and full display, Blanket Dances and Give Aways show a people's depth. It is a humble display of the best colors, a painting of generosity, where all is honored. Life is celebrated, and the unseen becomes visible. Gratitude is sung to the beat of others' generosity. These are the dances that reveal Native Americans' Namaji.

THE BLANKET DANCE

THE GUARDIAN

He placed the soft flannel blanket down on Earth Mother's lap. The good strong beat reminded the Elder of his purpose and strong connection. Dancing around the blanket, he honored each of the Four Directions.

For the first time in a long while, the Elder again wore his regalia. The bells. The buckskin. The bustle. The fringes remembered and swayed from his arms, as his feet stepped lightly honoring Earth Mother. Some fringes were shorter than they once were, some were now missing. Life takes away, the Elder thought. Now it is time to give.

As simple as the old days, the buckskin still soothed his skin like water. He knew the softened cracks running through the buckskin as though it were his own skin. Like his wrinkled face, his regalia had witnessed life.

He placed his moccasined foot tenderly on Earth Mother's skin. Soft on top, hard on the bottom, they still honored the Elder's feet with tenderness and strength. Having journeyed many trails, they led him easily around the Circle. All stood in honor of this dance, waiting for his circle to be complete, for then they would join in this honor dance, after greeting him, honoring him.

Lifting his feathered fan, the Elder saluted the Drum as the honor beats vibrated into him. The white flecks of paint on his face began to itch and reminded him of his task.

This dance was for Loon. This dance was for the loons who left this land, whose habitat was destroyed. Where rain, now acidic, confused thousands of years of instinct. Whose chicks were left unfed, for the fish were no longer edible. Where blacktop became illusionary wetlands, enticing the loons to land, crash, and die. This dance was for loons.

The beat moved the Elder around the arbor. Dancers began to join, entering in waves of generosity. Money was put down on the soft flannel blanket as each added their prayers for Loon. The Elder raised his fan to send the requests to Gitchi Manidoo. Then the dancers followed him, adding Namaji to this Honor Dance.

Soon the blanket overflowed with money. Money to help save the Loons from humans. Money to help fight greed. Money to help heal another injured Loon. Money to help purchase Earth Mother, who can not be purchased.

The old man had fought against this new way, fought against money, for it was not of his thinking. Yet, the old way instructed him to become a guardian of Loon. For Loon cannot speak for itself. And today, it was money that people listened to.

The generosity was collected, everyone danced, then the song ended. The Elder heard the silence of his heart. The spirit of loon would be heard.

In the Blanket Dance a blanket is humbly placed on Earth Mother's lap. The drum plays an honor song to honor Earth Mother. The Blanket Dance embraces the generosity of some to fill the needs of others. The blanket is put down on Earth Mother to gather the We-ness of the people in the form of donations for a worthy cause. Oftentimes, it may be a family in need, or a way to honor someone on their life journey. In the acceptance, the one honored is honoring those who give. In the giving and the receiving, we honor our unique role on the Sacred Hoop. All dance to the rhythm of giving.

The celebration of Powwow is expressed through song and dance. Yet, another important aspect is generosity and the exchange of gifts. Relationships are renewed and friendships are re-celebrated. When a gift is given, often one is offered in return. Generosity is visible.

Like the Blanket Dances, Give Aways express this tradition. The Give Aways are Blanket Dances turned around.

THE GIVE AWAYS

In this dance, the blanket is again put down on Earth Mother, but this time it holds the possessions of one who wishes to give. The Giver, a group or an individual, offers gifts to others. The gifts often include hand-made articles. In fact, much of a person's spare time is given to the making of gifts. From woven baskets, to bead work, from carvings to drawings, from quilts to cloth, the giver is free to give. In order to keep that which we treasure most, we must be willing to give it away. The best is offered to others. The giver invites all who attend to come forward and join the dance by receiving a gift. Give Aways are practiced out of gratitude and a sincere extension of Self.

Birthdays are fine examples of traditional Give Aways. The person celebrates his/her birthday by gifting the guests, rather than the other way around. It is a way to honor the people who came to share in the joy. It is a way to honor those who honor them. The Birthday person celebrates by giving, for we know that to give is the best gift of all.

FLOWERS BREATH

Flowers Breath remembered the first pair of earrings she had made: a red and white arrow tip design. They had dangled from her ear lobes, catching the glittering light of Grandfather Sun. Dancing, now, Flowers Breath remembered how proud she had been of these earrings! The drumbeat moved into her and reminded her of the day she had given the earrings away. Her first Give Away had been painful. How she had loved the earrings! How she had resisted letting go! But her mother had taught her the way, and she knew it would be done.

Then it all changed. Flowers Breath had watched as a tiny tot reached down, tenderly picked up the earrings, and lifted them up to see the sunlight move through the beads. She had watched as the little girl raced to her mother to show her this gift. She had seen the smile on the little one's face. It was the same smile Flowers Breath now wore. The pain had been instantly forgotten, as her heart filled with the greatest joy she had ever known! Stepping softly on the edge of the her very first shawl that now lay on the grass, Flowers Breath remembered this beginning. Then moving away, this honored royalty dancer told all who watched that this honor was far greater than her possessions.

This skilled fancy dancer beaded all the rest of that summer and right up until this full moon celebration, two years later. Prepared to give them all away, the beautiful earrings, wristbands, hairpieces and headbands had been made with joy. In the journey of giving, Flowers Breath threaded slender needles, carefully chose colored beads, designed many gifts. Now, nearing womanhood, she would complete this circle of joy once again.

As Royalty of this Powwow, Flowers Breath danced with graceful steps. Carrying herself with dignity, she twirled and lifted the shawl into the currents that Eagle shared. Dancing faster, Flowers Breath grew excited, knowing that her relatives were now placing the many beaded articles on the shawl. Here, in the dance arbor, where giving is the way, her gifts asked to be taken.

As Flowers Breath approached the shawl, now laden with her love, the young woman's eyes remembered the strings of beads that had once caught her eye. How many times did the tiny beads scatter to all directions as the strings were cut in the making? Looking now to the shawl at her feet, she saw the patterns of her heart and spirit.

As the Elder announced the moment, the young woman danced in place, waiting to see how her circle would grow. With great respect, men, women and children began to line up to select their gift. Flowers Breath was anxious to share her honor, to share herself with these people.

A woman selected the red rose hairpiece and held it up, recognizing the Spirit World. Flowers Breath remembered how long she had worked on this design to make the petals appear to fold. Flowers Breath accepted the woman's gratitude, and the next person moved to select her gift—the bright yellow and red earrings. They were made during the deep snowfall, Flowers Breath remembered. Next, a young boy selected the wristbands that pointed to the Four Directions. Flowers Breath watched as he too, held them in high honor, then he tried them on, thrilled to add to his regalia. As she shook his hand, she touched the wristbands one last time. Many young women and girls found their special earrings. Headbands were accepted. Hairpieces discovered. With each giving, Flowers Breath found something she could not explain. Finally, all was emptied, and a little girl with two long braids found her shawl. Twirling with delight at her new gift, the little girl ran to Flowers Breath to thank her for the gift. Hugging the little one, Flowers Breath had become the shawl of giving.

The circle was complete. The giving was accepted and Flowers Breath filled to overflowing with the smiles, delight, and love of the receivers. As her gifts were taken to new circles, part of Flowers Breath would touch many new worlds, would lift many hearts, and enter many silent places. And for this gift of connection, Flowers Breath said Migwetch.

TO GIVE

I overheard someone say today, "Indian giver." It was a passing comment from one stranger to the next. They moved in and out of my world, but their comment remained with me, pungent as rotting food. With great sadness, I wondered how many people have used the term "Indian Giver" and actually understood the truth.

People often use idioms without consciously knowing the origin or insinuation. Like many racial slurs and naive speech patterns (even of the educated), "Indian Giver," in the context of criticism, is simply discordant with the truth. If you ask the speaker what this phrase means, he may reach back to the story "given" to him and refer to Indians who "gave" their land to Europeans, but now want it back. This use of the phrase implies intentions less than honorable. It belittles the Native American. It attempts to taks honor from a people who have been greatly wronged. It is time for everyone to consciously recognize that "Indian Giver" means generosity of the heart.

Indian is the "We" way. This is a giving system. Tribal people are like bees in a beehive where their effort is for the common welfare of the entire hive. It is an effort of giving. The "We" way is necessary for survival. Materialism is the "me" way and leads to alienation and destruction.

IN THE CIRCLE OF PINES

The boy gathered sticks to feed the fire that would heat Mishomis Rocks. Knowing these stones needed to become so hot they would glow into the darkness, the boy helped in ways that he could. He knew that soon he would be old enough to enter the lodge and cleanse in this way.

But for now, he remained, outside, a boy helping support as his uncle taught him. He gathered dry bark that lay on the forest floor and made piles of many sticks, some small and some so big he had to drag them out. The boy collected heaps of pine needles, for he knew they were strong enough to make great heat.

As he gathered in the woods, not far from the lodge, he noticed a man sitting near a fallen pine tree. Curious, the boy began to gather kindling, gradually getting closer and closer to where the man sat. Entering a circle of white pines, the boy pretended to search for more wood.

"There are many dry needles over here," the man said. Without looking up, the man remained absorbed in his carving. The boy slowly approached this man whose hair was different than his people's. Somewhat fearful, but mostly curious, he neared the red-haired man. The boy wondered how his hair had become that color, when the rest of him was much like himself. They shared the same skin color and even their eyes were much the same. To the boy, this stranger was an intriguing distraction to his duty that day.

"Are you here for the sweat?" the boy asked, as he grabbed a handful of golden needles and put them in the bag he was carrying.

"I am here because I was invited," the man answered. Putting the knife away, the man looked at his wooden carving. From where the boy sat, it merely looked like a flat piece of wood, unrecognizable. Probably a beginner, the boy thought.

"Do you know my uncle? He is the one who will tend the sacred fire tonight." The boy sat back on his heels, squatting on the needles that covered the forest floor.

"Oh, yes. We have been friends for many years," the man answered. "Tell me, why are you not playing with the other children?"

The boy picked up a cluster of needles. Separating the five needles that were still attached at their base, he thought of the Star People. "My uncle is teaching me the way. He teaches me many songs and many stories when he tends the fire."

"Then you are fortunate," the man said. "When I was your age, I knew little of our tribal ways. I lived much differently than you."

"Where do you come from?" the boy asked, now beginning to understand why this man was like him, yet not like him.

"I come from my own people, many miles away. But many of my tribe had forgotten the way. Many had pretended that they were something different. They were afraid to be Indian. It was very dangerous to be Indian for a long time. I met your uncle at Powwow and he has taught me many things. It seems that you and I have much in common."

And so that night, the two sat and shared what they knew. The boy told the man about the Star People. The man told the boy how it is to grow up without tradition. Soon it was time to prepare for the sweat, for the fire had reddened the Mishomis Rocks.

"You have given me much, tonight," the man said to the boy. "May I offer you a gift in return?"

The boy felt proud, for he knew he was becoming like his uncle and the Way would continue. Understanding the exchange, the boy looked serious and answered, "Migwetch."

The man took out the wood that the boy had seen him carve earlier.

"Please remember me and put tobacco down that I may be more like you."

With great honor, the boy reached over to accept the gift. He looked closely at the carving made in the circle of pines. To his delight, it was a beautifully carved feather! Like the man, its truth could only be recognized up close. Its integrity was only visible when held near, and its delicate intricacies were only understood in the eyes of the receiver.

> They both got up to go their separate ways, and the
> boy offered the man the needles of five, offering the man
> his tradition.

The young need the old and the old need the young. This is the Circle of Giving. Listen with your heart when you are given a gift. In your listening you offer another gift in return.

THE CLAN SYSTEM

Clan systems speak of We-ness, not me-ness.

The clan system was the bond of the Native American Intertribal government. Food, shelter, and other needs were provided by the clan to specific clan members. There were seven original Ojibwe clans. The Loon, Crane, Fish, Martin, Bear, Bird, and Deer clans. Since everyone belonged to a clan, by birth and or marriage, there were no needy people. All were provided for. Each clan member was responsible to and for their other mutual clan members. Personalities were secondary within the clan code. Therefore, personal differences between tribes and individuals did not inhibit the functioning of the clan system's strength and order. Principles before personalities lead the way.

Traveling tribal members were welcomed to their respective lodges within other nations, which assured the traveler's needs were cared for[1]. Clan mothers were lodge leaders and guided them in an orderly fashion. To this day, clan mothers are respected for their firm but gentle adherence to their clan's codes[2].

The relocation of nations and subdivisions to reservations all but severed the fibers of this grand web. Today, the clan system has undergone resur-

---

[1]   Non-tribal dominant cultures have their own version of the clan system, often called the loyal Order of the Moose, the Lions, the Elks and the Eagle's clubs. A member of these national chapters can travel from state to state and be welcomed in a respective member club. Many of these organizations do much good for the plural society.

[2]   A clan member could not marry within their own clan. This insured blood lines would remain pure. Tradition tells that the deer clan violated this natural code and children of the clan were born with physical defects. It is also reported that because the people of the deer clan did not change their ways, the Creator destroyed this original clan for their departure from natural harmony.

gence and renewal. The clan system will, once again, bind the confederacy of tribal nations to assist in intertribal Mitakuye-Oyasin from shore to shore.

STORY GIFTING

Native American traditional story telling has transmitted the culture from one generation to the next for thousands of years. These traditional stories speak symbolically to educate and give. Popular animal characters move from story to story, teaching lessons, values and history. The lesson is not told directly, for it is to be received and discovered by the listener. I invite you to receive the following story. I invite you to discover the full meaning for you.

IT IS THE STORY OF FROG.

Long ago, Frog sat on top of a mountain full of himself.

Wanting more and more for himself, he sat there thinking of all the things he could give himself. Then his thinking got him thirsty, and the thirst got him thinking. Frog's webbed hands patted his lips as he looked around the mountain top. Seeing the cool water melting from the mountain peaks, he leaned over and began to slurp.

Savoring the delicious cold water, Frog thought into the future and feared he might soon become thirsty again. Afraid to leave even a drop, Frog began to drain Earth Mother of all her water. Frog drank and drank and drank and drank until all the water was gone.

Earth Mother's children grew worried. Brother and Sister trees were drooping. Fish were gasping for air. The two-legged, the four-legged, six-legged and eight-legged's throats became parched. From the Four Directions councils were held to find a solution for their thirst. From council to council, this great thirst traveled until the problem finally reached the Grand Council.

"Has anyone seen the water?" asked Mouse.

"I know where it is," said Crow. "I was flying high when I saw Frog drinking the cool delicious water from the mountain top."

"You are a trickster," said another. "How do we know you are speaking the truth?"

"Look at my feathers," Crow said. "They do not shine anymore, for even my feathers are thirsty. Although I may lie, my feathers do not!"

"He is telling the truth," said the chief. "Now, we must become of one mind, to solve this problem."

For the entire night, creepers and crawlers, winged and finned, two-legged and four-legged joined the talking circle. Each chose their words carefully, for their lips cracked and bled with each movement.

Grandfather Sun rose without his yellow buck skin glistening, for there was no more morning dew. His eyes were still partially closed as his rays peeked into the darkness. In that morning moment, when Grandfather Sun offered many paths in the sky, a decision was made.

Trickster Crow would be sent to talk to Frog.

Trickster Crow's feathers were too brittle for the flight, so he climbed the mountain, planning what he would say to Frog. When, at last, he climbed over the highest rock, Crow found Frog. Sitting on the very peak looking down, sweat beaded Frog's face as his mouth bulged, holding all the water of the world.

"Boozhoo Frog. How are you this fine morning?" Crow asked as he flicked some dust off his black-purple feathers. Relaxing with his back against a rock, Crow clasped his wings behind his head and crossed his legs.

But Frog only shook his head back and forth. Recognizing Crow as Trickster, he refused to talk.

Crow's eyes shifted in different directions, then finally settled. "Please, Frog. Please. Won't you give us just a little water? We don't need that much. Just enough to wet our mouths."

Again, Frog just shook his head in refusal.

Crow kicked the pebbles at his feet, disappointed that nothing so far had worked. Then the hard stones gave Crow an idea.

Picking up one, Crow pretended to eat. "Boy, is this bug delicious!" Munching, he continued, "You must be very hungry, Dear Friend. After all, no one can live on water alone."

Frog hadn't thought of that, and his eyes bulged out with the thought.

"I bet you'd like a nice juicy bug. Wouldn't you?" Crow asked, picking up a stone.

Frog nodded excitedly, wondering if Crow would help him eat it.

"Well, okay then. I tell you what. I realize it wouldn't be fair for me to get any of your water, since after all, YOU were the one who found it. So, this is what we'll do. When I place this bug between your lips, all you have to do is soften them and I'll pop it right in. That way, no water will dribble out. How's that?"

Frog nodded. His eyes bulged out even further, imagining bug's flavor.

"Close your eyes, so you can fully appreciate the delicious taste of bug."

Crow placed the stone up to Frog's lips and plopped it in his mouth without any trouble. Frog quickly swallowed, and the water and stone noisily slid down to fill his belly.

But what had looked like such a tiny bug, now filled Frog with a tremendous weight. Water sloshed and stretched Frog's sides. Water pressed up against Frog's nostrils. Water pushed his eyeballs out even further. Feeling terribly bottom heavy, Frog began to tip on the top of the mountain.

Trickster Crow backed up, looking with great concern at Frog. "Frog, you don't look so good. You look rather... sick. In fact, you look like my uncle did just before he died."

"Oh, my. Oh, my," was Frog's first words. "What can I do? Can you help me? Can you help me? Can you help me? Can you help me?"

"Well, there's one thing I could do," Trickster Crow began. "No. No. No. Forget it. It was a dumb idea."

Frog's webbed hands covered his aching belly as he rocked back and forth on the lonely mountain top. "Oh, please dear Crow, please help me or I will surely die."

"Do you trust me?" Crow asked, leaning against a ledge and cleaning out bark from between his beak.

"Oh yes! Just help me! I beg you!" Frog pulled at Crow's feathers, now more desperate for help than he had been for the water.

"Are you sure?" Crow asked again.

"Yes. Please. I beg you to take me out of this misery," Frog said, as tears welled up in his huge eyes.

Crow moved close to Frog's bulging middle and with his feathered wing patted his middle very gently. Then with one quick jab, Crow pecked a hole in Frog's side.

Instantly, water gushed out of Frog, as Crow jumped up to sit on Frog's head! From his high view Crow watched the water rush down the mountain, filling up the rivers and lakes, returning to all of Earth Mother's children.

Only then did Frog's belly completely empty of pain.

Frog was banished from the mountain, to live the rest of his days surrounded by water. To this day, if you listen with a sharp ear you can still hear Frog repeat, "Give it! Give it! Give it! Give it!"

TO SELF

Give Aways and Blanket Dances are gifts from Self to others. In order to give, you must first have something to offer. A tree cannot offer her colors until she has grown her leaves, nourished her growth, made her own food. You must find time for yourself in this busy world in order to give something that is uniquely yours. Unless you have devoted time and energy to your own internal balance, the seventh direction, you have little to offer others. The seventh direction, your personal color, is nurtured by Self. To see the colors of others, to experience the colors of the world, to offer your own color, you must first slow down and come to Self.

Listen to Turtle. His patient living offers wisdom. Turtle is intentionally slow so that he can investigate and see the wonder in everything around him. Turtle knows there are many lessons to learn in the forests and the lakes, in every leaf and rock. Learn the lessons of Turtle's teaching.

See with Turtle's eyes. Do not fall victim to seeing a leaf as just a shape, a rock as merely hard, a tree as only green, or water as simply wet. Turtle sees water as wet, and also as a home, as a pathway, as nourishment, as life itself. Turtle sees rock as support for the community, as strength, as Earth memory. Turtle knows that rocks are creatures like himself who can slow down and experience life on a deeper level of communication.

Feel the world like Turtle. Stick your head out to participate with life. Turtle does not go forward in life if his neck is not extended. Walk slowly across the sand, feel its warmth, find your direction, then make your own tracks. Spend time inside to understand who you are. Gift yourself the meaning of what is outside you and what is inside you. Be balanced in this exploration.

Become like Turtle. Enjoy a non-hurried journey. Take in the sights and smells of the beauty that surrounds you, of the beauty within you. Notice how Turtle wears his lodge on his back. His home allows him to stay and visit many beautiful places. There is no hurry to get home, so he can experience each stop along the journey without the rush of the world around him. Do not allow yourself to be plagued by the fast pace. Make your home within your heart, Ain-dah-ing, accessible at a moments' notice. In this way you will be able to experience the beauty of the journey.

Gift yourself, yourself. It is the best gift you have to offer.

TO OTHERS

We all have something to offer which is uniquely ours. You know something that others need to know. Brother Tree offers his colors at the proper time, in order to beautifully offer nourishment to all that will grow.

What colorful display can you gift others that will also offer nourishment? On your journey to becoming, find what you have to give, then offer it freely. What are your strengths? The longer your list is, the greater is your obligation to the Sacred Hoop of Love.

Recognize that what you give is for the good of all. What is your talent? Share it with others. What is your strength? Give it to others. What is your passion? Reveal it to others. What is your understanding? Teach it to others!

Like Earth Mother who offers her beauty with the colors of herself, do not hide your best, your beauty, your bounty. Your Seventh Direction is meant to be shared. Your hoop is designed to connect to the Sacred Hoop, to join your life circle with others'. In your connection, Mitakuye-Oyasin is shared. In the giving, receiving is possible. In the receiving, life continues. Participate in Life.

TO EARTH MOTHER

What is there to give Earth Mother? What does She need? What have you to give? How can you fill Her need?

Investigate your tracks. They will show you many things. Do you offer beauty and healing? Or injury and destruction? Be deliberate in your movement on Earth Mother's back. Walk softly on Her skin. Massage Her back, just as She massages your feet. Like turkey tracks in powdery snow, what pattern of beauty can you offer back to Earth Mother?

Realize that every decision you make will either hurt or help Earth Mother. It is that simple. What will you do? Keep this in mind as you move through the day. Become conscious of Her needs, of Her Life, of your needs, of your life. They are one and the same. You are part of Earth Mother, and you will one day return to Her; Her needs are yours. Your life is Hers. You and Mother are bound together.

Do you know someone who lives these words of Earth consciousness? Is there someone in your world that fully understands that we all share the same blue blanket? I have been spirit-blessed to know someone like this. Like a flutter of wings, your decisions are inevitably felt across the oceans, moving a little into a lot. Connecting with the gifts of the Four Directions, a better friend could not be found. Making life suddenly seem easy, affecting life so deeply, your splash is felt a thousand circles beyond you. Opening to each day, you wear happiness like Grandfather Sun wears his light. To you, my friend, I offer this poem. You are not only a remarkable friend to Earth Mother, you are also a remarkable friend to me. In your giving, you give to all. In your honoring, you honor your Self.

GIVING STAR

Giving Star,
You gift me all the things I could ever wish to give.
You teach me all the things I could ever hope to live.
You're a Star that Gives,
Giving Star,
You open up the space inside and sweet laughter flows.
You open up your Self and know what no one knows.
You're the Shine that Shows,
Giving Star.
But you'd never say that you do.
Giving more is how you grew,
And I wish that I could, too,
be a...
Giving Star,
I'd put you on a pedestal, but you wouldn't stay.
I'd shine more light upon you, but you'd turn my way.
You Light up the Day,
Giving Star,
I offer my space to you, and you make more room,
I gather flowers for you; you make World Perfume.
You're a Sun in Bloom,
Giving Star.
For that's just the way you are,
A Shining Earth Giving Star.

And I wish upon you, too,
To be more like you,
Giving Star.

LOVE

The ultimate gift is Love.

So what is love? Some say it is a feeling, a commitment, a connection, a desire. Yes. This is Love's beautiful pattern. Some say love is a multifaceted need, the answer to Life's grand question. Yes. This is what it is like to love and be loved. Some say love is the passion, the spilling of one's heart, the sense of belonging, the overwhelming joy of togetherness. Yes. This is the spirit dance of love.

But what is love? What is love's essence, its source, its vibration? What rhythm does love move to? Grow to? Dance to? Transcend to? What is love?

Listen to your drum—your own heart drum. You will hear love's beginnings. Love is as clear and resonant as your heartbeat. Love moves out into the world, just as your heart moves you out into the world. Love carries world nourishment, just as your heart gifts you health. Love celebrates all of life, just as your heart gifts your dance of celebration. Listen to your heart. Hear the strong good beat of life. You will recognize love. You will understand its source. In slowing down to Self, you will recognize the four beats of love: Respect, Honor, Dignity and Pride... Love is Namaji.

Stop. Feel your heart *respect* your asking. Pause and experience how life is honored within. Listen to the silence. Hear the *dignity* of each beat. Open to your Self and celebrate the *pride* of living.

Love is Namaji.

Namaji is the true connection to both the Spirit World and the Physical World. Respect, honor, dignity, and pride: Namaji. This is the balm for the world. Respect, honor, dignity and pride are love. Each radiates its own hue, its own beauty. Each is a beat, a source, of love.

Love is respect. Respect and notice the sacred in all, the purpose of all, and the connectedness of all. First respect yourself. Gift respect and you will receive respect, for it is a mutual life principle. Demonstrate courtesy. As part of One, respect All. Respect makes loving possible.

Love is honor. Honor is opening up to the experience of Life. As life is your greatest fortune, honor life by offering your best. Honor your roots, your essence, your vision. This is the color of concentration. Honor the past, the present, and future. Honor each other. Honor makes loving fully beautiful.

Love is dignity. Dignity is Self respect and Self honor. Dignity moves easily across the blue sky of honor and respect. Give dignity to all and dignify all of Life. Elevate the sacredness in all. This is how you dignify yourself. Experience this poise. Dignity makes loving powerful.

Love is pride. Pride flows from the Sacred Essence and gives you the courage to protect your values. Pride is the radiance of truth, the joy of knowing yourself completely. Pride is honoring your sacredness. With pride, embrace the circle of life, for love completes the circle. With pride, offer your best. With pride, celebrate the passion. Pride makes loving eternal.

TO ACCEPT

The Sacred Hoop embodies Mitakuye-Oyasin. For in our connection to each other, we accept and give within the Eternal Circle. In order for there to be a giver, there has to be a receiver. Without the student, there is no teacher. Without the listener, there is no message. Life continues as long as there is someone or something to receive its energy, its meaning, its quest for continuation. Learn how to accept, to receive, to honor the giver. Become the recipient and allow life to flow through you. Be the conduit to life's movement.

Native American traditional culture emphasizes interdependence. Unfortunately, with the erosion of cultural values and cohesiveness, many nontraditional people prize independence as the highest level of development. Unwilling to accept help from others, uncomfortable with needing others, unaccustomed to receiving the gifts others have to offer, society has replaced "We-ness" with "me-ness."

"I can do it by myself. I do not need anyone. I have achieved this. I am alone in my victory. I am alone in my defeat."

This lonely life is an illusion. Even if you insist you have accomplished something on your own, you have denied the reality that other people and forces have played their own part in your success.

TOGETHER

A father and son worked side by side gathering Mishomis rocks for the sacred fire. It was a hot day, sweat dripped from both their brows as they worked to gather enough rocks for the evening ceremony.

"Son, see that big Mishomis?" The man pointed to a large rock in the middle of a hilly clearing.

The boy looked up from his growing pile of nice size rocks. "Yes, Father. I see the one you mean."

"We will need that Mishomis for the fire tonight," the boy's father said, as he heaved a big rock onto the pulling board attached to their horse's harness.

The boy scampered across the clearing to where the Mishomis sat. It was much bigger than it had appeared. Settled into hard earth, it waited to be moved. The boy squatted, put his hands around its middle and with great effort attempted to lift Mishomis. Unable to budge it, the boy went back to where his father worked. "Father, I cannot lift the rock. It is too heavy."

"Yes, you can. You have not used all your strength," the father simply replied, continuing to stack the rocks onto the board.

So the boy went back to the rock and tried once again. This time, he used a stick and another rock to loosen it from the earth it had settled into. It took many scrapes on his hands before the rock was loosened and lifted slightly out of the depression of Earth Mother. Again, the boy squatted, put his cut hands and arms around its middle and with great effort attempted to lift the heavy rock. Mishomis loosened and moved a little. Sweat fell from the boy's brow onto the great rock. Still, he was unable to bring the rock back to his father.

"Father, I loosened the great Mishomis," the boy said panting, as he returned to where his father worked. "But I still cannot bring the rock here."

Again his father answered, "You have not used all your strength."

Frustrated, the boy returned to the rock and tried once more. This time he tried pushing it, letting Earth Mother carry it instead. Mishomis moved easily downhill, but became much too heavy to push up hill to where his father waited.

Once more, the boy returned to tell his father that he had failed.

"Son, you have not used all your strength," the man replied once again.

"But I have!" insisted the boy. "I used all my strength. I even let Earth Mother help me move the great rock. There is nothing more I can do. I have tried everything."

The father stood up and looked at his son. The man noticed scratches teaching the boy's legs, blood painting his hands, sweat washing his body.

"You have done well, son. Even so, you still have not used all your strength."

The boy began to cry, ashamed. For he thought he had done all he could. The father moved over to his young son, gently lifted the young chin with his big callused hand, and looked directly in the young eyes.

"You have not used all your strength, for you have not asked me for help. Do you not see that I am your strength, just as the horse is ours? Even Mishomis did not get into Earth Mother all alone. The great ice sheets brought Mishomis to this place. Nothing in life is accomplished by one. Everything in life is the result of many."

Then together the man and his son walked to where Mishomis waited. Together, they lifted the heavy rock as one.

It does, indeed, take an entire village to raise a child. As children of Earth Mother, come to see your role in the giving and accepting of the Sacred Hoop. Both givers and receivers are needed. We need both the empty bucket and the full well. We each participate in the success and failure of all. We each contribute in ways unseen. We each make an impact without knowing. We all are making memories for others. We are all smoothing out or blocking many paths. The world is a system... where the whole is greater than the sum of its parts. It is the invisible web that lifts the greatness. What have you woven lately?

Try this. Ask someone in your family or a close acquaintance what their best memories are. Give them time to remember. Give them time to celebrate. Talk about the moments. Celebrate together. You may find that you have played an important role in the making of that person's future. You may have contributed with your unseen webbing. Honor the receiver. Gift them Namaji. These memories accompany us upon our return to the Spirit World.

Now ask yourself, what are your best memories? Who or what was there to offer this memory-making to you? Who participated in the weaving of your life? Have you thanked them? Have you acknowledged their role in your living? Do you see your daily interdependence on another? Honor the giver. Accept their gifts.

My best memory always returns me to the Reservation. I would lay many nights, nestled in my bed by the lake's bay, listening to the woods, listening to the loons and whippoorwills, listening to the bull frogs and peepers. My brothers and sisters harmonized me to sleep. Earth Mother was my singer. I had opened up to receive her gifts.

Sometimes it is easy to accept. Sometimes it is difficult. Accepting Earth Mother's gifts may be easier than accepting the gifts of others. There are also life moments of great need. There will be situations that will require you to ask for help, to accept help, to honor the helper. When that occurs, it is time to put your false pride in your back pocket.

False pride is the belief that you are one person. False pride is grandiosity and places you above others. False pride is the denial of Mitakuye-Oyasin and denies your connection to others.

Connect and be the channel of giving. Accept the gifts given. Honor the giver. Honor the web of life. In so doing, you honor all.

KNOW WHAT TO ACCEPT AND WHAT TO KEEP

Do not automatically accept everything that comes your way. There are gifts and there are invasions. Know what is a gift and what is not. Gifts always make you more. Invasions always make you less.

Remember: keep what's outside you—outside you. Stress and tension does not belong in your home of peace. Allow shame and blame from others to run off you like water off a leaf. It does not belong within. Practice the skills and awareness of the warrior. Remember that initially, stress is outside of our body, as an event. If you brace yourself and become tense, you experience it internally as tension. To eliminate the tension, put the stress back into the external world, from where you took it. Deflect the stress externally so that you don't become tense internally.

Keep what is inside you—inside you. This is presence. Presence will allow you to identify the true gifts that come your way. With presence, identify the help you need and the resources available to you. Then accept the gifts with dignity. Be present with Earth Mother. She is there to help you. Be present with who you are, your Seventh Direction. Be present with those who would help you become.

Accept love. Accept compliments. Accept the gifts of the giver. Accept the beauty, the meaning, the message. Accept all that will help you become the vision of yourself.

A-QUA-O-DA

(Creeping Out of Water)

It was a big lake for an old man.

With the light of Grandmother Moon, A-qua-o-da's[3] body cut through the unusually warm lake, parting the quiet water. Gliding through a sparkling path, his silver hair spread out around shoulders that barely touched the water's surface. He stayed warm beneath the water blanket.

The old man did not swim fast. He did not need to. The Circle would wait.

And so he swam easily, his one arm and two legs moving to make up for what the other arm could no longer do. He had learned this new way of swimming many years ago. In the beginning, it was very hard to do this thing. To swim. His injured body, disfigured and out of balance, had struggled against the water, against himself. But A-qua-o-da had been determined to learn how to swim again.

Alongside the finned and the feathered, he had watched and learned. Pause, accept, move. Pause, accept, move.

Still, the old man's strong arm tired. So turning like an easy memory, the Elder floated and rested, as though on silk, watching a million stars get brighter. A-qua-o-da's legs effortlessly kept him afloat and rhythmically moved him toward the opposite shore.

---

3   Pronounced: ac-QUA-o-da and means, creeping out of water.

Pause, accept, move. Pause, accept, move. And in his own time, the old man silently crossed the lake.

A slosh on the water's surface interrupted the tranquillity. Hearing slick feathers slap, A-qua-o-da knew it would begin. Soon it would start.

Near the edge of the lake, the Elder waited. As silent as one can be and still remain afloat, he listened. The peepers from the shadows filled the night with their purple throat music. Then, more splashes from the darkened distance as feathers spanked the waters.

Finally, he heard it. The sound. Her sound.

Weaving the woods and lake into one warm blanket, her wail covered the night. The woods. The water. The wail. The blanket. It all reached to comfort him and A-qua-o-da knew it was her. It was Loon Sound.

Before his accident, when his arm was still whole, loons had sounded the same. Their chorus was another beauty of the lake, completing the forest, belonging to the lake and the woods. Now, it was more. Loon Sound—rich, deep, piercing, knowing. It was now his sound and completed him. Like the surrendering of forest floor into Earth Mother, A-qua-o-da's listening blended him into the woods.

Although A-qua-o-da's years of isolation had separated him from his people, it had also sharpened his senses. Nursing the injured loon, she had gifted him her special sound. Her sound. The old man knew this loon. He could not *not* know her. And as Loon wailed four more times to contact the others, the night finally opened.

The Elder swam to the shore as the night chorus began. He reached the shallow edge where earth tried to take over the water and smelled-tasted the wet, green water-soup.

The wailing intensified and became part of the smell, moving through the green-air with green-sound. Loons questioned and answered, wailed and laughed, shrilled and filled the night sky with winged emotions.

The Elder crept out of the slough like a dignified elk, leaving his night watering hole. Water glistened on his large chest, his hair still remembering the lake, his pants like velvet in the moonlight.

A-qua-o-da remained standing, and sinking slowly into the muck, he was sucked into the richness, pulled into its power, massaged with her thick softness.

As though in secret, his skin gradually dried as he stood there, pulled in, joined, listening. Listening. That was all there was. The listening and melting into Earth Mother.

Journeying further and further to the beginning, he found himself quiet inside, as the loon melody exploded outside. Like his home, Wee-ka-san[4], all parts of him gathered into a rush of awareness to rest in Ain-dah-ing, his home within his heart. Here, within, he understood himself. Here, the Elder could understand most things. Meaning entered in this listening.

Lake mud and Loon's song continued to soothe him, just as Earth Mother had offered him her medicine from the very beginning. Her songs, her touch, her welcome, her comfort, her teachings, all had been the medicine A-qua-o-da had needed when he had lost most of his arm. Alone with Earth Mother he forgot his disfigurement, for the lake had embraced him completely. The old man looked at the beautiful lake as the moon was now nearly overhead. To her, he would always be whole and she would cradle him. Would always be hers. And this understanding had healed him.

---

4   Pronounced: WEE-ca-san, and is the root of "Wisconsin." It means the gathering of the waters.

A-qua-o-da stepped out of the soft muck to hard land and beneath the jeweled night sky he headed to Loon's nesting place by the edge of the water. With his nearing, a frenzied shrill warned. Then, as if understanding, both the man and the wailing stopped. Within the silence, he had found what he had crossed the lake for. Stuck on some cattails that had stood guard to protect this wetland, it waited. The blanket—the soft red flannel shirt.

Seeing his shirt brought the past into the present. At the nearing of winter, two years ago, he had found Loon on a wet blacktop road, her legs bleeding and broken, her pain deeply cutting into him. A-qua-o-da had understood the pain and had wrapped Loon with his shirt. It had become Loon's blanket. The blanket had held her pain. The soft flannel had helped her heal.

A season later, Loon's legs were scarred but mended, and he had returned her to this wetland. Near the empty nest he had left the blanket for her to return to. For comfort, for memory. The Elder had visited her often at first, had continued to bring her minnows in the shallow warm protection of the bay. But then A-qua-o-da had found her on the nest with two eggs. Loon did not need him anymore. She needed to not need him, he had thought. She needed her own.

A-qua-o-da picked up the shirt, remembering many things. His one hand brought it up to his nose and smelled the woods. The clean dirt. The dried leaves. The wind. Now it was his turn to give to Loon. To give back to Earth Mother. The red shirt would become a blanket, once more.

The Elder found a small tear in the sleeve. Pushing his finger through and using his teeth, he tore it. A single wail cut through the night. Holding two pieces, one in his teeth, the other in his hand, the old man understood "me" must become "We."

"The loons must not die from people's greed, and I must not die in my own loneliness," he chanted in his tribal tongue.

The Elder placed the sleeve back near the cattail to the East Direction, knowing Loon was now his extension to the world, and put the blanket-shirt on, singing in harmony to Loons' chorus.

And like a raindrop entering and becoming an expanding Sacred Circle, A-qua-o-da crept back into the big lake, felt his body extend to the shores, and swam back to the rhythm of the loons.

Like A-qua-o-da, find that in the giving, you transcend healing. Giving closes the circle, for it is the last step in accepting the life you are given. Free from the concerns of Self, it is time to offer yourself.

In the giving and receiving, come to see that the Sacred Hoop is a great moving circle. Like A-qua-o-da, put your own blanket down to collect the hearts of your people. If it is to give to others in need, then give. If it is to heal Earth Mother, then, like A-qua-o-da, swim your own dark waters so that you might save her.

Earth Mother awaits our gifts. Will acid rain, destruction of habitat, poisons, and harassment be Loon's last memory? Won't you give A-qua-o-da your hand and offer your attention, your time, your gifts to our one Mother? It takes many lives, it takes our collective strength to make a difference. It begins with you...and you, and you, and you....Let us become WE! Please join me in making a new memory for Earth Mother.

Place your own blanket down on Earth Mother's lap to gather donations to save the loons, the wolves, the seals, the trees, the rain forest and all other life. It is the "WE" that we save.

Celebrate the Circle! Dance! Extend to the shores of your world!

DANCE WITH EARTH MOTHER

"Walk your path amidst beauty," says the Navajo.

PART THREE

EARTH DANCES

Our Elders' prayers have been heard!
Eagle is off the endangered species list!

Earth Mother is also a Grandmother.

She has been a mother for a very long time. As Mother, she gently nurtures. As Grandmother, she wisely guides. With Mother joy, she has hoped. With Grandmother sadness, She has wept. Tired, She waits for our assistance. Softly, She whispers to us. Patient, She awaits our listening. With arms open, our Grandmother invites us all to Her.

How will we treat our Grandmother? Will we honor Her? Will we respect Her? Will we hold high Her dignity? Will we value Her? We hold Grandmother Earth in the palm of our hands, just as we cradle Her grandchildren. Will we help our Grandmother or will we continue to hurt Her?

We cut down Her limbs, yet She offers us shade. We slash Her soft skin, yet She still does not withhold Her spectacular views. We dirty Her waters, and She spreads a clean white blanket over Her sleeping children. We injure Her hopes for the future, She offers us healing in the now. See how Turtle carries Her medicine from one continent to another; from the lake, to the river, to the ocean, from the Arctic, to the Antarctic, and all that is in between. Turtle carries our Grandmother's good Earth Medicine, from sea to sea. Earth Mother extends Herself to honor us. To respect us. For dignity. For pride. Join Turtle and spread the good medicine of healing and celebration! Let us return Namaji! May we express our love for our Grandmother Earth!

With our time, our effort, our commitment, our accountability, it is time to give back to Earth Mother. Namaji: dignity, honor, respect and pride belong to Her. These are Her robes. It is time to respectfully clothe our Grandmother with the garments She, Herself, has woven.

As concrete and asphalt separate people from land vibration, our sustaining connection to Grandmother's maternal womb erodes. Under the concrete and asphalt, She cries for us. Grandmother wants to massage our feet again. She longs to comb Her healing Four Winds through our hair. Grandmother needs to feel our bodies on Her lap. Until we reconnect to Her soothing touch, until we return to Her Earth Embrace, society will continue to erode.

The mental, physical, emotional, and spiritual diseases that permeate our society stem from a separation from our precious life source. Like the moose who have locked antlers with each other, we are separated from Earth Mother's sustenance when we lock horns with daily conflicts and distractions. Cut off from their life source, the stubborn moose die from starvation and exhaustion. If we don't free ourselves from attachment to things that separate us from Earth Mother, our species will die. Earth Mother is life for moose, as She is life for humans. We are born from Her soil. It is Her winds that warm us, Her plants that sustain us. It is Her rock that remembers us. She is our Mother. She is our Grandmother.

For even as the water and sky reflect the other's essence, love needs your reflection. Become the reflection of love. Offer our green-breathing Plant Brothers Namaji. Offer the winged and the swimmers, the creepers and the crawlers, the two-legged and the four-legged, the six and eight-legged Namaji. Offer Earth Mother—Her valleys and hills, Her rivers and lakes, Her inside and outside—Namaji. Offer one another Namaji[1].

Earth Family needs an understanding and gentle touch. Greed, competition, and violence covers Earth like a piercing blanket of painful thorns. Only five hundred years ago, this land was a paradise. What has happened? Why

---

[1]   Nuclear waste storage and nuclear testing inside Earth Mother is not Namaji. It is disrespectful and destructive to our Mother.

have we abused Her so? Why have we allowed this abuse? Why have we not loved Her in the same way that she has loved us?

Love is Namaji. Abuse is the absence of love. It is time to extend our love to Grandmother again. Return to Her. Connect to Her. Like the Sun Dancer, we must contemplate and develop bravery, fortitude, generosity, and wisdom in order to fully love. These four aspirations will guide our moccasins, as we learn once again to step lightly on Earth Mother's back.

BRAVERY

Love is brave. Bravery is a gift of reaching Ain-dah-ing.

Ain-dah-ing, your home within your heart, is accessible through the awareness of your breath. Slow down to life and experience the calm of Ain-dah-ing. As you experience Ain-dah-ing, the place of peace, you will understand that even death cannot touch you. Once you have experienced this freedom on a personal level, you will be able to extend this love out beyond Self.

Connect to the power of the Great Spirit, and discover that all things come into focus and balance. Allow this global perspective of Life to empower you. Overcome obstacles with this Great Love. From this center, you will receive inner strength. Inner strength will offer you courage.

MASH-KA-WISEN

Bravery is the ability to tap one's Mash-ka-wisen. Mash-ka-wisen, or inner strength, in the Anishinaabe language means to be strong and to accept help. Freed from the expectations of self and others, you will able to recognize what is important in life. Little concerns will remain little. Big concerns will be assertively confronted[2]. Mash-ka-wisen guides you to your center, where you will be able to view both the spirit and natural worlds as your love flows freely. From this vantage point, your perception will be more expansive, more accepting, more open to the multitude of possibilities. You will

---

2   Refer to Chapters 4, 6 and 11 for more on assertive choices.

come to intuitively understand things that were once confusing, see vistas that were formerly outside your view. Engage your Mash-ka-wisen and look at life's problems without avoidance. Engage Mash-ka-wisen, and fear will not control you.

Mash-ka-wisen neutralizes life's fear. Fear is the great trickster. It will cause you to freeze, flee or fight. When you freeze in reaction to fear, you empower it and it looms over you, creating shadowed monsters. When you flee in reaction to fear, you ignite it, and it chases you down. When you fight in reaction to fear, you are pulled into it, and you are beaten before you begin. Fear goes as you go.

But if you face fear, understand fear, and respond (rather than react) to its source, then fear is of no consequence. Without inner peace, fear is the master. Tap Mash-ka-wisen and you will master fear. Mash-ka-wisen comes from a place of knowing, where all is in perspective. This serenity and understanding frees us from the bondage of fear.

RELEASE YOUR FEARS

If you are presently being controlled by fears, you can release them and then fill up with Mash-ka-wisen. I invite you to participate in the following exercise. Release yourself from your fears, to be free to heal our Grandmother. You will need a quiet place to sit in contemplation, some paper and pen, a little tobacco and sage, and some string.

Identification is the initial step in all healings. First, identify what it is you fear. Write your fears on your piece of paper. Look at the paper. Read them. Experience them. What do you really see? Do you see anything but ink on your paper? Or are they more? Have you empowered your fears, by giving them a large part of your life? Come to see that your fears are merely ideas. Fear is reacting to ideas that have not yet happened—and may not happen. Fear is always in the future. Even if your fear comes to pass, instantly it has transformed into a circumstance. Circumstances are tangible and have definite possibilities and solutions. Ideas are intangible with indefinite endings that cannot be resolved. Are you letting future ideas and "what ifs" rule your present circumstance? Will you allow these fearful ideas to control you?

Fear is like Grandfather Sun refusing to set, simply because he is afraid he may never rise again! See that you can take the risk and let go of your worries! Allow yourself the peace of letting your worries sleep until tomorrow. Then if tomorrow does or does not come, deal with them then. Learn to live in the present.

Now that you have identified your fears and have refused to empower them any longer, cut a piece of your hair and place it on your paper. Create a tobacco tie, by adding a pinch of tobacco and a sprinkle of sage. Then roll this up, so that your fears, essence, respect, and cleansing are all in one bundle. Then bind this bundle with string.

Take this tobacco tie to a place where you will not be distracted. Let Earth Mother assist you in releasing your fears. In the woods, on a shore, under stars, in a cave, come to center, to Ain-dah-ing. Then in Earth Mother's presence, quietly burn your offering. Celebrate as your tie ignites and you watch your fears ascend to the Spirit World. The Spirit World will know your fears by your hair, for your hair contains the story of your uniqueness. Our ancestors await to help you release your weaknesses. Like working a thorn out of your body, expect that it may still hurt as it is being removed. Allow the Spirit World to provide you with endurance. Allow Gitchi Manidoo to take these fears from you. Allow Mash-ka-wisen to fill the spaces where your fears once lurked.

With like bravery, we need to protect Earth Mother. With Mash-ka-wisen, we need to neutralize the intimidation and fears that are rampant on the Earth, causing reactions such as wars and violence. Safe within our place of peace, there is no threat to Self except that which threatens Earth Mother. When we die, we will return to Her. What happens to Her, then, is our future. What will we leave behind for our future? Fear and complacency? Or bravery and Namaji? Freed from fear, we can do much good.

FORTITUDE

Fortitude is mental endurance. It is perseverance, longevity, and dedication. Have you dedicated yourself to your own well being? Do you love your Self?

When you would rather give up, have you experienced the satisfaction of self-discipline and self love? This is your gift to Self.

Now extend this endurance to Grandmother. Love Her with like fortitude. Be fiercely determined to help heal Earth Mother. When you think you have nothing left to give, see that you are only limited in your giving by your thoughts. Your heart knows things which your mind does not have access to. Reach within your center, and a new well-spring of giving will rush to meet you. When set backs and bad news threaten to discourage you, become like cedars after a heavy snow: be resilient and bounce back up to face the new challenge! Experience the satisfaction of Earth Love. Realize that Earth Mother waits to return to Her healed Self.

COMMITMENT

Fortitude embraces a spirit of commitment. Commit to honor Grandmother. Commit to respect Her. Commit to offering Her dignity and pride. Prepare yourself to commit. Give yourself time to think about what it is you wish to commit to. This decision needs to come from you alone, not your friend, spouse, children, or others. This is your commitment, your time and your energy. How do you want to invest yourself?

Take the time to write your thinking down. We tend to commit to things that are grounded, rather than the ideas that float around escaping our attention. Make a top-ten wish list for yourself, your community, and your world. Consider the intangible gifts you would like to give these three areas. Earnestly consider your list. Find the common threads that run through all three. Now find tangible ways to begin to achieve these gifts. Which ideas could you turn into action? How could you turn a wish into an event? Brainstorm possible ways to achieve them. Find another person or persons who think like you. How could two or more of you achieve these things? Take one item at a time. Prioritize and set goals.

Now, write down the reasons why you haven't done this before, what has prevented you from committing. Take time to do this now.

Perhaps you have found laziness, fear, or hopelessness preventing you from giving as your heart wishes you to. It is time to listen to your heart. Listen to the drum and discover what you can do. Balance yourself and you will find that many things will change. You will find that you can discipline yourself, for now you understand the steps to achieving goals: visualize, believe, practice, and become what it is you need to become. Reach within your Mash-ka-wisen, as you develop breath awareness and you will find the source. Making small differences in your life will help you to understand how big differences are possible. Like a pebble in the water, your actions can reach the shoreline of others.

Become responsible to your Self and your world. Live the life of an adult. Grow up. It is time to do what you can and must do. It is time to fulfill your unique purpose. It is time to commit to your world.

GENEROSITY

Without the Wind Spirit's generosity, seeds could not travel the Earth to plant new life. Without the Water Spirit's generosity, all of life would die. Without Grandfather Sun's generosity, there would be only a cold, dark absence. Without your generosity, I would not be able to survive. For I rely on you. You rely on me. We are all interdependent. Honor Earth Mother by offering your best. Do not be stingy in what you give, for when you give to others, you give to all. Do not waste your gifts. Generosity is deliberate. Find ways to be generous to Earth Mother. What can you do to help Her heal? Offer your time and hard work. Honor Her with your sweat. Dignify Her with your attention. Respect Her with your choices. Give pride back to Her with your love.

Offer as much as you can from yourself, and you will find that your bucket empties to help fill many more. Be generous to Earth Mother. Generously offer Her Namaji. Like the seeds that are carried for endless miles as they cling to the hides of animals, bring to Earth Mother what you can carry. You have much to offer, many places to go, for you carry your own seeds of experience, talents, and purpose.

Native people are now generously buying back as much land as possible. The land is not bought for "me," greed, destruction, or "progress." Tribes are honored to be guardians of this land. This land is for the future[3]. The land is

---

3   Some tribes are currently pursuing water treaty rights enforcement. These waters go beyond the boundaries of the reservations, as originally stated in their treaties. As guardians of the waters, higher tribal water standards would ensure the aqua-food-chain is protected for all.

for "us." As tribal people understand, no one can really own Earth Mother. They "purchase" Her in order to acknowledge Her freedom. Earth Mother is honored with this generosity.

Many non-Indian people are also buying or leasing land. But, unlike many who buy land for self-profit or conspicuous consumption, these generous people are purchasing the future. Protecting and helping Earth Mother return to Her Self, helping Her heal, is perhaps the most generous gift of all!

There is much you can do. Contribute to Earth Mother's reclamation. Become vocal in your commitment to Earth Mother. Find a specific cause and participate in its fulfillment. Pick up garbage that litters Her trails. Recycle until it becomes habitual. Plant new growth. Honor Earth Mother. Return Her to Her natural self. Allow Her to fulfill Her purpose.

WISDOM

Consider the effects of your actions. Consider the effects of your inaction. Both are your personal decisions. Only when we are able to reflect on our decisions, and are able to be fully Self, are we enlightened. Once, carrying many pounds on my back and climbing a steep incline, I spotted a candy wrapper on a pristine wilderness trail. In my laziness I ignored it. I have since passed by people's garbage that litters the streets, yet this one wrapper continues to have a far greater impact on my memory. Here was a chance for me to return Earth Mother to Her Self, for these miles of protected reserve were once clean of human exploitation. Foolish, I did nothing. To this day, I still wonder if another had, not more strength than I, but more wisdom, to reach down and pick up the wrapper. This decision of inactivity still haunts me, and may still impact our Earth Mother.

Consider the effects of the world's actions. Consider the effects of the world's inaction. Participate in your world. Recognize your purpose and contribute to the common "We." Come to know the world and become wise. There are many little wrappers, but there are also many people. If everyone decided to participate in the climb, to reach down and clean up the debris from our Earth Mother, our streets and trails would be clean.

Consider the effects of universal actions. Consider the effects of universal inaction. With a higher state of consciousness, may you flow with the Universe, rather than against it. Come to know the Universe and become one with all. What affects are we having on the universe? With streets so full of litter, will we allow our garbage to be sent out into the Universe? Is outer space being cluttered with space debris and probes? What will our actions do to the Universe? What will our inactivity (not protesting) mean to the Universe?

"A great learning must occur," says the medicine man.

Without the listening there is no message. Without the student, there is no teacher. It is time to humbly listen with the spirit of the student. What must you learn? What listening must you do? The wise person knows when to make or take a new trail. It is time to take a new direction with Earth Mother and the Universe. It is time to get off the fast lane and move onto the Red Road of Namaji. It is time for us to pick up the litter in the world!

An opening must exist before it can be filled. I invite you to become receptive to the truths that beg for your attention. I invite you to honor the filling. May you fill and offer your wisdom to the world.

EARTH FAMILY: MITAKUYE-OYASIN

What is night? Is night when the sun is setting? Is it the moment the sun is completely set? Or is night fully night when the moon is high up in the sky? Is it when the first star is visible? Which of these is night? Is night one of these? Or all of these? Where does night begin and end?

What are you? Are you Yellow? Red? Black? White? Is the night sky yours or the others? Does color determine who will see the stars? Just as the night gradually offers its silence without beginning or end to all colors, gradients of uniqueness blend us all together. We are all one family under the same night sky.

What was before night? What was before light? Where do the winds come from? Where is vapor born? Where is color found? The source is One.

Mitakuye-Oyasin means we are all related. You are my brother. You are my sister. I am yours. We are all part of Earth family.

MITAKUYE-OYASIN

Earth Mother
Loves Her Children.
We are all related.

From the Finned
To the Feathered,
From the Legged
To the Rooted,
Creepers and Crawlers,

We are all Her children.
We are all related.

The Weak and the Strong.
The Rich and the Poor.
The Young and the Old.
Swift and Slow.

We are all Her children.
We are all related.

With Love and Hate, Joy and Pain,
Life and Death,
We are related.

Yesterday, Today, and Tomorrow,
Here and There,
You and Me,
We are all Related.
We are all Her children.

SHARING THE BREATH OF LIFE

Where was your breath one month ago? Think about it. Follow it back. Discover the connection. Was your breath in a penguin, a zebra, a panda, or a polar bear? Was it in an elk, a fish, a hawk, or a snake? Whose breath is it? Did your breath come from a tree that gave itself, so you could have a next breath? Or did your breath come from a cactus, a bamboo shoot, a fern, a flower, or a spruce? Whose breath is it? Was your breath in Yellow Man, Red Man, Black Man, or White Man? Whose breath is it? Did it come from the East, South, West, or North? Were the winds warm, cold, wet, or dry? Whose breath is it?

If you can follow your breath, you can find Mitakuye-Oyasin[4].

Wherever it was, from whatever it was that breathed it, come to see that part of them is now part of you. Who, then, is the dominant? In accepting the Breath of Life, you have accepted all that has come before you. In the giving of your breath, you are giving it to another. In this exchange, you embrace the Universe and become One within each other. We all share the same Breath.

On the Sacred Hoop of Life, we are all an equal radius from the center, which is Gitchi Manidoo. Come to honor this truth. It is freeing. It is loving. With this understanding you will be free to give to Earth Mother, to all Her children. For you will understand your role on the Sacred Hoop of Life.

EARTH DANCES

EARTH DANCERS

Deer bounded. Fox skipped. Rabbit hopped. Eagle soared.

Rock looked out from his cracks to the Earth Dancers that passed by. Even Grass knew how to sway with the Four Winds. But Rock could only watch as the dancers moved to the Whispering Needle Songs. He could only pretend it

---

4   To order *Follow Your Breath* audio tape, call 1-800-983-0600 or write to the publishers of this book.

was him, stalking to the beat of the Thunderers. He could only wish to be part of the gentle rhythm of Earth Mother's cycles. Rock saw furs, feathers and skins shimmer in sunlight. He stared as the beautiful animals moved to the timeless certainty of the Beat of Life.

"But I cannot dance. I must only watch," thought Rock now on the edge of the Dance Circle.

Rock watched Animals and Plants Earth Dance. "They move like Water," he thought. Tails balanced great leaps. Wings flapped majestic flight. Ears twitched momentary presence. Flowers opened into day movement. But Rock could do none of this. For he was Rock.

Rock was unaware that Grandfather Sun peered in. He was unaware that Grandmother Earth looked out. He was unaware that he was moving ever so slowly toward the good beat. As he paused in the midst of his slow memory making, Grandmother Earth gently pushed Rock out into the world of dance.

Earth Dancers stopped in their movements and crowded around Rock as he entered the Dance Circle.

And all fell silent... there was no movement, no song, no dance. This time, it was Bear, Deer, Grass, Flower, Eagle, Butterfly, Fox, and Squirrel that watched with awe as Rock moved. Out of the quickness of time, Rock moved. Slowly, he changed, to feel the beat of life.

Still Silence filled all present.

Suddenly, Four Winds lifted grasses and dancing furs. Grandfather Sun pushed heat onto Rock's face, then disappeared. Soon, Water Spirits began their rhythmic Sky-Drumming onto Earth Mother, returning movement and song. A small bit of Rock lifted to touch the vibration of the dance, and quietly this part of him began to roll off.

With great-slow rolling joy, Rock danced beautifully into the moment. Falling ever so softly onto the lap of his Mother, part of Rock blended into Earth Mother's embrace. Earth Dance completed, Rock became Soil. The circle was prepared for all who now dance.

So when you dance, dance lightly. Remember and honor Rock, who now massages your feet. May his dance become your joy. May your dance become his honor. Let Rock experience your dance, each time you honor his moment. See how Rock left himself behind in order to offer you a path. Understand that Rock dances slowly, contrasting, revealing, your movement and beauty. Thank Rock for his part. Know that the Earth Dance is for all.

Some stories say animals taught people how to dance. When dancers put on their regalia of animal skins and feathers, when they hold sweet grass, and claws of the winged, the spirit of each plant or animal is being honored. Powwow dances honor Earth Mother.

The many different dance styles honor the uniqueness of each dancer. Some dances are reserved for women, some for men, some for children. Yet, all acknowledge the truth of Mitakuye-Oyasin. All are gifts to those who will accept. All step to the beat of Namaji. All manifest a great love for Earth Mother.

Each dance celebrates the interconnectedness of people to Earth Mother and Sky Father. Each dance celebrates a lifestyle that challenges the thinking of Western Industrialization. Every dance celebrates an inherent dependence on cycles and honors the Sacred Hoop. Native American dances honor Earth Mother as the movements speak of and honor Her, each with a unique history.

DANCE WITH EARTH - YOU ARE NOT ALONE!

Eagle comes to fly overhead to bless the ceremony with his presence, guidance, and approval. Participants dance proudly at Powwow, for their presence celebrates and honors the Creator.

Fly with birds. Swim with fish. Travel with animals. Grow with plants. Imagine with stars. You are not alone. It is time to dance alongside our Brothers and Sisters and honor their existence.

Tonight, I invite you to go outside and pick out one star. Just one. Befriend it. Communicate with it. Talk to it. Discover how meaning pours into this star as you give it your time and attention.

All relationships begin with deliberate attention. Think of your pets, your family, your garden, your music. Learn to create relationships with the world around you. Practice giving attention to your world. Practice honoring Earth Mother. In this way you will create a web of caring. In this way you will care about the future of each member. In this way you will care about the future of all.

It is my guess that ducks think about water a lot. Earth Mother is three-fourths water. We are nearly three-fourths water. What do you think about? Realize you are a child of Earth Mother. In the discovery of who you are, you will find your mind and heart will shift to your life source. It is my guess you will think about Earth Mother and Sky Father, Cousin Water and Cousin Fire, a lot. From the attention, you will practice. From the practicing, you will become.

What you believe, you practice, and what you practice you become. What are you practicing? What are you becoming? What do you believe?

Don't run from the truth. Can you outrun the truth? It is amazing how many people deny who they truly are, but look for themselves in escapes and distractions. Like running out of the rain in order to take a shower, they miss the joy of the Creator! Experience Life! Don't run from the truth! Experience who you really are...a precious child of Earth Mother!

Above all, follow your happiness. Discover your connection to life and you will discover the relationships that await your time and attention. In this becoming, your purpose will spill to fill another's bucket. In returning home, you will find your joy.

Earth Mother, Sky Father, Grandmother Moon, and Grandfather Sun all dance in a circular motion with the dancers. So connect! Sing! Celebrate! Earth! Dance! Drum! In your dancing, may you be as happy as Deer bounding through the quiet woods. And in your resting, may you be as happy as Snake on a warm rock.

MEN'S DANCE

His soft touch is his strength.
He honors Her this way.
His dancing tells the story.
He returns to Her soft clay.

His feet become the stick
Her skin becomes the drum.
His movement are the words
And tell where we come from.

Earth Mother requests a concentrated effort, a deliberate conscious awareness of Her needs. Traditionally, Native American men provided for and
protected the family as both hunters and warriors. Their concentrated effort,
their deliberate conscious awareness, ensured all were cared for. As a
periphery support of the hub on the Wheel of Life (the women), men honored their roles on the Sacred Hoop.

Men's traditional dancing originates from the celebrations and reenactments
of hunting or war parties. The Grass Dance, the Crow Hop, and the Sneak
Up are three dances that honor Earth Mother, each with its unique style.
Each are danced with traditional regalia, where the dancer blends with
Song, Beat, Earth, and Sky. All of life is honored, as the spirits of our Brothers
and Sisters also participate in the dance.

THE GRASS DANCE

Rising and falling colors met to blur the contour of his dance. Red and yellow yarns intertwined, as white and black yarns accented each beat. Sparrow Hawk watched carefully, trying to pick out each unique movement. She had seen her son's dancing so many times. Yet each dance was different, a fresh step always surprised and pleased her. She stood on the outside of the Circle, watching carefully, following his movements proudly.

His high step was his strength. His soft touch was his beauty. He drained all of the weight into one foot and pulsed a connection to Earth Mother. He tapped one foot behind on the soft green grass and honored her.

The mother's son swayed with the good strong beat. Moving with the very vibration of the world, his dancing was hypnotic. Yarns fell from his arms, his chest, his back, his legs. Together, he became the high moving summer grass.

His strong, powerful legs fooled many looking on, as he suddenly looked like he would fall. Sparrow Hawk felt many around the arbor watching her son, honoring his dance. She was pleased that he was now able to further extend himself. With incredible balance, his dancing reached out to honor all at the ceremony.

The multicolored fringes swayed. As he moved on to another step, the fringes were still moving from the step before. Sparrow Hawk wondered if the fringes still taught him about Life's movement.

Then as though rushing to catch up with his steps, the yarn cascaded around him like a great waterfall, so loyal to the dancer. The fringes massaged him, just as his soft steps massaged Earth Mother.

Sparrow Hawk looked at her son and remembered securing the scarf on his head as he had prepared for his first big dance in his yellow and red regalia. How proud he was of his moving fringes! How proudly he held his beaded medicine bag! How tall he had stood that day!

Standing just as tall, Sparrow Hawk followed his moving fringes. She watched as his outstretched legs hopped forward. Bent, balanced, and intense, he followed the straight song understanding its language. It was his language. A language without words. A language without discussion. Around the Drum, he had listened so many days. Like a sponge, he had absorbed the sounds until they were part of him. Until they had filled his opening with familiarity. Until finally, he was the song. The yarn jumped as he danced to the beat. The fringes he wore knew the drum's language, too. All were one.

A sharp turn and a sudden drop reminded Sparrow Hawk of her son's recent maturity. Watching his head subtly nod to the good rhythm, she knew these steps had prepared him for the great changes fatherhood would soon demand.

His dancing accelerated with the beat until the four colors bled into one another. Each separate strand danced with Mitakuye-Oyasin. Like the fading sunset, he was now a wonderful swirl of dancing color!

Then, for her eyes alone, his fast dance seemed to slow down. Like a colorful leaf floating to the ground, she saw each fine movement. Time blurred to separate his colors once again. Each movement became a moment as she watched his head, shoulders, back, feet, legs, and arms dance in a fluttering balanced pattern. Reaching, circling, pulsing, folding, he honored all.

"Does he know how beautiful he is?" Sparrow Hawk wondered.

Then soothing her thoughts with his layered movements, the present collapsed into the past. For a long instant, her boy was young again with his falling colors. His yellow yarn hesitated, unsure, then raced ahead—so excited.

Then blinking, her eyes saw him again as he was that present moment. Male fullness revealed in mature movement. Like a bird's feathers filling out, his dance filled her view. His entire regalia danced a burst of colors. There was nothing else for Sparrow Hawk to see. Nothing else to hear. Just the beat, the song, his dance, her great Love.

Then just as she had caught up with time, a quick step took him forward to the very edge of her view. Here, he became more. Looking at a young man, her eyes reached and instead she saw him old. With these borrowed eyes, Sparrow Hawk saw her son, now an Elder, still dancing, still honoring Earth Mother. She saw the circling completed, his high steps still proud, his movement flowing into the North, his dignity extending to all who watched.

The song was almost over, his burst was nearly finished. The beat gathered strength to stop, while his step looked for the end. Then all at once, it was done. Together the man, the dance, the song, the grass bowed to honor the last beat of the Drum.

The Grass Dance is the oldest remaining Northern Plains dance[1]. The tempo ranges from very slow to very fast[2]. Grass Dancers do not wear bustles, but usually wear a roach and spreaders[3] on their head. Cascades of yarned fringes adorn their regalia. Originally, it may have signified a celebration of victory.

The dance may have also represented a warrior flattening the grass for a ceremony or to prepare a place of rest. Like the deer or wolf, circling around

---

[1]   As a wedding gift, the grass dance is said to have been passed on to the Sioux.

[2]   Straight songs have vowel sounds (ya, hey, hi, lay, etc.) that correspond to specific tones and notes.

[3]   A spreader usually holds two feather plumage at the top of the head.

and around until the grass is flattened, may you prepare a place to sleep, to rest, to re-energize yourself and your world[4].

What have you to prepare? What ceremony for Earth Mother can you participate in? What Earth Dance can you celebrate?

WHAT ARE YOUR STEPS?

Like Grass Dancers, work to remain connected to Earth Mother while you tap the Spirit World. As you move, remember that you live in two worlds. May you honor them both. Work to be flexible when life expects more from you, demands more from you, asks more from you, needs more from you.

Accept the sudden turns in your life as part of the dance. Remain balanced and strong. As life is unpredictable, learn to dance to the unpredictable. That is how remarkable balance is born. Fold and collapse when you must. Don't be there, if it is not appropriate. Live life in the descent as well as the ascent. Relax, stay grounded, and centered. These are the steps to a good dance.

DANCE WITH THE WIND

Dance with the winds of change. Have you recognized where the winds come from? Be flexible with your steps and you will be able to celebrate the changing movements of life.

Find a tree top view during a storm. What do you see from this height? Can you see the waving, the bending, the balance, the flexibility of the wind? Isn't the storm a thing of beauty? Celebrate Life's movement, as all of life is transitory. See that there are always choices. Choices can become memories to cherish, to place in your medicine bag. Remember, your decisions will follow you like the fringes on your dance regalia.

What is your career path? Make out your life's mission statement. Sit down and look at what you learned about yourself in Chapter 1. What is your joy?

---

4   If you scare a deer out of its bed unintentionally, you can honor it by laying in its bed. In fact, the deer may even watch you and honor you as you lay in their bed.

What are your strengths? What do you want to be remembered as? What do you need to do with your life? Write this understanding into a mission statement. Post this statement about what you wish to do with your gifted life and who you hope to become, where you will see it. Know yourself, and you invite the world in. Be a stranger to yourself, and you cannot greet the world. Know what your purpose is. Know who you are.

Engage Bimadisiwin, your fate, free will, and purpose, and live a good life. What is your direction? Where do you point? Like the Four Directions, your life is pointing you to the things you need to become. Are you obsessed with innocence of the East? Then ask yourself what beginning is begging you to honor. Are you drawn to the growth of the South? Then ask yourself what you need to develop within. Are you fascinated with the mysteries of the West? What journey must you take? Are you attracted to the wisdom of the North? Ask what giving you have to do.

What is your growth? Growth requires both acceptance of nurturance and the giving of Self. What gifts have you accepted? What manifestation of growth have you given? Without the give and take, there is no movement. Without the movement, there is no growth. Vibrate with this necessary exchange. Grow and become!

Notice that love opportunities abound. Love self, others and Earth Mother. Do this and your dance will be of the wind, carrying your essence to the Four Directions, circling you out into the world.

Yield like the grass in the wind. The "wild" horses on my reservation weren't wild, they were free! Their manes danced with the wind. Tribal people were not wild, they were free! Our stories and cultural inheritance ride those same winds!

We all have ancestors. Where were your ancestors five thousand years ago? No matter what your ethnic bloodline, continental origin, or language, all of us have ancestors that were dancing to the drums. Go back to your beginnings. Consider your history. All history is tribal! All of our ancestors were drumming, dancing, singing, living with nature, rather than against it. It has only been in recent times that restriction and separation from nature has taken place. Your history is as traditional as my history.

Today's norms are comparatively short lived and change frequently. Yet, the people are always the same. The difference is that Native American and other indigenous people have held onto and valued Old Age wisdom. My roots, your roots, their roots, our roots, all join together in the depth of Earth Mother's soil. Mishomis has seen all and knows all. Greet Mishomis and you will greet all our relations.

Look beyond today's fleeting moment. Can you see that we are all joined with the longer and stronger legacies of our ancestors? That we are all essentially memory-walkers? That in our hearts and spirits, we are all tribal people? Come and celebrate this truth! It is the truth that leads to we-ness and free-ness!

Embrace your own freedom and dance to your own beat! That is your right. That is your privilege. That is your obligation to the Spirit World. You are in this world, not to be shackled, but to dance with the Four Winds! See how the dancer's layers of fringe gently sway like prairie grass on a windy day. Let the winds move you into your future, and offer you whispers of your past. Be prepared to stop your life when your beat stops you. Fully experience this life, and honor all. Be completely connected to the beat of life and any moment will be a good moment to go back home to the Spirit World.

Then bow your head to honor the Drum.

CROW HOP

Like Crow hopping, Split Hoof moved to each beat. His body met the slow, pronounced rhythm as easily as rain hitting Earth.

With great care, Split Hoof placed his foot down on Earth Mother's skin, honoring her. With great hope, his head and shoulders shifted positions into Sky Father. Each abrupt movement honored the Four Directions and the Wind Spirits.

His Eagle feathered bustle moved with its own life and honored the Sacred Hoop. Even Eagle remembered Brother Crow, honored Crow[5].

Split Hoof now danced with Crow, their spirits mingling in the Circle, in the beat, in the song. Circling him with good medicine, Crow offered lessons without Split Hoof knowing. Crow was with Split Hoof, filling him with Crow life.

Split Hoof touched the sweet grass braid that hung from his side. Gently, he stooped to touch Earth Mother. Split Hoof's foot stepped on a stone in the Circle. With strength he lifted his foot to honor Mishomis. He heard the Buffalo bone breastplate sharing its sound. Split Hoof shared his Seventh Direction with all present. Knowing the honor beats, he raised his Sacred Willow dancing stick high and honored the Drum's Spirit, honored the Great Truth.

The song moved. At times, Split Hoof dipped down low and came back up. At other times, he honored Crow with his deliberate step. His single bustle moved him, and directed all eyes into the very core of Split Hoof's heart and spirit, coming together in his design, the design of his Seventh Direction. Dancing in this way, all connected.

The song ended, yet Crow remained with Split Hoof. For Split Hoof entered as One, and left as We.

CROW'S COURT

The strict Crow Hop beat leads us down the path of Crow and reveals a sophisticated judicial system. In the world of Crow, as in the Crow Hop, clear expectations beat a strong and deliberate message. Responsibility, accountability, commitment and honor are expected from each member of the tribe.

---

5   The first bustles were made of Crow feathers, then were modified. From tribe to tribe and over time, bustles evolved into the customary Eagle Circle Bustle often seen today. Many bustles are made of a wide variety of decoration that includes: quill work, bead work, colored tape, paint and fringes.

A crow will be taken to court if he violates this code. There, he will be found guilty or not guilty. Crow's natural laws ensure this species' survival.

Learn from the Crows' Court: The crows all circle together and discipline the Sentinel Crow who allowed a predator to get past without warning the others. The Sentinel Crow did not do his job, he did not shield the rest of the flock. Like the Crow's court, take care of your old business before you go on with your life. If stresses have gotten past your sentinel warrior's shield, first deal with them and then move on. Discipline yourself to do what you must! Then always be prepared to use your warrior shield if necessary.

What can we learn from Crow? As dancers of Life, we have our unique flexibility, yet we need to follow the natural laws of the universe, stepping lightly down to the given beat, following the natural order to the song of life. As life will certainly go up and down, we must meet the challenge and honor Earth Mother with four Anishinaabe teachings. <u>Sweet grass</u> teaches us gentleness. <u>Rocks</u> teach us strength. <u>Animals</u> teach us to share. <u>Trees</u> teach us to tell the truth, small truths, even if they are only to Self.

We are the guests of Earth Mother. If we are good guests, we get to stay. If we violate the natural laws of nature, we will no longer be welcome here, and our species will not survive. Work to be both strong and gentle. Share what you can. Be truthful with yourself, others, and Earth Mother. Truth is freeing.

We are now standing in Crow's Court. How do you plead to pollution and environmental damage? Guilty or not Guilty? How active or inactive have you been? What will be your verdict? Our verdict? What happens to human kind, depends on how kind humans are!

THE SNEAK UP

This traditional dance, The Sneak Up, reenacts brave deeds. The events of hunters or warriors are retold. During the tremolo[6]—a rapid beating on the drum—the dancer may kneel on one knee, or meander about making his

---

6   Also known as the ruffle.

body quiver fiercely, looking for tracks of an animal or enemy. A sudden quick burst symbolizes an encounter with the enemy, requiring great dancing energy. The dancer makes each movement count, for he understands the moment is quickly over. Dancers never dance backwards during this style, for that would symbolize retreating from the enemy. Each round of sneak up is played four times.

Today's warrior stands alone in a difficult situation, to tend their children's fire. Today's warriors are environmentalists. They are today's healers. Today's teachers. Today's givers. Today's nurturers. For today's war is poverty of spirit, mind, body and emotions.

What will we give to our children? How will we make each moment count? When will we notice the tracks that are before us? Behind us? Will we pay attention to the lessons of yesterday? Like this dancer, we must not dance backwards into the hands of our enemy, human weakness. We must look to the future and prepare a good life and a good land for them.

Children need roots, something to cling to, like corn soup or fry-bread, traditional stories and memories, ancient rituals of love. Begin your own traditions. It may be as simple as getting an ice-cream cone at your favorite dairy, or a prayer that your family speaks together. The key word is together and the power is in its simplicity. Give roots to your children and you will be feeding them well.

As the Sneak Up Dance plays four rounds, let us honor this sacred number. There are four directions. Four seasons, four moons, four guests on Earth Mother: human, animal, plant, mineral. There are four life cycles, four colors of people, four elements: earth, air, water, fire. There are four aspects to our being: spiritual, emotional, physical, and mental. As we honor this truth, may we also honor each member of each sacred group. May we protect and honor each as part of One. As Powwow lasts four days, the dancing is experienced for four cycles of Sun and Moon.

SNEAK UP

He would do it right this time!

Before his dream—before the laughing man—Red Stone walked through the woods too loud, too fast, too separated. This time he moved slowly, quietly, connected. Holding the carved stone image in his hand, he knew what he must do.

Having been named for his skilled carvings of soft red stone for pipe bowls, Red Stone was never without a pipe to carve. His designs had grown up alongside him, from simple lines, now to beautiful and complex birds. To others, his purpose had been clear.

But to Red Stone, what had once been fun, had become tiring. Four seasons of carving Mishomis had taken Red Stone away from Nokomis[7]. Away from Grandmother.

And so returning to her, that day he had run through the woods, had crossed the clearing, to reach the great Mishomis, to escape. Standing on Big Rock, seeing Big Water in the distance, Red Stone had finally felt free. Alive, he felt as though he would be able to fly. So, like many times before, he had jumped down with boyish playfulness onto the lap of Grandmother Earth.

As he landed, Grandmother Earth suddenly moved! It seemed that She had jumped up to meet him. In the next few moments of trying to understand, Red Stone thought at first that Nokomis was angry at him for leaving his carving behind. He did not at first understand what had happened. He did not see it as it was. At first, he did not hear it, smell it, feel it. Only when the pain shot through his ankle, when that moment moved into another, did he understand. Red Stone had landed on White Tail.

---

7   Pronounced: no-KO-mis and means Grandmother. Here it refers to Grandmother Earth.

As the deer jumped up to escape Red Stone's landing, the young man's foot had twisted. Now, feeling the pain, hearing the snap, watching White Tail disappear off into the lushness, Red Stone instead felt shackled to the base of the hard rock, where just before he had felt free.

The crawl back to village had taught him much about the Creepers. So out of habit, during the first days of his healing, Red Stone had carved Creepers and Crawlers on the pipe stone that had waited for him. Even with his birch bark cast, he was still unaware of what healing truly meant. With good spirits, he returned to his stone. But when the Creepers were finished, Red Stone began to discover how time chained him down. Confined to his lodge, his spirits turned to anger. Putting the stone down, he decided once again that he would not carve.

Long days without walking made Red Stone hungry for Nokomis. Long nights of dream-walking fed Red Stone with Mishomis.

Every empty-day, Red Stone would imagine the jump differently: White Tail would not be there. Red Stone would run through the clearing again, smell the cedars, hear the chipmunks. And always, he would return to band, and tell others he would carve no more. And the Creepers and Crawlers would not become the artwork in his beautiful carvings.

Each dream-night, Red Stone would reach the great Mishomis. Then Big Rock would mold himself into the image of a large man. Looking at Red Stone, the man would laugh hysterically, as the young man jumped onto White Tail. Over and over this dream circled. Even White Tail laughed to remind him of his foolishness. Then Red Stone would crawl away from Laughing Man, doomed to carve the Creepers and Crawlers once again.

And each morning, Red Stone looked at the carving of his accident, and hated his dream, hated his life.

Finally, determined to end the carvings once and for all, Red Stone took the stone and cut slashes to gouge out his anger. This time Red Stone did not plan to make anything but ruin. But instead, the stone easily shifted images, into the face of the Laughing Man.

Eyes, big and hollow. Nose, pointed and sure. Mouth, eternally laughing.

Red Stone looked at the image he had created. Confused, he did not know at first what to think, to do, to feel. Then, looking carefully into the image, Red Stone suddenly realized the Laughing Man of his dream was not laughing at him at all. For the Laughing Man was Red Stone!

He understood! It was time to laugh at himself! Looking at the stone shape in his hand, Red Stone suddenly saw the foolishness of what he had done. The eyes showed him to look before he jumped next time. The nose told him that winds can take your scent away. The Great laughing mouth taught him to find the humor in it all.

Red Stone saw his own foolishness, his own mighty joke, his own great joy right in front of him. He would carve, when he was ready, when he had first filled with Earth Mother, when the carving slipped into its own shape. For only then can it be what it is meant to be.

Red Stone held Laughing Man in his hand. Feeling the familiar impressions, the young man smiled. Stepping softly, with the wind in his face, Red Stone would do it right, this time. Hearing his own heart beat, his steps were light. Looking before him to find the shape that does not fit, he would find what he was looking for. Looking before him, his new steps would take him where he must go.

Freezing to mold himself into the woods, she would not see him. Head down and sneaking up, Red Stone knew that this game needed completion. Then finally touching her White Tail, Red Stone found his next carving.

As White Tail bounded off through the woods, Red Stone laughed and laughed! Holding the healer in the palm of his hand, he laughed and laughed some more!

AWARENESS OF LIFE

The Sneak Up offers many teachings on awareness and life-consciousness.

Awareness includes your thoughts, feelings, understandings, beliefs, impressions, responses, intuitions, dreams and sensations. Awareness is your experience of life. Consciousness develops when you reflect on your experiences. For many people, much of their day is spent thinking about some aspect of wants or needs, such as hunger, thirst, sleep, distractions, and money. Learn to exercise your conscious awareness to a greater depth. Emotional, spiritual, physical, and mental consciousness needs your attention, too. Physically reconnect to Earth Mother. Let Her umbilical cord of world vibrations heal you, guide you, fill you, teach you.

Like the warrior, be aware of all that is going on inside you and outside you, the very moment it is happening. Like the Sneak Up dancer, make the most of every moment, for they are soon enough over. Like Red Stone, stop your Self long enough, and humble your Self true enough, to learn from Earth Mother.

Know what it is to be a Creeper. Get on your belly and you may discover the gems. Stop yourself and eliminate all distractions. Quiet your mind. Discover the path. And in the journey, discover that ultimately you are alone. Discover that silent solitude is good. Unearth your gems.

Even alone, you are not alone at all, for all the Earth has shared in your Great Mystery. In this mystery, discover who you are. In this silence, offer back your breath. In solitude, reach for your great connection. Listen to your dreams, your heart, your song, your laughter. Do this and your awareness of the life within you and without you will expand.

I have never seen two birds collide. Have you? Birds fly swiftly through Sky Father without the need for traffic controllers. Why is this? They are aware. Aware of their surroundings, aware of themselves, their abilities, their intentions, their destination, their possibilities, their choices, their purpose. Before attempting to fly, it would be best for you to be aware of your abilities, your intentions, your destination, your possibilities, your choices, your purpose.

Notice the variety of ways Earth Mother has replanted Herself. Maple trees transform into little helicopters. Cottonwood seeds lift their own future with their soft gentleness. How can you continue to replant growth within yourself? How will you transform your giving to the future? How gentle will you become to offer your gifts of Self to Earth Mother? Become aware of you. Become aware of your surroundings. Become aware of the changes you can make through your own interaction with this world. Be honest and authentic in your offering. Respond, rather than react, to what is there. Discover the possibilities. Then choose the best course of action. Free your own soft seeds of truth to all Four Directions. Your awareness may implant, grow, and offer gifts somewhere else.

What is boredom? Boring people get bored. Look into an elk's eye and see the reflection of contentment. Look into the eyes of someone who has laughed throughout life. Like Red Stone, find your own humor. Discover the contradictions. Find your own contentment. Look within and discover your own answers. Do not rely on others to fill you with enjoyment. Enjoy yourself! I guarantee, if you search for these things, you will never be bored again. I also guarantee, you will never be boring again!

What is happiness? Happiness is finding that root beer tastes similar to blueberries. Happiness is honoring the joy of life by giving. Happiness in finding the joy in each moment. In the giving, you will find happiness. In creating, you will discover happiness. Happiness is wanting your past, present and future just the way it is, was and always will be. Not wishing for the other. Understanding that your life fulfills One Great Purpose.

Train your unconscious mind. Like traditional Ojibwe people, learn to remember your dreams[8]. Learn to participate in your dreams. Learn to listen to your

---

[8]   Many traditional and new songs, as well as dancing, have been inspired through dreams and visions.

dreams. Find the common threads that run through your dreams, for they weave a pattern that speaks to you. Opening the door to your unconscious promotes insights that expand into conscious awareness.

Awareness changes patterns, just like the sun rises and sets. When you think the sun has set on your conscious mind (sleep), it has actually risen on your unconscious thought, giving your dream world the sunlight of honor. Elders considered their dream life as essential as their daily life. They understood the power offered in their dreams. Listen to your dreams. Discipline yourself to listen. Dreams are integral to imagination. Imagination is essential to creation. Dreams are from the Creator.

Allow your dreams to teach you about yourself, your world, your confusion, your understandings. Your dreams, like Water Spirits, wash away the debris your mind collects during your waking hours. The dream state of consciousness is as meaningful as your waking hours, offering you symbols of recognition and teaching. Those who practice dream-listening, have learned to listen to the silence. They can listen to their deepest self, therefore understanding themselves intimately.

Likewise, pay attention to the waking hours, your waking decisions and the waking dialogues that go on inside you at each moment. Learn to listen to yourself when you are awake. Notice what your entire Self is telling you. Remember to listen to yourself as "we." What is your tense shoulder trying to tell you? What is your preoccupation asking you to resolve? What are your emotions signifying? What attention does your spirit crave? You will probably find it easier to listen to your dreams. People who exercise self-reflection can more easily dive into the pool of the unconscious, for they have recognized their image and are not unfamiliar with what they see.

Experience the golden moments that dwell between wakefulness and sleep. Here lies a feast of symbols, understandings, images. Attend to a few and you will discover much about yourself. It is the journey you have taken since you left the East—the path that leads to the other side of yourself and back again. Here you will find the things about yourself that you have brought back up and down again, time after time. This state of consciousness, closest to your awake, yet pulled up from sleep, is the familiar path that guides you to yourself.

Higher states of consciousness, are rooted deeply to the unconscious. The deeper you are able to journey into the Self, the higher is your transcendence out. A higher state of consciousness results when you have listened to the truth of yourself and your world, when you are able to listen to the silence, traveling the Red Road, walking with Namaji.

There are many ways to train your unconscious mind. Through meditation and breathing exercises you can open the gateway to the inner You. Through creating art, you can tap into your unconscious wisdom. Through watching fire's dancing flames, you can teach your mind and heart to focus. Through sitting still and doing nothing, you can become the flame and merge with all.

THREATS TO LIFE AWARENESS

Awareness is threatened when our past experiences block the view of our present. Get unstuck! Live in the present and you will free yourself from the past.

Awareness is threatened when the future takes priority over the present. Come back! Live in the present and let tomorrow take care of itself. Do what you can do today. That is all there is. That is all you can do.

Awareness is threatened when we flood our mind, emotions, body, and spirit with food, alcohol, drugs, and other addictions. Food is medicine and should be respected as such. Eat when you are hungry. Stop eating when you are not. It is that simple. Drugs and alcohol become illusionary awareness enhancers, yet cause you to miss out on the best that life has to offer. Drugs are like fingerprints on your mind's eye. They create a smudge on the mirror of your mind. A dirty window blocks the sun light from entering. Soon these images steer you sideways, distracting you away form the Red Road, into the ditches of misery and regret.

Look into a clear, clean mirror to see who you really are. Be content like an elk, taste your own blueberry sweetness, enjoy your internal journeys, and transcend to your own heights of giving. Only in this way can you contribute to the universe. Only in this way is your giving authentic and honest. Be who you are, and you will enjoy your own company. Have a root beer and celebrate! You have arrived!

WOMEN'S DANCE

Her steps are patient.
Her movement, flowing.
Her gifts are graceful
Her silence, knowing.

Her dance is beauty.
Her honor, regal.
Her voice is lifting,
Her wings, the Eagle.

Put your ear up against a sea shell, and you will hear Creation. Feel the soft cattail down in the meadow that warms little feet[1], and you will touch Creation. Swallow the clear water of Earth Mother's stream and you will taste Creation. Smell the scent of wild rose, and you will smell Creation's perfume. See the love in a mother's eyes and you will understand the secret of Creation.

Women are highly respected members of Native American culture. Within each woman is the sacred power of birth. In the gifting of another life, women honor and serve both worlds. For woman is the connector of old spirits to new bodies. Pain gives birth to both temporal and spiritual existence.

---

[1] Traditional Ojibwe babies were often surrounded with the soft down of cattail to both insulate the from the cold and provide emotional comfort.

In a mother's sacrifice, she is gifted with a mother's joy. Her maternal dance easily slips into the cadence of the good beat of the Drum. As her heart echoes this same beat for the baby she carries, her heart understands and teaches her child the rhythm. Her spirit understands and teaches the dance. Her body remembers and teaches the Circle. Her mind soon forgets the pain of Oon-da'-di-zoo-win[2].

Honor the women in your life. Honor the soft secret of Creation that they embody. Discover their unique role on the Sacred Hoop, as they dance the steps of life. Gift all mothers Namaji. Gift Earth Mother Namaji. Return to their sweet embrace of love.

From the women of this world, learn of Earth Mother's great love for you. Like a newborn who places his ear against the soft skin of his mother to reconnect, to remember, to fill with love and life, place your ear against Earth Mother, and return to Her great beat.

Listen... Her rhythm is everywhere. Put your ear against Earth Mother's good heart.

Listen... to the rhythm of the Water Spirits. The babbling creeks, the powerful waterfalls, the rippling lakes, the constant ocean tides are her pulse.

Listen... Her rhythm moves the wind. As leaves rustle, hear the ruffle of the sneak up.

Listen... In the thawing of her soil, hear the steady beat of worm wiggling.

Listen... In the thunderers, hear the strong honor beats of Life.

PESHTIGO RIVER SONG

I met you many years ago,
To see your music-view.
I hear your song has changed.
For your melody is new.

---

[2] Pronounced: ON-da-DEE-zoe-win and refers to the birthing process.

Your water's edges rose and fell.
While Mishomis sings his tune.
The Water Spirits moved some rocks
to feel Nokomis Moon.

But I still recognize your beat
I hear Mishomis song.
Your Water washes over me
Earth Mother, you dance strong.

Earth Mother teaches us of birth, death, and rebirth. Dignified Elder Oak offers new life to seedlings. Even our bodies, blending into Mother's soil, will someday offer new life. Mother's endless services of cycles sing a song of Mitakuye-Oyasin, of our interconnectedness. All things are in eternal progression. Sacred and eternal, our purpose fulfills the greater purpose.

Discover your purpose. Engage your purpose. Contribute to the cycle of life.

WOMEN'S DANCE STYLES

Native American women's dance styles illustrate the beauty of Namaji. Women's dance styles are poised dances of gentle sound, uplifting sight, and regal steps. Dances include the Fancy Shawl Dance, Traditional and Jingle Dress styles. Each speaks to a different aspect of the Hoop of Womanhood, honoring the whole woman, demonstrating Namaji with each step.

FANCY SHAWL DANCE

Popular with young women and girls, this dance style respects and honors the agile and balanced female energy. Requiring complex footwork, quick leaps and spins, the Fancy Dance becomes a whirling sight of feathers, ribbons, sequins, and color. Dancers wear an embroidered, beaded, or sequined shawl over their shoulders, as they hold the ends stretched out with their hands.

With hands on their hips and elbows extended, or with arms stretched out, spreading the shawls into beautiful wings, these women dancers become birds in flight and butterflies in transformation. The long fringe on their shawls is never allowed to touch the ground. The fringe comes alive with uplifting awareness of the Spirit World.

HER SONG

Sing With Birds was ready to dance for her Self.

The Eagle plumage in her braided hair added a softened honor to her morning shadow. Yellow and lavender bead work on her moccasins and shawl sparkled in the morning sun. This morning, it was Sing With Birds turn. Last night, she had danced for her brother, Evening Sky. Today, she would dance for herself.

So moving through the East entrance of the arbor, Sing With Birds stepped back into the dance. The guest drum played a good song and Sing With Birds remembered how Evening Sky had sung. The air was fresh. The grass, dewed. The sun, new.

Catching the beat as easily as Deer bounding at a moment's notice, the girl slid into the rhythm, fled into the moment, moved into the song. Sing With Birds remembered the good strong heartbeat that soothed her. Her beaded moccasins lightly touched Earth Mother. Her easy movements twirled her into the ones to follow. Returning to the gentle caress of her Mother's touch, Sing With Birds relaxed into the massage of Drum vibration, stepping lightly, dancing easily, moving quietly.

Then the beat quickened. Voices sang with great strength. The strong beat honored her.

Sing With Birds moved into her fast steps, as her Spring energy led into Summer steps. Her knees lifting, her shawl twirling, her fringes swaying, her steps touching. Sing With Birds knew her dance, like Wolf knows her run. Powerful, sustaining, timeless. Sing With Birds could feel her dance, like Eagle feels the wind. Lifting, changing, soaring. Sing With Birds became her dance, as Rose becomes the flower. Beautiful, opening, gifting.

She met the beat, excited to be alive, honored to be dancing. She met the song, hearing her brother's spirit, honoring his life. She greeted the day, seeing the beauty all around her.

Sing With Birds danced the Circle. Celebrating Life, She danced as agile Deer, flew with wings of Eagle, opened like Yellow Rose. Her face honored the new morning. Twirling and stepping, rising and shining, Sing With Birds danced. The birds sang, the sun warmed the dew, and the air was refreshed. She was the beat. Sing With Birds was the morning. She was the song.

The Fancy Shawl Dance reminds us to return to the energy of youth in order to remain in balance. What have you done lately to return you to the East and South Directions? East is the direction of sunrise and the color yellow, the new life of spring awakening from its deep winter sleep. What joy have you returned to? What needs to be awakened in you? South is the direction of summer, of exploding experimentation and invigorating growth spurts. What new growth have you? What twirling does your spirit need to do? Meet the fast beat with agility and balance! Allow your spiritual fringes to lift you high, up to your own personal transformation! Your wings will take you to greater heights! Once you have discovered your possibilities, put on your wings and fly!

Take this moment to re-identify the twirling your Spirit wants to do. What have you forgotten? What joy must you return to? If you don't know, recall what you used to enjoy doing. Take out the old records, for the songs hold your memories. Take out the old toys, for they hold your joy. Take out the colors, for they hold the color of your expression. You are never too old to enjoy, twirl, dance and sing!

WOMEN'S BUCKSKIN DRESS DANCE

Regal. Elegant. Dignified. Ageless. The Traditional Women's Buckskin Dress Dance honors all of Earth Mother. With the folded wool blanket and fringes cascading down her arms, this Traditional Dancer embraces world comfort to her heart. Wearing the skin of deer or elk, she honors the gift of another life. In her right hand she holds an Eagle Feather Fan and honors the Spirit World. Porcupine quills, cowrie shells, and elk teeth decorate her dress and the spirits of All dance alongside her on the Sacred Hoop. Wearing an Eagle Feather in her braided hair, she points to Ishpeming .

With the graceful beat of Mitakuye-Oyasin, the dancer holds her head high as she dips slightly. This repetitive up and down motion allows her fringes to sway to the rhythm of the Drum. Preventing the fringe from touching the ground, she acknowledges the Spirit World.

Fringes sway,
drawing your spirit in.
inviting you to join her journey
around the Circle.

Fringes sway.
Follow her regal steps, her dignified gate,
her deliberate understanding
of the strong beat.

Fringes sway.
Her eyes are certain. Her gaze is calm.
Looking to the horizon,
She sees clearly.

Fringes sway,
helping you see her poise.
Teaching her quiet dance,
her quiet way.

Fringes sway.
She dances an easy pace of peace.
Follow her steps and see
Fringes sway.

This dance style embodies pure connectedness. The fringes on the blanket sing of interdependence and ask us to join this dance. The feathers in her hair honor Mitakuye-Oyasin, honoring the winged brothers and sisters. Her adorned dress wears the spirits of all, and asks us to honor this truth.

Learn to wear Mitakuye-Oyasin in your daily attire. Honor all as you walk through life. Gift Namaji to all of our Brothers and Sisters. In this way, you honor yourself. How do you show that all that inhabits the earth is related? What fringes do you wear that speak with the silent movement of Mitakuye-Oyasin? How can you quietly wear the drumbeat of peace? Consider what you wear today, revealing how you feel inside. Does it speak of your commitment to your world? How do you honor Earth Mother with your clothing? Yet, we wear more than our clothes. We wear our inner world on our outer faces. What have you put on today? What does your face wear? Do you wear peace or strife? Hope or despair? Love or hate? Wear the robes of Namaji and honor Her, blend into her colors.

Look at Earth Mother's children. They have learned to blend with her. Walking Stick blends into Brother Tree. Grasshopper blends with Grass. Snake blends on Rock. Otter blends with Water. How do you blend with Earth Mother? What merging can you do? How can you become One with the Earth?

Become your truest Self and your walk will be as dignified, as graceful, as complimentary, as purposeful as the Woman Traditional Buckskin Dancer. Become walking trees, grass dancers, rock crawlers, and water ripplers. Like the traditional dancer, with Namaji, recognize your role on the Sacred Hoop of Life, dance, sing, and celebrate your Brothers and Sisters!

Women as Teachers

The Traditional Woman Dancer offers many teachings, for woman is the first teacher. In the beginning, Woman teaches the heartbeat of life, holding her baby both within her womb and encradled by her arms. Then teaching love, Woman teaches baby's first smiles. Listening and talking to her infant, she teaches sound and silence. Teaching patience, Woman gifts the child's language. Teaching acceptance, the listening is returned. And the heart beats strong.

Quietly, Woman teaches. By her example, we learn. Because of her acceptance, we believe. Through Woman's patience, we pause to wait. With her giving, we accept. Through her soft simplicity, the difficult is made easy. Because of her forgiveness, we also give. As Woman understands, we, too, learn. Follow her swaying fringes and discover what learning occurs within you. Honor Woman and her ways. Follow her teachings of give and take.

SACRED SISTERHOOD

Women Buckskin Dancers move in the same direction. Female energies are not interfered with, for there is no conflict. She dances her beautiful dance with pride. They dance together as One. Each dancer's sacred essence flows in the same direction, coming together in a stream of consciousness. Like a river dancing, this is Sacred Sisterhood. All become One.

Unlike the Sacred Sisterhood of tribal dances, much conflict and distrust threatens the Woman of today. Raised to nurse her insecurities, rather than nourish herself, she is always searching for self-sufficiency. Feelings of inadequacy control her moments. Competition poisons many of her relationships. Self-centeredness, comparison, fear, dependency and expectation, lure her decisions, plague her waking hours. Not being enough, not doing enough, not knowing enough, not having enough, haunt her dreams. Taught that she should be more, do more, know more and have more, Woman is not content with who she is. Insecurities evolve. Wanting safety, she tries to protect her fragile flower within, and grows her quills.

Like the delicate seed that protects its inside with its outside thorns, Woman must discover the kernel of beauty and growth that lies within her. Yielding to life's movements and trusting the world to provide the nourishment that is needed, the seed opens itself to become its destiny. Likewise, Woman must shed her piercing and unrealistic expectation of Self and judgment of others, for it distances her from relating to others. It distances Woman from becoming what she must. It distances her from the Spirit World of peace. With thorns still attached, Woman will remain guarded, distanced, and alone. Her sharp edges will isolate her from experiencing life.

Woman must listen and nourish herself. Opening up to Earth Mother, she will be able to reconnect to life itself and find the opening of her own shell. Here, in the safe comforting arms of Earth Mother, spiritual presence and spiritual freedom is close by. Here, Woman will see who and how she must become. She will understand what she must let go of, where she must plant herself.

MINKPAW

Minkpaw put tobacco down as she thinned out a cluster of wild roses, who were competing for root space and sunlight. She gently removed them from Earth Mother's cradle and placed them in her birch bark basket. Entering the woods, Minkpaw knew where she would take them.

The elder tree waited. Minkpaw walked through the woods thinking about her own recent decision to return here. It had been hard leaving the life she had known. Long nights had been her companion as she considered her choices. Finally, having made a list of both the benefits and the burdens, she had come to see that here was where she belonged. Here, in the comfort of the forest, Minkpaw was free to be herself. Where green and blue surrounded her, Minkpaw returned to her calm.

Reaching the old tree blending into forest floor, Minkpaw stood still, listening to the quiet, smelling the freshness, enjoying the solitude. With the opening out to Sky Father, and shade of Brother Trees, she smiled knowing that this place offered good growth. Gently lifting the rose plants from the basket, she noticed how roses' roots still were intact, ready to accept this gift. Although slightly injured, Minkpaw was certain the roses would soon sprout new growth.

Moving to her knees, the woman tenderly replanted the seedlings into the good rich peat of dignified elder tree. Patting the soil around the roses' roots, Minkpaw envisioned the growth. She knew that here, roses would be able to see and communicate with one another, yet not need to compete. Here in the comfort of woods, open to Grandfather Sun, roses would fulfill their own maternal instinct, spreading their seeds, enjoying their grand-children's future.

Minkpaw brushed off the good dirt from her knees, picked up the birch basket and thought of the path that had returned her to this place. Knowing that these roses were not wild, but free, Minkpaw followed the trail that led back to her home.

Woman must let the Four Directions bring her new winds of change. She must honor the Water Spirits cleansing and movement. If each separate water droplet tried to maintain its separateness and worked to be better than the next, lakes could not open, rivers could not flow and empty, oceans could not fill. Woman must feel the presence of Water Spirits, for there can be no natural flowing movement if one is trying to outdo another. I ask the Woman who now hears this, to trust Sister's swaying fringes, Sister direction, Sister connection and Sister honor.

I ask Woman to connect to Sacred Sisterhood. I ask you to honor these teachings.

Life is full of uncertainties. If we don't trust, we cut ourselves off from possible rewarding experiences. Full of ourselves, we miss the teachings of the Universe. Trust Sisterhood to offer the path ahead. Trust yourself to be good enough as you are. Trust Earth Mother to offer her teachings that all creation is sufficient.

JINGLE DRESS DANCE

The Jingle Dress Dance Style began with the Ojibwe in Wisconsin. The origin of this dance is very old and is based on a story about an Ojibwe Shaman's daughter who was very ill[3]. In a dream, the man was told his daughter would get well if she wore a dress that had a sea shell hanging from it for every day of the year. The medicine man did as he was told and created this dress for his daughter. She wore the dress and she was healed.

This Ojibwe Jingle Dress Dance has migrated to other tribes across the country. For within the regalia, the cycles, the seasons, her seasons, her cycles, are honored. A jingle for each day of the year reminds us of the circle of life, the circle of Earth Mother. As women traditionally do not wear bells, the tinkling sound of the shells has become a wonderful way to give voice to feminine celebration and joy. With braided hair and high beaded or sequenced moccasins, the steps in this dance are light and graceful.

Today, rolled up chewing tobacco tins replace the shells. The tins are sewed in a chevron design and the cones strike one another to create a pleasant and subtle tinkling sound.

THE SIDE STEP

The honor beats moved Winter Green to salute the Drum.[4] With her left hand on her hip and her right hand raising her feathered fan, Winter Green understood her dance. With her heels together, her short side step would take her around the Circle, would connect her spirit to the Spirit World.

Winter Green knew it was the little steps in life that mattered. They were the ones that counted, the ones that moved her life forward. Her tight form fitting dress reminded her of her straight up and down movement. Life would always go up and down, she thought, remembering

---

3   Stories may vary slightly.

4   The Side Step is a specific style that Jingle Dress Dancers are known for. Other Jingle Dress Dancers may dance in a similar fashion as the Fancy Shawl Dance.

the lessons. Each time she danced, Winter Green would reach something new. The Dance would teach her.

This time, it was the sound. Stepping to the rhythm of the Drum, the cones on her aqua-colored dress jingled in time with the drumbeat. It was like before, the sounds were the same. Yet this time, Winter Green was different. She listened with different ears. Like a mother hearing her baby's cry, Winter Green heard her sound amongst all the sounds that encircled her. Staying with it, she listened only to her cones tingling. They rang into her, touching her heart, her spirit. Vibrating, the jingles made her unique sound. The sound from her heart.

Suddenly, Winter Green understood that the song of the waterfall began with the Spirit of the Creator. The sound of the forest began in the Heart of the Seed-Carrier. The melody of the universe begins with the Song of the Singer. That the pounding of her heart begins with the Beat of the Drummer. The tinkling sound filled Winter Green with joy and called the Spirits to join her celebration. The jingles had honored her.

Again, the honor beats sounded and Winter Green's feathered fan arched her tribute to the Drum. As though gliding across ice, Winter Green's whole foot moved her to the next moment. As she shifted sideways, she honored the clouds overhead that mirrored her movement. Not in a hurry to get there, Winter Green effortlessly journeyed around the Sacred Circle, in love with the sound of herself.

Here in the now, she was the channel between Earth Mother and Sky Father. Winter Green rooted, reached, and saluted both directions. Jingling her distinct sound, she offered her Self.

WOMEN'S ASSERTIVENESS

The Jingle Dress Dance sounds women's presence. Like Winter Green, women must be able to sound their intentions. Acquaint yourself with who you are and what you believe your purpose is. Practice the skills of stepping into life, inch by inch, and you will go far. Listen to your own jingles. Hear your own song.

Effectively communicating, your presence can be known and experienced throughout the world. Be open, honest, direct, calm and specific in your communication. Become comfortable with who you are.

Learn from Tree. Tree is neither passive nor aggressive. Tree is assertive and yields her sap to root level in winter and asserts herself in summer growth. Like Tree, discover the yielding, the timing, the knowing, the sensitivity needed in order to fully become.

Learn to yield. Yielding is not being passive. It is being sensitive to energy flows and extending wisdom. Allow the winds of change to flow through you, rather than against you. Be flexible with what is happening today. Yield to the circumstance, yet rooted with who you are. What do you need to yield to?

Discover the wisdom of timing. Honor the seasons of your growth. Do not rush your growth. Do not dismiss the urge to develop. Be present. Grow and become naturally. Recognize the forces and opportunities that encourage you to be yourself in the moment. Experience the joy of growing into your vision. Allow time to flow through your inner core, budding the life within. Respond when appropriate. Make wise decisions in the now.

Know who you are and what your purpose is. What is your vision of yourself? Who do you see yourself becoming? Understand your abilities and tendencies. Acquaint yourself with what is around you. What environment would nurture your growth? What hinders you or distracts you from your vision? Like Tree, exercise circular thinking. Tree grows inside, out. How can you grow upward and outward? Grow into a balanced view, extending all around, and you will be prepared to offer your gifts of shade, strength, and beauty to those you encounter.

Appreciate and honor your gift of sensitivity. Do not discard this gift. Sensitivity heals. Assertiveness is not brutal, it is sensitive. It is not an automatic "yes" either. Recognize when "no" and "yes" is appropriate, become sensitive to what is needed. Insert the word "no" into your vocabulary. Learn to use this word without guilt. "No" can strengthen your understanding, assisting you to set limits and boundaries, as all trees shape themselves to a defined maximum height and width.

SPIRITUAL IN THE NOW

Stay in the present. Honor each small step in life, for as they accumulate they move you forward on your journey. Life is a journey. Honor your journey, for the journey is your direction. Honor your direction, for it points to the most meaningful views of yourself. Discover your own sunrise and sunset. Move with clouds to the next moment and like Winter Green, you will reflect peace as you sound your joy.

Return to the shade of the Pines, and like Winter Green, you will root strong and grow with your own unique fragrance. Allow Earth Mother to nourish you, as a woman, as a person, as a Spirit. Discover your connection with all who have taken this path before you. May your roots understand your connection. Let Earth Mother remind you of who you are and which direction you are taking.

Look for the moccasin tracks of your ancestors who have walked this path. Come to know that you are not alone in your values, choices and decisions. A sense of belonging is good medicine.

Be the empty channel through which the Creator swifts Spiritual currents. Flow with, not against the current of Love. The Creator has needs, too. Writers and singers, builders and healers, teachers and students, talkers and walkers, are needed by the Creator to fulfill the purpose of the Universe. Claim your talent!

Iron Legs, from White Earth Ojibwe Reservation, once said to me, "I'm not a talker. I'm a walker." Walking from coast to coast, this Elder and his walking shoes, understands that each step counts. His walking has brought attention to his values. His commitment to action says more than all the words in this book. These words mean nothing unless you and I experience them, and transform them into action. We must not just talk the talk, we must also, walk the walk, and dance the dance!

These words are written with the prayer that we will find ways to experience them and transform them into action. Walk these words with your little side steps to life. Learn from Crab's side-step actions. Your mind is about as flexible as your body is. Become able to walk through life with side-steps, as well as forward, and knowing when to step back. You will then be able to take a circular approach to life. For a circular approach is in harmony with the Universe.

Stay with the present, with what is happening now. Discover the celebration of calling in the Spirits with the sound of your own joy! Root in to Earth Mother, reach out to Sky Father, honor both worlds and offer your best! I can't wait to hear the beautiful tinkling of your jingles!

SISTER CEDAR'S GIFTS

A Spirit came and talked to me
and said I must go find
Sister Cedar's giving Self
or I would lose all that is mine.

So I left that night and heard a voice
tell me where to go
I searched the narrow valley near
the river's overflow.

There was not much to guide me, though,
just a green-laced curtain wall.
I could not see beyond its hands,
its branches were so tall.

So I left the valley and traveled to
a mountain for me to climb.
I heard an echo of a flute,
Its melody - so fine.

But Sister Cedar wasn't there
and I was overwhelmed.
Would I just cease - no longer be?
For she wouldn't show her Self.

I traveled to the deep dark woods
but could not see a thing.
Just sweet smells of something near
reminding me of Spring.

So I pleaded with the Spirit
to help me find the way
Where Sister Cedar sings her songs
Her home, of night and day.

She had not left, for in my dream
I saw her trunk and root.
Within her growing locks of hair
Spirit offered me her flute.

And beyond her reaching, giving arms,
She invited me to climb
the soft green branches I had seen,
Her view, another time.

Her smooth perfume of Springtime Woods
encircled me with scent.
Sister Cedar was always there, I found,
no matter where I went.

"I was the wood you burned last night,
the home for Brothers' nest,
I am the shade you sat beneath.
It was me who gave you rest."

"But you did not know my Spirit,"
said Sister, to me, clear,
"And now it is time to take away
all that you hold so near."

I bowed my head in open shame
for not knowing Sisterhood,
and waited for the certain pain
of her vow, but I misunderstood...

For, Spirit took away my shame,
Spirit took my sadness, too.
Spirit took my fears, my limitations,
and filled me all anew.

I became the song. I became the view.
I became the scent of Spring.
Sister filled me till overflowing
With her Cedar offering.

SNAKE DANCE

Friend on the Red Road, may I enter your skin.
For your spiral trails whisper my journey within.
Friend on the Red Road, may I shed my skin.
For your clear view of life shows where I begin.

Snake has often been an innocent victim of humanity's judgment, prejudice and suspicion, when really Snake simply wants to coexist. Snake's inherent warrior skills that developed to protect self, have been misjudged. Snakes attack humans only when they are frightened or threatened.

Our long slender friend sadly reminds us that society often favors the rights of the perpetrator rather than protecting and defending the victim[1]. As a victim of people's fears, misunderstanding, exploitation and dominance, Snake has endured many life cycles of other's loathing. It is time to honor Snake for his unique purpose, teachings, and patterns of beauty. It is time to see Snake as Snake. No more, no less. Snake deserves this light of truth.

Like Snake, tribal people have been victimized. Now, with minorities becoming the majority, a great segment of the dominant society is being victimized by greed, fear, crime, and misunderstandings of the world in which they live.

---

[1] Headlines are full of cases where today's criminal is protected and even supported, while the victim is further injured economically and emotionally. The brutal exploitation of conquerors were conveniently "translated" into heroic feats to be glorified. Victims have been disgraced by this extensive deception and massive fear of the truth. Whose rights should be favored? The perpetrator or the victim?

Through the lessons of Snake, may we open ourselves to the truth of Mitakuye-Oyasin and the vital role each member plays.

The Snake Dance is a celebration of our life's journey. It is a profound teaching of Self and the World. As we dance from the East to the North, we are reminded of what it means to be here on Earth Mother, participating in this dance of life. Rich with meaning, the Snake Dance offers understandings of life and death, of choices and direction, of the Drum and of Creation. Follow the Four Directions of the Spirit, as the story of living is honored. May the Snake Dance open you to the possibilities of coexistence, of cooperation, of life and of death. May Snake offer you a path of honor and teach you of yourself.

NIGHT BIRD

Night Bird's eyes searched the darkened sky. Journeying the endless possibilities, his eyes followed the constellations to where each one led. And like picking a special, succulent berry from among the many, his spirit selected, reached, embraced, and merged with one unique star. Remembering the stories he had heard of the Star World[2], his heart and spirit followed the meanings his chosen star taught him. He would dance his first Snake Dance, believing and trusting that tonight's journey would gift him the knowledge of the Star People.

The beat began. Shadows moved across the dance arbor. Except for the soft beat and eagle bustles whispering, bells and jingles gently singing, all dancers were quiet. Night Bird's moccasins softly moved him to join the dancers. Like a fine mist, anticipation spread through each dancer, covering the night air with mystery. Self-secrets guided in each dancer. Night Bird was swept into the circle of colors,

---

[2] It has been said that the stars represent all thoughts. The Creator sent the stars forth as he searched for a place to put life. The knowledge of the Creator is endless, as are the stars. Therefore, if you are to seek knowledge, you would have to know every star. The Star World lodges the Seven Grandfathers (powerful spirits) who watch over Earth's people. Their gifts of wisdom, love, respect, bravery, honesty, humility, and truth reflect their brilliance in the night sky.

feathers, skins, ribbons, fringes, bells, and jingles. Without words, this dance would tell the story of each. With Mash-ka-wisen, all would face their circle of life and death.

Entering this remembering, the two honored dancers respectfully led the long rhythmic group of dancers into the Great Circle, as head of the Snake. Hundreds of dancers coiled into position as one great system. Pulsing, vibrating, touching, their spirits joined in a colorful design in the darkened circle. Like one long vibrating snake, the dance began. This circular mix of moving colors swirled together, their movements coloring the dance, the shadows following their movements.

Winding around this Great Mystery, the long snake of dancers coiled around the very center of timelessness—the Drum. The beat of life. Eternal and ever present. Night Bird heard his own heart pounding inside. Reaching to connect to the Great Spirit's Drum, his steps were soft, his movement fluid, his posture proud. Wrapped and protected with the support of those around him, Night Bird's feathers supported his silent spirit, dancing him into becoming.

His dancing joined his companions. In the lifting of his moccasin, he was aware of each dancer's separate journey. In his soft steps, his life became part of a weaving, joining all others on the Hoop of Life.

Coiling out of the East, the group of dancers spiraled into the beginning, honoring the sacred power of birth. In the darkness, Night Bird recalled when he had returned to his people on the reservation, like an infant, just four years ago. He had arrived home, broken, unsure, separated, self-absorbed. Searching for himself, he found tribal tradition. Looking for a new way, he discovered old age wisdom. A light fog slowly settled in and Night Bird could only see that which was near him. Now, as he healed and danced, he began to understand that there are many answers yet to discover, many questions yet to ask. Within this soft cloud, Night Bird entered the tunnel of truth. He now danced with courage, that he might see in this misting darkness.

The Spirit of Snake called to him, like a song remembered, enticing the dancer with memories of his beginning. Like a helpless baby, Night Bird remembered his thick dependency. Like a snake coiled up, motionless, he glimpsed his infant view, heard his infant tongue, listened with infant ear, and touched with infant limits. Dancing with a strong remembering, Night Bird had watched others' steps, he had learned the dances, the movements, the ways, the stories. And Night Bird honored the East.

The head dancers led the colorful snake to unravel its long, lean, cylindrical body into a beautiful moving pattern, while the dancers' spirits remained joined. Beautifully moving, Snake slithered into the beat. The fog slowly cleared and like evening ocean waves, rhythmic regalia followed the lead dancers to a sea of understanding.

Night Bird vibrated in his own wave of sound and movement, as he united with the S-shaped ribbon-line of dancers, looping and curving across the arena. The unwinding dancers completely uncoiled, as the rhythm vibrated into the secrets of each dancer, unveiling them, discovering them, entering them.

Like each dancer around him, Night Bird separated and danced in his own personal circle, journeying <u>South</u>. Here, Night Bird rooted to Earth Mother, to soak in Her nourishment. Remembering Her, he honored Her gifts. She had healed him with Her gentle winds. She had soothed him with Her warm sands. She had honored him with Her beautiful views. She had remembered him in Mishomis' heat of the sweat lodge. And then his frenzied dancing of the South direction began.

The Snake shook with enormous energy. Night Bird recalled how quickly the teachings of his tribe had filled him in his sobriety. The learning had rushed in, like a michi-zee-bee[3], making his blood rush with passion!

Now, Night Bird spun in a circle, his body shaking. In a matter of moments, he embodied the memories of the turbulent emotions of early recovery. His arrogance emptied into regrets for the decisions that had hurt his family. Recognizing and being responsible for his mistakes, Night Bird let go of the past, and spun into the excitement of a new future.

With rapid spins, he soon caught up to his new identity. Still whirling, his vision became new as he worked to acquire balance.

All so fast! All so powerful! All so recent!

Night Bird intimately understood this direction of innocent and misdirected youth. He had returned to encircle the Hoop, to gather the nourishment of the South direction. And Night Bird honored the South.

The song slowed, leading the head dancers into the <u>West</u> of their spirits. The dark sky reminded each of their beginning and end. The pulse slowed to carry each into their heart. Night Bird followed and the dancing became less erratic, more thoughtful. The shades of unique color were no longer blurred. Each dancer's shape became clear once again.

The head dancers led the line of relatives West. Dancers steps became serious, their movement deliberate. Snake stilled. Night Bird relaxed into the unknown. The Great Mystery of his life—the addiction, the pain, the surrender and the healing— joined all the dancers into the Grand Web

---

3   Pronounced: MICH-ee-ZEE-bee and means greatest river.

of Mitakuye-Oyasin. From the West there must be the mystery. Contemplating Snake, Night Bird knew he must also live close to the ground like his brother. Slowing to feel the quiet spirits of the present, Night Bird embraced the sacredness in all things commonplace. The world around him would became his teacher.

Like light seeping in from the edges, Night Bird's circular vision brought all realms of possibility. The stars overhead sprinkled in their understanding. Night Bird saw the shadows of his past encircle the drum. Each beat gave Night Bird the courage to observe and feel it all, the pain he had both endured and inflicted on others. Growing into and accepting his movements, his direction became clear. Maturing even as he danced, Night Bird's vision widened. Suddenly, Grandmother Moon was visible behind some clouds. Looking down on the family of dancers below, the Stars and Moon smiled and reflected their light on the backs of the moving Snake.

The path opened in front of him and Night Bird saw his past choices, his future, his gifts, his honor. Understanding he was all of this, both the light and the dark, Night Bird was prepared for his next step. He was prepared to be Snake. And he honored the West.

The head dancers led the group to the <u>North</u>. Like Snake, it was time for Night Bird to shed his own skin, to leave his past behind, to crawl out into a new future.

Night Bird's movements followed the dancers in front of him and slowed. A feeling of great excitement contained within each dancer, oozed out into the darkness. Night Bird's pace eased so that each step joined his quiet heart, the deliberate drumbeat, the present moment. And in this keen awareness of Self. Where thought no longer demands attention, Night Bird began to surrender his limitations.

Like two visions focusing into one, the spiritual and physical worlds began to merge. Meaning was reborn. The rhythm carried Night Bird to the middle way, the Red Road. Shedding the anger that had once poisoned his emotions, he took the first step out of his old self. Molting into his own experience, Night Bird was aware of the other hundred skins being shed around him. Casting off the control that had once intoxicated his mind with a sense of false power, he empowered himself with another true step toward a new life. Discarding the apathy that threatened to slip his spirit back into his old addicted self, he moved further into Earth Mother's lap. Slipping out of his old body, Night Bird was experiencing a beautiful rebirth. Shape-shifting with others in this Snake Celebration, he honored the North.

The singers voices lifted all into the heights of the evening sky, higher and higher. The mystery was at hand. Night Bird was nearly free of himself, free from hate, free from fear, free from both good and bad. Approaching the sacred tree limb that had been carefully placed across the dancer's circle, all watched to honor this young man's journey.

This was his moment!

Dancing with all the energy of his Spirit, Night Bird's regalia fluttered, ready to fly. Twirling into all directions at once, his dancing vibrated and quickened. Lifting his feathered fan with Namaji, he honored all that had helped him reach this River of Life. Night Bird felt the pull to cross into the Spirit World, to shed his life, to enter a new form. Then, as though crawling completely out of his skin, Night Bird shook himself free! Pausing in silence, his regalia stilled. For a brief moment, there was no sound, no movement. Then, with a great cry of triumph, the man jumped over the tree of life!

Night Bird turned and the stars twinkled in the mirrors of his regalia, to remind him of who he once was. And he was grateful, thanking Snake for this dance. With a breath of love and respect, Night Bird turned to honor the next dancer's moment, feeling whole, centered, balanced and complete.

And Snake moved on.

COILED EAST

Snake teaches us that we exit the Spirit World and enter this physical dimension through birth, the East door of life. Some snakes enter this world as an egg in a shell. Other snakes leave the Spirit World similar to us, from the door of one's mother. The mother's door is both symbolic and literal, and its dual nature begs us to look inward to where we came from.

What is on the other side of the mother's door? What does the door swing into? Follow your physical birth back to the womb, and you will be led to the tiny coiled egg you once were, and finally to the genetic memory of that which you would become. This is the memory that we have forgotten. For what we previously accepted as the beginning, is really only the beginning of a memory. What have you forgotten? Where did you begin? Just like baby snakes shed their outer layer of skin after birth, we, too, shed our remembrance of the Spirit World when we entered this physical dimension. Once we have passed through this door, it swings shut. Eventually the door completely closes unless we are willing to return to the East, to our "beginning." At rare times we are offered a momentary memory of the other side. This is meditation—the listening, the opening to this dimension.

Just as Snake initially took a coiled position and remained motionless, as infants, our motion was also restricted. Each of us was bound by our infant limitations and depended upon our mother for survival. Mother was our umbilical cord to the Spirit World from which we came. Mother's milk and care nurtured and nourished us until we could become more mobile and less restricted, until our forgetting was complete. The beginning coil of the Snake Dance represents this embryonic stage, the 'forgetting,' and the eventual worldly replacement of our experiences. From infancy to age six, nearly 90% of our adult

personality patterns are defined and developed. Our physical scales are pat-
terned with a new view of reality, replacing the memories of the Spirit World.

Ironically, our outer world view has been shaped by an internal urge to
return to the door of our memories. Like water that rushes to discover its
beginning, we search to remember our essence, who we are meant to be.
Rocks obstruct and challenge water's direction. Winding tributaries lead
water to diverse places. Cold winds freeze and prevent it from moving.
Likewise, personal conflicts (rocks), distractions (tributaries), and demands
(cold winds) deter us from our journey back home. Only when water pauses
long enough, becoming a still pool of meditation, does it allow the Sacred
Circle to transform it back into vapor. Then water recognizes its true essence.

Many of us may not be willing to slow down to this remembrance, so a
constricted life view may develop. This view will be perceived through
mental filters[4]. Compensatory behaviors and attitudes shade and color our
personal version of reality as we experience it. Whatever we experience in
our inner world reality—joy, frustration, sadness, fear, hurt and other emotions—develops from our interpretation of our external circumstances. One
child falls down and cries, experiencing more discomfort than wonder.
Another child falls down and gets back up, experiencing greater wonder in
the experience than discomfort. Given the same situation, two people will
interpret it very differently. For, like water, their understandings has followed
different tributaries of life.

The coiling represents the dependency of childhood, the urge to grow into
itself, the innocence of recent forgetting, and the joy of trying to remember.
This stage of life is our personal shading of reality, from the colors and
textures we have both been given and have chosen.

Take this time, now, to slow down into the still waters of yourself. Allow
yourself to forget what you have recently learned. Let the rocks be there. Let
the moving waters rush past. Let the warm winds free you. Recognize there
is no place you must go. Follow your breath to the place of peace. In the
gentle breath of your quiet self, return to the door of the East. Circle back to

---

4   Known also as defense mechanisms.

your spiritual essence. It is here, in the peace of knowing, that you will remember what you have long forgotten. And the door to your beginning will open once more. Peer within and know your essence. You are loved and connected.

FRENZIED SOUTH

The frenzied twirls of the Snake Dance represent the southern direction of adolescence[5]. In the flurry of life, discover what gifts you gather as you dance into the South. Carry your essence across the continent as you learn about your power. Celebrate the youthful energy of the South Direction!

Adolescence, the transition between childhood and adulthood, is temporary for most people. The erratic spinning in the Snake Dance eventually dissipates before the dancer loses his balance and falls from exhaustion and dizziness. The psychological, emotional and physical turmoil of adolescence are times for rehearsal, experimentation, and the collection of your identity. Here, peers are sought out for validation. The fancy spinning and dancing is performed for their approval. Conformity is paramount. As Snake shifts direction, from side to side, the shifting of adolescence (from child to adult and adult to child) expresses this transitional life phase. Accept this in self and others as part of the dance to the South. Just as you expect snake to shift in its path, expect adolescents to frequently change their directions (and moods), for that is the way of the South.

The real challenge of this phase of life is the movement through it. Twirling with hormonal preoccupation, most adolescents would prefer to have privileges without the accompanying responsibilities. It is the responsibility of their families and community to help adolescents balance their privileges with accountability. It is our job to remind them of their path. A definite transition needs to be enacted, either in the form of ritual or a meaningful passage. In this way, the adolescent will be able to accept and adjust to the changes happening within.

---

5   Adolescence has often been described as 'hormones with feet!'

An adolescent recently told me, "The only thing you have to do in life is.... live!" In her maturation, she has come to understand the distinct beat of life. "Living" is much more than breathing. The Snake Dance points to the balance needed in order to fully live. Physical, emotional, mental, and spiritual balance must be practiced by both young and old—adolescents and adults—in order to fully live. Without this balance, one is merely pretending to live fully.

The South is the direction of change, growth, and passion. Take time, now, to dance! Twirl with your own excitement! Giggle! Honor the passionate growth that yearns to take place in you! Discover what you have yet to learn. Take on a new project, discover a new talent or interest, and rush into its power and passion with the energy of an adolescent! Here is the twirling secret of youth!

DIRECTIVE WEST

A more deliberate, focused pattern emerges as the dance of adulthood is approached. Like a mountain peak in the distance, West is a stabilizing point of reference. The dancer's perspective moves from the infantile "me" to the co-existing "We." As "life" has previously been experienced, West is the time to understand "living." West is a time of great internal insights. Emotional and spiritual questions beg for resolution, but instead of answers, more questions emerge. This is the time of depth and darkness, the night of the spirit.

At the western point in the dance, the movement becomes less erratic and more directive. The dancer is offered the lesson of living close to the ground like Brother Snake. The dancer will return to Earth Mother's vibration in order to find comfort inside the dark. Work to be grounded in nature's realities[6]. Adulthood is a time to discover your unique purpose. Let the world be your teacher. Open up to not-knowing. Then you will be able to see your place in the universe. Celebrate the Great Mystery of Life!

---

6   Consider the benefit if the bureaucrats in Washington would trade places with the park people for a week or two. What effect would sleeping on the ground, engaging Earth Mother's vibrations and the Star People's energies have? Upon their return to Congress, they might have a renewed sense of reality—based on fact rather than fiction. I'm sure a new set of environmentally favorable laws would soon be forthcoming and a sense of "We"-ness rather than "me"-ness would prevail.

The dance of the adult takes on a deliberate cadence and direction, harmonious in its movement. The frenzied-ness of adolescence unwraps into a more planned, patient presence. Exercise your patience. Exercise your presence. Be deliberate in your daily movements and choices. Tap your Mashka-wisen in order to face your fears and weaknesses. In this stage of the dance, the dancer is in complete awareness of all that is going on inside and outside of him/her.

Like the dancer, during adulthood you need to become self-determined, self-directed, self-motivated, and self-sufficient. You need to be able to validate yourself as living your life in accordance with your self-designed aspirations. Honor the great possibilities and choices you have each day. As an adult, you are a free spirit, living your life rather than deferring to someone else's expectations of you.

Practice reflecting throughout your day. Become aware of everything you do. Often we live without this awareness. As you walk down your path, return to healthy self-consciousness. Expand this to include others on your path and the path itself. Notice the way your foot steps down on the grass. Move with deliberate intention. Become aware of how your body feels, the wind on your face, your relaxed posture. Notice the colors around you, the earth beneath you, the clouds above you, the experience inside you. Become aware of all that is you and surrounds you. Challenge yourself to notice the unnoticeable. See what you can see. Hear what is present. Expand your experience to include all that is present in the now! You will be astounded by all that you have been missing! There is much to honor as you journey through this life.

Honor your own steps of the West.

REFLECTIVE NORTH

The branch placed across the Dance Circle at the Northern point represents the River of Life that we will be required to cross as we return to the Spirit World. At this time in the dance, we reach our Elder state and our body movements are slowed. For as we become older, we acquire more mass and experience less physical energy.

As Snake prepares to rid himself of his old layer of skin, he loosens the scales at the front end of the body, along his lips[7]. Crawling completely out of his skin, Snake sheds a transparent, colorless skin. This transparent, discarded skin reminds us that our life is colorless in the beginning, and that "We" are the paint brush that colors our lives with our choices and decisions. Be careful what actions, choices, and decisions you make, for they will determine your passage.

As you cross the River of Life and leave your physical skin behind in order to return to the spiritual realm, know that you are ultimately responsible to only two entities: yourself and your Creator. We will all enter the Spirit World, shedding our transparent skin, naked for review.

The final step and vocal expression of the dancer declares that there is no death. Like the rising of the sun, to its setting, life and death are simply a change of form. The Eternal Circle only exists. Death and Life are opposite sides of the same reality, just as sunrise and sunset balances the East and the West.

What do you want to take with you to the Spirit World? What can you take with you? What is your vision? What is your dream? These are very important questions to ask now, before the River of Life urges you to cross its waters.

As this life is both a physical and a spiritual journey, your challenge is to honor both worlds in your daily choices and actions. What do you want to accomplish in your life? How do you want to live? Have you thought about this? Can you put yourself into the North Direction of the Snake Dance, for this moment? Can you look back on the life you have not yet lived? Like the sensitive tongue of Snake, use this vision of the North in order to determine your future and your past.

What memories, experiences and emotions do you want to take with you when you go back to the Spirit World? What do you want to give through your

---

7   Just as Snake sheds its skin, birds molt feathers, animals shed fur, and people shed their skin every month, learn to shed your 'shoulds' and the old patterns and beliefs that are no longer of any benefit.

life while you are here? What do you want to take from life? What do you want to leave behind? How will you be remembered? How will you be honored?

What death must you die in this life in order to move on? What must you surrender? What habits and behaviors must you shed? What direction must you move in order to live life fully as a balanced individual? What shoulds must you shed?

Native American tradition teaches us that the Spirits will recognize us by our Indian name when we return to the Spirit World. What name will you be recognized by? Will it be Giver or Taker? Will you be known as "Me" or "We?" Your opportunity is now, to determine your future. The choices are always yours, as your free will is the most precious gift you have to offer. How will your free will translate once you have arrived on the other distant shore? Will it be translated as Abuse or Namaji? Can you approach your Creator and relatives with your head up, clear eyes and clean hands? Proud to have walked life's path?

SUN TRAIL

A small band of people had been growing weak, as the buffalo where they hunted were now scarce. After a long futile day of searching for food, the hunters gathered around the white teepee at the far end of the encampment. The white teepee stood out from all the rest, not because of its painted Sky symbols, but for its occupant, who was known for his wise decisions.

Approaching Big Cloud's home, the small band knew they would now need to travel to find food. Together they would look to Big Cloud for his direction. All knew his heart listened well to the world.

"Big Cloud, come out and join us. We need to know your mind," said one member to the skinned teepee.

Big Cloud pushed the flap aside to join the people who gathered near his lodge. The big man was larger than two of the others. Tall and broad, his height moved him further out to Sky Father.

"I have seen Golden Eagle, Ganu today," he finally spoke. "Let us hear our Brother's mind." Then Big Cloud went back inside his lodge.

The next day Golden Eagle appeared as the small band traveled south. As young boys shouted the news, the group stopped to watch Ganu circle overhead. Four times the Golden Eagle hooped above them. Big Cloud stood silently and watched until finally Eagle flew into the sunset.

"That was no message from our Brother," spoke one who was in a hurry to continue on their old path.

"Brother Eagle only came to give us his approval," agreed another. "I say we continue on."

Big Cloud honored their voices as his own and made their words his. "Your ideas are good. Yet, perhaps there is more to the circle flight of our brother. What was his mind in the hoop?"

"Yes. Let us not forget the four winds on which he rode," said another, encouraged by Big Cloud's observations.

All sat around the circle listening with open hearts. "But Ganu disappeared into the darkness," the first one reminded the group. "What could be the reason for such a direction?"

"The Great Mystery asks us all to journey to the dark places," Big Cloud answered his brother. "It is here where the light is born."

"Then the sunset is our destination!" realized one.

"Golden Eagle is our guide," agreed them all.

So the small band shifted their course to the West, crossing rivers and hills to a place they could not see, loyal to the Red Road, loyal to the golden Eagle. The group remained on the Sacred Path, until one day they met others who were also following the sun trail.

"Boozhoo," greeted Big Cloud. "If you are going the way of the Sun, you are welcome to join us."

And so in this way, year after year, the small band grew in number as they continued on their trail. Strong bonds were made. Good fun was shared. Time caused their teepees to fray and frazzle, but their tattered lodges were quickly mended. Together the growing family continued on their way.

One morning, the group awoke to find Big Cloud's teepee empty. Loving him so, the now large band of travelers searched the hills and the rivers, but Big Cloud was not there. Hundreds of hearts searched the forest and the path behind them, but no one could find Big Cloud. There was no sign of the big man. The prints of Sky symbols on his yellowed teepee were fading.

That night, as all prepared for sleep, a visiting ball of white light was seen leaving the sun trail, moving to the Milky Way. The next morning, the large band of travelers put tobacco down and respectfully left the teepee of Big Cloud behind and continued to move on to where the sun sets.

EXTEND NAMAJI TO ALL

The Snake Dance teaches that we must honor all. From the birds to the fish, the animals to the plants, the minerals to the crawlers, the water to the sky, our dance of life must be lived with Namaji for all... for all honors us.

Like snake, get on your belly and feel the vibrations that travel through Earth Mother's soil. Discover your connection to the world. Honor the sacred in all and elevate the essence of each to their rightful place of honor. Learn to look at the world as "We." To do this will forever change you. It will forever change your world.

See the sacred in all—the "We" in all—and you will have come to understand the very essence of the Snake Dance. You will embody Mitakuye-Oyasin. You will be a living example of Namaji. When you move through the day, move with the dance of snake. Take Snake with you on your journeys. In this way you will come to honor the beginning of life, the energy of youth, the awareness of self, and your spiritual journey to wisdom. With "We" in the forefront of your mind, every day, you cannot help but gravitate to a higher state of consciousness. Here, you will change. Here, you will influence others by your very essence.

Take the mind of Snake and you will be sure Earth Mother's soil is kept clean. Take the journey of Snake and you will understand your purpose in this life. Shed like Snake and you will leave behind that which no longer serves you. Feel with the senses of Snake and you will see with your heart the beauty that cannot be experienced by your physical senses.

In the extension of Namaji, you will extend your Spirit. In the giving of Namaji, you gift yourself. In the experience of Namaji, you become Namaji and all becomes sacred.

THE RED ROAD OF THE SNAKE DANCE

Like Night Bird, as you prepare to cross the River Of Life may you discover that you have been carried along its current all the while. As Life is fragile, come to see we are always near death. We do not realize just how close the River is, until the Wind Spirits splash us personally with the directions of life. Look and see that at any moment you may enter the River of Life to cross to the other side.

The Red Road is the path of the Snake Dance. Like the color of our blood, the Red Road reminds us to honor the life that flows through our spiritual veins. It is this same River of Life that offers all that we need to live. As you cross to the other side, like Night Bird, you will turn to see the path you have chosen. May it be the Red Road, the path of freedom, moderation, balance, and Namaji. Stay with this direction and your destiny will be positive and fulfilling.

The Red Road is the Sacred Path for living in harmony with the natural order. Flow with nature, rather than resisting it. Stay with the River. Follow the course. Honor the turns. Stay on the Red Road. It is the narrow path between dark and light, that neither enters virtue nor evil, but views both sides clearly. From here you will discover the infinite possibilities, for the source of timeless Creator energy is in the center of the Medicine Wheel.

Flow with the River of Life. Walk the Red Road. Live with Namaji. Dance and celebrate! And your growth will equal your service to others. Like Brother Tree, grow inside up. Grow out to the Four Directions. Root in to Earth Mother. Extend out to Sky Father. And travel in to your Self. Your journey here will prepare you to cross the River of Life.

The Snake Dance creates confusion in those who think they know and understand life's course. Let go of what you think you know and understand. Experience the moment of the dance. Flow with the energy of the River. Dance the path of the snake. Enter Snake's skin. Let Snake teach you the lessons of life and death, the Sacred Hoop, the seven directions of your journey, and of your connection to it all. Befriend Snake and you will be a friend to ALL.

DANCE THE CIRCLE

PART FOUR

THE HOOP DANCE

"See far around you," says an Ojibwe Elder.

THE SACRED HOOP

One Circle. One word. One vision. One truth.

Native American tradition honors the Circle, for here lies the secret of life itself, the spirit of the Creator. The Hoop Dance is about the Circle. The Sacred Hoop is the circumference of the Medicine Wheel, a healing symbol of balance[1].

We live above circles, beneath circles, within circles, through circles. Earth Mother, Grandfather Sun, Grandmother Moon, and the Stars are all circular. The seasons are cyclical. The water cycles. Life carries us around the Sacred Hoop. The Seven Directions point to the circular way of life.

All dualitys are constant companions on the Hoop of Life. One merges into the other, and back again. Life blends into death. Death blends into life. Day circles into night. Night circles into day. Separation and connection are constant companions, as are emptying and filling. The circle joins all cycles, balancing each energy, so that all becomes one. Never ending, never beginning, the Sacred Hoop is the vision of Eternity.

---

1   For more information on the Medicine Wheel, see *Listen to the Drum: Blackwolf Shares his Medicine* and *The Healing Drum*.

The Sacred Hoop reminds us of the visible cycles of each day. It also symbolizes our connection to the invisible cycles, as the circumference of the Hoop circles an invisible center. The Sacred Hoop represents the eternal configuration of the Creator. It constantly renews itself. The Hoop Dance is a way to honor this understanding.

Originated with the Great Lakes Tribes, the Hoop Dance is a specialty dance[2]. No two people dance the Hoop Dance exactly alike. Dancing to the beat of the drum, the dancer's vision of the Sacred Hoop is expressed through the intricate designs created by his/her body and many flexible hoops[3]. Like fish that swim through kelp and algae without getting tangled, the agile Hoop Dancer flows through the hoops, understanding the need to honor that which has become an extension of their experience. The Hoop Dance is a dance of Namaji, for all is honored, all is taken into consideration within the hoops of this dance.

Using his or her entire body, the Sacred Hoops are embraced with the dancer's entire Self. The dancer reveals the possibilities of the hoops, honors all with the intricate designs, acknowledges the connections of all life and the truth of the Sacred Hoop. As the dance begins, the dancer carries in one hoop. Gradually picking up more and more hoops, the dancer weaves his understandings of life, patterns, and movement within the dance. In the end, the dancer is literally covered from head to foot in many hoops—covered with the vision, the truth, the spirit of the Creator.

ECHO-MAKER

It had rained.

It had rained and the rain had brought it all inside. The dancing, the drumming, the singing, the spirits, were all inside. Inside a big building, where the wooden floor was no longer the Earth, where the cement canopy was no longer a tree-laced sky. Inside. Separated from the green

---

[2] Both men and women may dance this beautiful dance. It is danced by one person, while others watch.

[3] The hoops are approximately 2-3 feet in diameter, made of a flexible wood or plastic, sometimes florescent. The number of hoops used and the composition varies from dancer to dancer. Smaller hoops are used by smaller dancers.

grass darkened by the night. Inside. Separated from the soft clean breathing plant brothers whose winds lifted his fringes. Inside, separated from his own spiritual soaring. Like Eagle in a cage, Echo-maker's spirit was contained inside.

The dancers waited. With their colorful regalia circling the enclosed dance floor, instead of the arbor that opens to eternity, they waited. With the spotlight on the floor, instead of Nee-ba-gee'-sis on Earth Mother, they waited. All dry and warm, instead of refreshed with glistening rain drops, they waited. They waited for Echo-maker to dance the hoop, but round did not fit square, inside, separated from Earth Mother.

Echo-maker tried to begin, but his legs could not move. He listened for the beat, but could not feel its rhythm. He tried to pick up a hoop, but the hoop could not be lifted. He looked over, reached over, to where the other hoops waited, but he could not travel the distance.

Then Echo-maker understood. This was a dream. He tried to move through to the other side in order to remember. Momentarily awakening in his bed, he still slid back down into the dream. Connected to both the past and present, the timelessness, of each, Echo-maker viewed both his dream and his awake.

Inside asleep, Echo-maker saw a bright circle of light appear by the waiting Hoops, rising up like the rays of Grandfather Sun on brilliant mornings. Echo-maker looked over to honor this sight and saw his Elder, sitting in the middle of the hoops.

The young man shouted over to where the light began, hoping that perhaps his strong voice would reach the old man's ears. "I cannot dance!"

The white haired Elder held the beam of light in his hands. "Are you sure it is you that can not dance? Or is it your path that can not be danced?" the Elder echoed back.

"But the present is my path," Echo-maker replied. "And I cannot dance this present."

"The present is not to be neglected," the Elder whispered as he set the sun down. "It is to be honored."

"But, my present path is inside this building, separated from Earth Mother and Sky Father!" Echo-maker looked at the walls that imprisoned him. "I cannot dance inside these walls!"

"Your path will either neglect or honor the present," the Elder repeated.

Echo-maker watched the old man place a stone dish in front of him. Reaching inside his medicine bag, he brought out kinnikinnick to fill the earthen opening. "Can you see my prayer?" the Elder asked the dancer.

"Your prayer is from your heart. Your heart is inside your body. I cannot see your prayer," the dancer replied.

"Look closely and you will see the vibration of my heart." The Elder picked up the sun, lit the kinnikinnick and fanned the fire with his breath. Echo-maker watched as the fire glowed. He sniffed as the smoke lifted the sweet scent. "See how my breath has now become a prayer," the Elder continued. "With this smoke I offer myself, then I am gifted another breath in which to complete the hoop." As his prayer lifted, the Elder merged into the invisible.

Echo-maker wanted to awaken, rolling over in his sleep. But continuing the dream, he knew there was an answer somewhere inside the old man's movements. Remaining within his dream, he decided to follow the prayer. The circling smoke led Echo-maker around so that he could view all sides of the dream-building. Empty walls, stifled sound and closed feelings separated Echo-maker from Earth Mother and himself.

Still following the dream-smoke, Echo-maker left the building to follow the prayer. Still inside his dream, but out of the dream-building, he found a path, but now, the floor was the forest and the canopy, the clouds. The path that all had danced before and would dance after him became Echo-maker's path of connection, of his spirit. And his dream continued.

With deep respect, Echo-maker moved through the old man's smoke-prayer to find and pick up his hoops. He then placed the many hoops, on the soft damp dream-grass... some to the East, some to the South, some to the West and some to the North. He knew that he would honor each hoop, only by honoring first the spirit of his ancestors, his dream of past connection.

The dream-song began and Echo-maker held one hoop, easily dancing to the rhythm of the Drum. The dream-rain kissed his face and Echo-maker was glad. Four separate hoops remained behind as reminders of the Four Directions. He would not pick them up this night, as they provided Echo-maker the center where he would dance.

At the very center of the Four Directions, at the center of life itself, Echo-Maker dream-danced. His two strong hands held the first hoop in front of him. As though stepping into Life itself, Echo-maker stepped in and through the hoop, smudging himself with the circle of life. Having honored this first hoop of Self, of his Seventh Direction, Echo-maker was ready to honor all of the Sacred Hoop of Life.

He would begin this honor for Earth Mother and Sky Father, for without them, Echo-maker would have no song. Without a song, he would have no dance. Without a dance, he would have no beat, and without a beat, Echo-maker would not be.

With the first hoop around his waist, his center, Echo-maker danced from the center of the Four Directions to the place between North and East, where one hoop waited. The hoop of Earth Mother was resting lightly on the damp green grass. Echo-maker wondered what it was like when Earth Mother was new. He honored Her beginning where the lines between the North and East blurred. Now dancing with great energy, he stepped into this hoop, acknowledging his dependence on Earth Mother. Echo-maker lifted this second hoop with his foot until his legs wore it like a bracelet. Bringing the hoop up to join the other at his waist, Echo-maker rooted to Earth Mother with each step.

Remembering the winds, Echo-maker dream-danced a diagonal path between South and West to honor the hoop of Sky Father. Warm beneath his covers, the sleeping man continued dancing, covered in heavy dream-movement.

His foot lifted under the next hoop, stepping in and pulling it up to meet the two hoops at his waist. As this third hoop had waited between the directions of growth and insight, he knew this hoop would lift his dance to great heights. Echo-maker dream-jumped and dream-whirled, creating designs with the three hoops and his arms and legs. With a quick turn and a powerful kick, Echo-maker twirled with the power of Sky and Earth. Circling around, he honored their contribution to his dance, to his very life.

Next, dancing to the South, Echo-maker honored the cycles of life. He picked up two more hoops and honored the seasons, the beginnings, the innocence of this dream.

Moving easily within his dream, each hand now held two hoops, connected to each other by one center hoop. As his arms extended wide, the five hoops wove together and stretched out in a horizontal chain, revealing the web of all directions. Knowing that all power is inherent in the Circle, Echo-maker stepped into the hoop at each end and he became the center of the interconnected hoops. Spinning with this great understanding, Echo-maker stepped out of the hoops, moving them to line up vertically. Here, the five hoops honored Sky and Earth.

Echo-maker finally dove into each separate hoop. Moving in and out, Echo-maker worked to connect the separate. With Namaji, he moved through each hoop. Touching the soft wet dream-earth with his dream-feet and feeling the open expanse of the dream-sky, he danced lightly and persuaded the circles to join together. He did this until the hoops merged inside each other at connecting angles, creating a circle within. All at once, Echo-maker magically stepped out of the hoops. With great pride, Echo-maker held up one beautiful sphere. His breath circled, in and out, gifted and offered back. His prayer to unite all people, all animals, all plants, and all minerals with a hoop of love vibrated in his hand. The essence of the Creator was honored.

Dancing in the center of the four directions, Echo-maker first lifted the sphere to honor Earth Mother, then raised it high to Sky Father. Saluting each direction in turn with the sphere, his knees stepped high.

Placing the dream-hoops down, Echo-maker then danced toward the South. Picking up the hoops of growth that still waited there, he began donning their meanings, for the hoops became his regalia. Dancing to the North Direction, he bent over to pick up the hoops of wisdom. Dancing to the East, he added hoops of renewal.

His legs were covered with the north teaching the south. He was ready to dance through the difficulties of life. He remembered the words of the Elder and twirled around so others could see how the hoops danced his dream. Echo-maker was aware that this life, this dream-moment, was only one of many hoops.

Finally, dancing to the West, Echo-maker felt the strong beat of Earth Mother through his hoop-covered legs. Although it seemed impossible, the dream-dancer picked up many more hoops. Putting these on his arms, his chest and back, Echo-maker became a great living hoop of love. Twirling with interconnected hoops. Honoring the Sacred Hoop. Dancing the cycles of all things. Like wings, his arms expanded out and then drew close together. Like Eagle, wearing circled-feathers, he flew.

Again, the dancer stepped in and out, through and into the many hoops on his body. Again, blurring the separation of the hoops, he created a spherical design. Again, he stepped out of its truth. Tossing it up, he caught its integrity. Setting it gently down on the wet dream-grass, the dreamer honored the connection.

Echo-maker picked up two hoops. Whirling them around on one arm, the hoops created a figure eight, each replacing the other's momentary experience. Like a bee, each understood the path the other had taken.

Then the dream-song ended. For the dreamer awoke to rain hitting the skin of his teepee. The memory of his dance was near, the movement as real as the sound on his teepee, and understanding brought into his present. Echo-maker opened his eyes to his vision, to the power of the hoop. He knew his prayer would be his dance. His steps would honor the path. His song would complete the hoop. And his dream would become his vision.

HEAL THE SACRED HOOP

It is time to heal the Sacred Hoop. It is time to heal Earth Mother. She awaits our decisions. It is time to treat Her with dignity, respect, honor and pride. Let us return these to Her and honor the children of the future with the decisions of today.

Animals and plants do not need us. We need them. Without us, Earth Mother would return to a healthy balance and all would flourish. The only medicine that can cure the world is the hoop of love. Join the hoop of love by living Namaji.

Return to Old Age Wisdom. All of our ancestors had this wisdom. The lessons of truth encircle Earth Mother. Reach up and capture the meaning of tribal people. Open up to the lessons of yesterday. Hear the stories of our people who talk of when the Earth was new. Honor the future by connecting to your past. The only hope for Earth Mother lies in the memories of Mishomis and the truth that rides the four winds.

NEW UNDERSTANDING OF OLD WISDOM

I have been one of thousands of people who have visited the White Buffalo Calf[4]. Tobacco ties, colorful ribbons, feathers, and other gifts from thousands of miles away have been carried to Wisconsin in order to honor this birth. Native American prophesy states that this birth affirms that we are at a crossroads. Either all colors will come together to heal the Sacred Hoop or we will face global disaster.

Leaders from around the world are now joining to pray and celebrate the mending of the Sacred Hoop. From the United Nations to Six-Nations, the prophesies of the White Buffalo Calf have been presented by Elders to political leaders. On June 21st, 1996, World Peace and Prayer Day, people around the world prayed for peace and balance.

May this be a beginning of Nations praying and joining together in the support of world harmony. May you join in the prayers and become committed to healing the Sacred Hoop.

Whether you are on the inside or outside of the dance arbor, tribal people and all others on the Sacred Hoop face the same world dilemma. We are all children of this aching Earth Mother. We are all responsible and accountable

---

4   In August of 1994, a White Buffalo Calf was born in Wisconsin. Native American prophesy states that when the White Bison returned, she would "unify the nations of the four colors: Yellow, Red, Black and White."

to Her. Recognize your part in either the destruction or the healing of the Sacred Hoop.

It is easy to live Namaji. All it takes is an open heart and an open mind. Recognize the inherent honor to all the children of Earth Mother. Come to know that everything has a spirit. Develop a relationship with everything around you and you will begin to care about the future of the Earth. Return to Earth Mother and honor Her. In this way you will embody Mitakuye-Oyasin. You will live Namaji. You will become an active link of love on the Sacred Hoop.

May we all gain a new understanding of Old Age Wisdom. There are limits to what Earth Mother can give us. Whenever something is taken, something must be given back. Earth Mother's limits require a balance. We all have the right to non-polluted fresh air, water, and earth. She has the right to offer this gift. It is time to give back to our Mother from whom we have so thoughtlessly taken.

Destruction and pollution must stop! A new direction must be taken! Testing the effects of nuclear bombs is no test! It is a clear violation of our Mother's integrity! Continued eradication of endangered species and habitat must be halted!

There is an Anishinaabe saying that states, "The Circle comes around." Everything is connected and has consequences.

If Earth Mother is not given a chance to heal, She will rid Herself of us. Her Water Spirits will cleanse Her of filth. Global warming, due to a tear in the atmosphere approximately the size of Europe and the effects of burning fossil fuels, has increased the global temperature. This, in turn, is melting the great ice sheets on the North and South poles at an accelerated rate. If this continues, intercontinental flooding will occur. And Earth Mother will flush the toilet!

There are many ways to conserve energy. There are alternate ways to use energy. Unbridled greed has led to plundering vast volumes of resources and energy. It is time to move forward with environmental awareness and alternatives. Without this action, you better carve a canoe!

CIRCLES OF DIVERSITY

Are you aware that your life is one hoop of many hoops? "See far around you," says an Ojibwe Elder. Practice circular thinking. Move outward to the "we," rather than inward to the "me." Like the Hoop Dancer, recognize that many diverse circles intersect with your life circle. Have you honored their beliefs and practices? Do you respect the ideas of others? Can you see that you are but one of many flowers in the field? That flowers of distinction create a beautiful field of sight and scent?

Diversity is an integral aspect to the Hoop Dance. As the dancer intertwines the many hoops, this awareness and appreciation is lifted to the height of honor. Honor the diversity of each tribe, each culture, each people. Honor the diversity of your Seventh Direction.

Native people are not all alike. Each tribe has its unique traditions and dances, stories and history. All people are not alike. We each bring something unique to the Sacred Hoop, both individually as persons and collectively as a people. May we celebrate this truth of distinction and honor the uniqueness of each other.

INTERTRIBAL DANCE

The Intertribal Dance at Powwow recognizes diversity among tribal people as well as other ancestries. The Intertribal Dance celebrates these differences by connecting each dancer to the other. It is a reconciliatory dance. In this dance, all people are welcome to dance, regalia or not, Indian or not. As the diverse group circles the great beat of life, the hoop of love is proclaimed in dance. The Intertribal Dance links uniqueness to uniqueness. Here the web of life is recreated. Each fiber is honored as important as another. The Intertribal Dance weaves a pattern of Mitakuye-Oyasin, for the Intertribal Dance acknowledges the great connection to all children of this Earth Mother.

SHE

She stood on the outside of the Circle, aware that She was different from the people who danced. On the outside She watched.

With Sun overhead, She watched many dances that day. Alone and learning, She listened to good songs. In her quest to understand herself, the woman stood on the outside looking in. Like a lone wolf, She watched and listened and waited.

Sun journeyed West. A good strong drum began to play. It was different than the one before. Yet, the voices were still strong and confident. Clear and pulsating. The Elder announced an Intertribal, announced that all could dance. Part of the young woman wanted to dance. But part of her wanted to stay there—on the outside, safe, not connected. Watching. Listening. Waiting.

Like looking for her own ancestry, She walked to a spot with a good view, distanced from the pulse. Like her own uncertainty, She settled herself on cool earth with her back against a familiar tree, watching an unfamiliar dance. Listening to the outer sounds with her keen ear, She did not listen to her own strong voice.

Again the Elder encouraged all to dance. Never having danced this way, She was afraid to join others whose movements were easy. She watched as their feet touched the ground lightly, rhythmically. Their subtle movements made the dance look easy, yet She knew it would be difficult. Difficult to let go of her rigid self. Difficult to allow the beat to enter her, even as it now entered them. Difficult to let go of what She thought the dance should be. Difficult to let go of what She thought She should be.

Blue became gray. Still sitting in her comfortable spot on
the easy slope leading down to the arbor, She watched as
others joined the Circle. People from other tribes danced
the Intertribals. White, Yellow, Black, and Red people from
around the world all joyously entered the arbor, glad to be
connecting with their relatives. From her view, She felt
curious of their bond. She watched them move over the
Earth, on the lap of their mother. Still, on the outside She
remained. Watching. Listening. Waiting.

Then She looked west, discovering what She had been
waiting for. In the quiet moments of Sun disappearing, She
finally understood. Her ancestors had journeyed West, just
as She now looked West. West was the direction of all. And
it led her to her Self in her darkened world.

Stars replaced Sun. Finally, the Elder announced that the
last Intertribal would be played for the evening. Having
finally heard the beat within, She would dance.

She moved shyly toward the circle. Half walking, half
dancing, She moved to the edge. Coyote passed. Eagle
flew by. Shawls and feathers. Bells and jingles. Hoops and
fans. Differences danced passed her.

Feeling her way into the rhythm, She was at first too
excited to understand what She was doing. At first, She
was too self-conscious to be aware of the others that
joined her. Hesitating inside, the beat reminded her that
She was near the edge of letting go. With her beginning
steps She was too full at first to empty.

Then draining into Earth Mother, her foot felt the strong
beat. It was her beat, her Grandmother's beat, her relatives'
beat. It was the beat of all. Without thinking, She, too,
became the prayer of the dance.

The young woman felt her back straighten. She felt the power of Earth Mother enter her from below. She felt the rhythm match her heart. She began to empty. She began to join.

Carrying herself with pride, respect moved her steps. With dignity she connected to this great gift. An Eagle whistle blew and She was caught up in a wave of spiritual energy. Moving her. Carrying her. Honoring the young woman, it lifted her as though She were wings.

Filling up with life and living, melting into Earth, finding the beat, honoring all that circles the endlessness, She was truly part of the circle.

Dancing, She looked over to the tree where She had waited. She noticed that the circle extended out past the dance arbor to those that stood on the edges looking in. And like rings in the water's surface, the hoop circled out further and further, to the very edge of her view. Inside and outside, the woman understood that She was always part of the Sacred Circle that She now danced.

DRUM-SING-DANCE

The drum is my dance is my song.
My song is my poem and my poem is my prayer.
My dance is a prayer in song.

We are all drums. We can all sing. We can all dance. We can all become Earth Dance Drums. We are at future's doorway. What we do today will determine tomorrow's condition. It is time that we all dance our lives with Namaji. If you have forgotten this wisdom, please take the time now to practice the art of loving. Namaji is the love-vibration that moves through us. Namaji is the great good gift of connection.

As a good song first depends on a strong drum, first you must sound your own drum. Evidence Namaji for yourself. Your drum—your cadence with life—will determine what your dance will be. Begin your life-dance with a strong beat. Heal your wounds. Balance yourself in the ways of the Medicine Wheel. Return to Earth Mother and allow Her vibrations to heal you. Tap Mash-ka-wisen and face your fears. First you must honor all of you, strengthen, heal, and balance yourself. When you can hear your heart beat strong, your song will become.

Then practice your life-song. Like the singers of the drums, many moments need to be invested before the song will lift the fringes of the dancer. Invest yourself in yourself. In this way, you will offer your best to the Hoop of Life. With Bimadisiwin, contribute your part to the Sacred Hoop. Discover your purpose and practice what you will become. Don't be a bird without a song! Sing! May your song heal others! May your song echo the Universe!

With a strong beat and a beautiful song, it is time to unfold the wings of your dance. Celebrate life as you journey around the Hoop. Make each moment a ritual of internal dancing, of celebration and honor! Hold a ceremony of gratitude when you catch a fish, use the medicine of plants, eat and drink. As Earth provides plants, animals and food as medicine, recognize the essential link between humans and nature.

Then drum, sing, and dance to honor this link. Heal, become, and celebrate! Like the Elder of Echo-maker's dream, become the prayer sent to Gitchi Manidoo. Prayer lifts your Spirit to Ishpeming, the High Place, so the Spirit World can see your heart more clearly. When it is time to fly, fly! Like Blue Heron that circled the beat of my heart, the Spirit World moves around and through us, as we drum, sing and dance.

Become the drum that vibrates the Earth with prayers! Become the bird that heals the Earth with song! Become a dance that gifts the Earth with celebration! Become Earth Dance Drum and join the Hoop of Love.

HOOP OF LOVE

The Great Spirit in me honors the Great Spirit in you.

The Sacred Hoop connects with love. Love is the Sacred Mystery from which the East of beginnings is born. All of creation is of love's essence, for we all enter from the same door. To love all is to see the sacredness in all, the sacredness in Self.

All is sacred because the Giver is the Creator. The Great Spirit is pure love. May you become an open channel for love to flow through. May you practice giving and loving, for the only cure for Earth Mother—to mend the Sacred Hoop—is love. Love joins all together so that differences are no longer threatening.

See the world with eyes of a child and recognize the essence in all. Touch the world with the soft wing tips of a dove and offer peace. Listen to the world with the understanding of Mishomis and offer healing.

Then dance for the Creator, Gitchi Manidoo. At the center of the Great Mystery, the Great Spirit awaits your dance. As you dance the circle around your life source, may it be the Hoop of Love. May your dance heal. May your steps reveal and reflect the Creator's essence at each sunrise and sunset. May your dance offer visions. And may the universe open to you as you dance the Hoop of Love.

THE UNIVERSE AWAITS

Do you know where you belong? Have you reflected on your place in life? Do you know what you can do?

See your place. See your role. See your sacredness. This is the joy of the dance of life.

Take this time to discover your place in the universe. Take a piece of paper and trace your hand. At the very center of your drawing, in the palm of your hand, sketch the country or state that you live in. Next, pin-point the city or area you live.

Look at your picture. This is your world. This is your door to the universe.

Become a warrior and tend Earth Mother's fire in your world. Join the philosophy and action of Native Americans who, for thousands of years, have been and continue to be, the guardians of Earth Mother. You are Her keeper. You are Her guardian. If that means signing petitions to halt pollution, then do this. If that means defending waterways, wetlands, and habitats, then defend them. If it means bending over to pick up trash, then grab a bag. Find accessible ways, realistic ways, to vibrate love for our Earth. Write a mission statement alongside the drawing of your hand. Commission yourself to be a warrior to defend and protect Earth Mother.

If and when you move your teepee, you are commissioned to defend Earth Mother in that new environment. Wherever you go, your responsibility to protect Earth Mother accompanies you. In this highly mobile society, it is imperative that this attitude of responsibility goes with you. Design your pledge and commit to honoring Earth Mother.

Like a painter who can see the image before it has been finished, visualize your world image in the colors of healing. Like a sculptor who can feel the creation before he has carved it, pick up some soil and feel its potential. Like a writer who knows the story without words, know that your role in the story of life is being written by you. See it! Feel it! Live it!

Now return to your drawing. Take a pencil and with the width of a finger, trace around the outside of your image. Now you have two hands, one inside another! Repeat this procedure many times, until you run out of room on your paper.

Like your drawing, the Universe emanates outward, in hoops of love. What you do with one hand today, you may also do with two. What your two hands do today, may reach hands beyond yours. What you do in your world, reverberates in another. Do you now see that you are indeed an integral part of the Hoop of Love? What footprints will you leave behind? What gifts of healing will your hands give to the future?

As the pulse of the Universe massages your bare feet, Her joy is your privilege. May another pair of feet also walk along the shores of your world and feel the same gift of life. May you ensure the sands are clean, the air is pure, and the waters are clear.

As you touch Earth Mother with your feet, you hold the Universe in the palm of your hand.

WHEN THE EARTH IS NEW, AGAIN

They call it progress.

An hour ago I heard the buzzing chain saws, the steel-loud bulldozer. I walk over the uprooted green brothers and sisters, laying in the now dark colored sand, strewn with ripped bark. Sawdust sprinkles the forest floor where earlier this day, Brother Deer's hoof prints spoke to his path.

Just this morning, the top colored sands were sugar white. I had picked ripe red raspberries. I had tasted their sweetness. I had listened to Chipmunk. He had given me joy. I had watched Porcupine climb a tree. Porcupine had taught me lessons.

Ants now scurry to bury their eggs and drag off their dead. Strawberry and raspberry plants will no longer be here for Brother Mu-kwa. What will he eat? Where will he go for food? Sister Cedar and Brother Spruce still bleed, oozing their sap from their ripped stumps and limbs. And who is there to mourn their devastation?

In the deep cleated tracks from the iron horse bulldozer, I put down tobacco, to console Earth Mother. To offer my prayers for Her torn flesh. Cut logs lay on piles like fallen warriors, waiting to be pulled out of the forest, to the road, to the paper mill... to a wastepaper basket.

I look down from the stump I sit on, I see small maples and spruces who somehow escaped the blade of the iron horse. They wonder where their neighbors are. Already the leaves of the unlucky ones begin to whither as their sap blood hemorrhages. I hear a bird calling her brood. How many bird homes now lay on the forest floor?

My dog looks puzzled as he sniffs the devastation. Will our children ever know what the forest was like? I wonder.

All is in a bleeding, moaning, desperate state. I sit there for a long time. I wonder for a long time. I do nothing for a long time. Then I hear a buzzing sound once more.

It is Mosquito.

Offering my bare arm, I offer the world all that I have. I offer the world hope. Carrying my blood, may Mosquito heal the Universe. And when Earth is new, again, may Mosquito circle once more.

I'm the Drum.
You're the Drum.
We're the Drum.
Earth Dance Drum.

GLOSSARY

Word	Pronunciation	Definition
Ain-dah-ing	AH-da-ning	Home. Referred to as home within our heart.
Anishinaabe	a-ni-shi-NA-bae	Those who were the ancestors of the tribes now known as Ottawa, Potawatomi, and Ojibwe.
Benaysay	be-NAY-say	Thunderbird.
Bimadisiwin	be-ma-DEE-zee-win	To live life to the fullest. To become and fulfill one's fate and purpose. To engage free will. Sometimes spoken by Elders to mean: to live the good life.
Boo-zhoo	Bou-zshoo	Hello.
Earth Mother		Recognizing the female, creative, nurturing qualities of the earth.
Ethnostress		The loss and grief experienced by conquered people.
Flag Song		An Indian anthem.
Four Directions		The Four Directions of the medicine wheel: East, South, West, and North.
Ganu	ga-NU	War or death eagle.
Gitchi	GI-chi	Great.
Gitchi Manidoo	GI-chi MON-ee-doo	Great Spirit.
Gitchi Migwetch	GI-chi ME-gwich	Big thank you.

Word	Pronunciation	Definition
Ishpeming	ISH-pe-ming	Refers to the High Place.
Kinnikinnick	KIN-ee-kin-ik	"Much mixed." Is a tobacco based mixture also accompanied with other herbs, primarily: cedar, balsam fir, sweet grass, calamus root, sweet non-fern, sweet gale and mints. Other mixtures may also include bear berry, sweet goldenrod, rose petals, sage, willow bark, red ooshier bark, sweet clover yarrow and tobacco. Used in Native American sacred ceremonies.
Manidoo	MON-ee-doo	Spirit.
Mash-ka-wisen	mash-KOW-sin	Inner strength.
Medicine Bag		A Native American healing pouch that contains a variety of herbs, medicines etc.used to connect to the participant to the Spiritual Realm.
Medicine Wheel		A Native American healing wheel to represent balance in one's life, as well as a symbol for life cycles. The Medicine Wheel has three parts: the circumference (the Sacred Hoop), the center (Gitchi Manidoo), and the Four Directions (East, South, West, and North).
Michi-Gami	MICH-ee-GAM-ee	Great water. The root word of Michigan.
Michi-zee-bee	MICH-ee-ZEE-bee	Greatest river.
Midewinin	mi-DAY-win	Sacred Medicine lodge of the Ojibwe people.
Migwetch	ME-gwich	Thank you.
Mishomis	mi-SHOO-mis	Grandfather in the Ojibwe language. Is also a term for the spiritual healing stone.

Word	Pronunciation	Definition
Mitakuye-Oyasin	mi-TAHK-wee-a-say	We are all related.
Mu-kwa	MA-kwa	Bear
Namaji	NA-MA-GEE	The highest Anishinaabe principle: respect, honor, dignity and pride.
Nokomis	no-KO-mis	Grandmother.
Ojibwe	O-jib-wa	Known variously as the Anishinaabe, Chippewa, Ojibway, Chippeway, Otchipwe, and refers to the large tribal nation residing in many now upper midwestern states and large section of Canada.
Powwow	pou-WOU	Pau-wau or pauau is Algonquian for a gathering of medicine men and spiritual leaders in a healing ceremony. Early European explorers mispronounced the name as pow-wow and believed it meant any large gathering of Native people. Powwow is an outgrowth of the spiritual and social dances of Tribal people. Powwow refers to a gathering of Indian people, a four day celebration of dancing, singing, drumming. It includes feasting, giveaways, and a social celebration.
Red Road		The guiding principle to stay between virtue and evil, to have a positive focus.
Roach		A warrior's hair piece made from deer tail, porcupine or horsehair with one or two feathers in the center.
Sacred Hoop		A Native American symbol for our journey in this life, as well as our connection to the Spirit World. It also illustrates the cycle of all things.

Word	Pronunciation	Definition
Sahgeen	San-GEEN	Love and respect.
Seven Directions		Represents the seven directions for one's life: East to the Eagle, South to the Wolf, West to the Buffalo, and North to the Bear, into Earth Mother, out to Sky Father and Yourself - the seventh direction.
Seven Generations		Native American philosophy that states all decisions must be considered within the context of the next seven generations.
Sky Father		Recognizing the conceptual, supportive qualities of Sky.
Smudge		The sacred act whereby the participant releases (through burning) the spiritual essence of the sage and wafts the smoke over oneself. Becoming one with the Spirit world through the gifts of this world is the purpose. This act is done with Namaji and with sacred intent. Sage symbolizes cleansing, sweet grass symbolizes filling up with the Spirit World. Cedar symbolizes the sending of prayers. Tobacco symbolizes gratitude and opening the door to the Spirit World.
Star People		The belief of the Anishinaabe people that our ancestors reside in the stars after they die and watch and guide their children below.
Straight Song		A traditional song without words. Vowel sounds such as hey, ya, hi, accompany specific tones. A lead singer leads off with the first line and is eventually joined by the

Word	Pronunciation	Definition
		group. Attention to pitch and tone is the beauty of the vocals of this type of song. Northern singers use powerful, high falsetto voices.
Sun Dance		A Native American ceremony where dancers pray and fast for four days while dancing in the sun form dawn to dark. Prayers and ceremonial rituals support themselves, their families and their tribes.
Sun Trail		The journey we take in this life to complete the hoop. Beginning in the East of birth and ending in the West of death, the Sun Trail is a celebration of the life we are gifted.
Turtle Island		The Earth of North America. In the Ojibwe creation story this land rests on a turtle's back.
Vision Quest		A Native American ceremony where the participant abstains from food, light, etc. in order to obtain a spiritual vision to guide his free will in directing his purpose. Sometimes conducted in pits, mountain tops, or near a waterfall.
Wee-ka-san	WEE-ca-san	This is the root of "Wisconsin" and means the gathering of the waters.
White Buffalo Calf		In August of 1994, a White Buffalo Calf was born in Wisconsin. Native American prophesy states that when the White Bison returned, she would "unify the nations of the four colors: Yellow, Red, Black and White."

INDEX

SUGGESTED READING

Benton-Banai, Edward. *The Mishomis Book: The Voice of the Ojibway*. Saint Paul, MN: Red School House,1988.

Campbell, Joseph. *The Hero With a Thousand Faces*. (3rd. Ed.) New York: Bollingen Foundation Inc.,1973.

Densmore, Frances. *Chippewa Customs*. Saint Paul, MN: Minnesota Historical Society Press, 1979.

Frankl, Viktor E. *Man's Search for Meaning: An Introduction to Logotherapy*. Boston: Beacon Press Books, 1959.

Freesoul, John Redtail. *Breath of the Invisible: The Way of the Pipe*. Wheaton, Ill: The Theosophical Publishing House, 1986.

Gibran, Kahlil. *The Prophet*. New York: Alfred A Knopf, 1968.

James, Wharton. *Learning from the Indians, 1908*. Philadelphia: Running Press, 1973.

Jones, Blackwolf & Gina. *The Healing Drum*. SLC, UT: Commune-A-Key, Publishing, 1995.

Jones, Blackwolf & Gina. *Listen to the Drum: Blackwolf Shares His Medicine*. SLC, UT: Commune-A-Key Publishing, 1995.

Ross, A. C. *Mitakuye Oyasin: "We are all Related."* Kyle, SD: Bear, 1989.

Steinmetz, Paul B. *Meditations with Native Americans: Lakota Spirituality*. Santa Fe, NM: Bear & Co., 1984.

Summers, Caryn L. *The Girl, the Rock, and the Water: Rediscovering the Child Within*. Mt. Shasta, CA: Commune-A-Key Publishing, 1994.

Sweet, Denise. *Days of Obsidian, Days of Grace*. Duluth, MN: Poetry Harbor,1994.

The Sacred Tree: Reflections on Native American Spirituality. Lethbridge, Alberta, Canada: Four Worlds Development Press, 1984.

Warren, William W. *History of the Ojibway People*. Saint Paul, MN: Minnesota Historical Society Press, 1984.

ABOUT THE AUTHORS

Muka-day-way-ma-en'-gun, Blackwolf, is the Indian name given to co-author Robert Jones. He is of Ojibwe heritage and lived on the Lac Courte Oreilles reserve during his formative years. Blackwolf frequently visits his home to renew and further the Anishinaabe way.

Blackwolf achieved sobriety in 1977 within the fellowship of Alcoholics Anonymous and has enjoyed continuous sobriety since that time. He holds a Bachelor degree in Psychology, a Master's degree in Guidance and Counseling and has accomplished post graduate studies in Addictive Disorders. He is a licensed psychotherapist, a Certified Addiction Specialist and has published in professional journals. He maintains a private clinical practice and speaks nationally about Native American healing techniques in personal growth.

Gina Jones is of Mohawk ancestry. She, too, has enjoyed continuous sobriety since 1979. Holding a Bachelor's of Science degree in Education, Gina is a language arts teacher in the elementary school system. She presents training on Reading and Writing Workshops for educators in Wisconsin.

Gina writes in her free time on her own projects, as well as in conjunction with her husband. She has published poetry in literary publications and is looking forward to publishing other material, including children's books and young adult novels.

Blackwolf and Gina are involved in Anishinaabe activities and participate in the Powwows of many tribal nations. Their dream is to promote global healing through their conscious activities such as the Earth Dance Drum Society. Their first books, *Listen to the Drum: Blackwolf Shares his Medicine* and *The Healing Drum* have received critical acclaim worldwide.

COMMUNE-A-KEY PUBLISHING AND SEMINARS

Commune-A-Key Publishing and Seminars was established in 1992. Our mission statement, "Communicating Keys to Growth and Empowerment," describes our effort to publish books that inspire and promote personal growth and wellness. Our books and products provide powerful ways to care for, discover and heal ourselves and others.

Our audience includes health care professionals and counselors, caregivers, men, women, people interested in Native American traditions—anyone interested in personal growth, psychology, recovery and inspiration. We hope you enjoy this book! If you have any comments, questions, or would like to be on our mailing list for future products and seminars, please write to us at the address and phone number below.

ORDERING INFORMATION

Commune-A-Key Publishing has a variety of books and products, including other works by Blackwolf and Gina. For further information on our books and audio tapes, or if you would like to receive a catalog, please write or call us at the address and phone number listed below.

Our authors are also available for seminars, workshops and lectures. Please call our toll-free number for further information.

Commune-A-Key Publishing
P.O. Box 58637
Salt Lake City, UT 84158

1-800-983-0600

EARTH DANCE DRUM SOCIETY

Earth Dance Drum Society is an international family of people who are dedicated to the healing and survival of Earth Mother. In drum, dance and song, all which have ever existed, all which now exists, and all which shall exist, unite as one mind to respect and honor Earth Mother. We acknowledge that all beings have a right to continued and sustained existence within Life's web. We ask Creator to bring each individual of each species into balance, so that we may fulfill our special purpose within Universal Rhythm.

Migwetch,

Blackwolf and Gina

If you are interested in joining *Earth Dance Drum Society,* please send your name, address, phone number and any suggestions to Commune-A-Key Publishing at:

Commune-A-Key Publishing

P.O. Box 58637

Salt Lake City, UT 84158

or call

1-800-983-0600